POINTS OF DEPARTURE

POINTS OF DEPARTURE

*Rethinking Student Source Use and
Writing Studies Research Methods*

EDITED BY
TRICIA SERVISS
SANDRA JAMIESON

UTAH STATE UNIVERSITY PRESS
Logan

© 2017 the University Press of Colorado

Published by Utah State University Press
An imprint of University Press of Colorado
5589 Arapahoe Avenue, Suite 206C
Boulder, Colorado 80303

All rights reserved

 The University Press of Colorado is a proud member of
The Association of American University Presses.

The University Press of Colorado is a cooperative publishing enterprise supported, in part, by Adams State University, Colorado State University, Fort Lewis College, Metropolitan State University of Denver, Regis University, University of Colorado, University of Northern Colorado, Utah State University, and Western State Colorado University.

ISBN: 978-1-60732-624-3 (pbk)
ISBN: 978-1-60732-625-0 (ebook)

Library of Congress Cataloging-in-Publication Data

Names: Serviss, Tricia, editor. | Jamieson, Sandra, editor.
Title: Points of departure : rethinking student source use and writing studies research methods / edited by Tricia Serviss, Sandra Jamieson.
Description: Logan : Utah State University Press, [2017] | Includes bibliographical references and index.
Identifiers: LCCN 2016049466| ISBN 9781607326243 (pbk.) | ISBN 9781607326250 (ebook)
Subjects: LCSH: English language—Rhetoric—Study and teaching (Higher)—Research. | Academic writing—Study and teaching—Research. | Report writing—Study and teaching—Research. | Research—Methodology.
Classification: LCC PE1404 .P574 2017 | DDC 808/.0420711—dc23
LC record available at https://lccn.loc.gov/2016049466

Cover illustration © vs148/Shutterstock

CONTENTS

List of Figures   *vii*
List of Tables   *ix*
List of Appendices   *xi*
Foreword by Karen J. Lunsford   *xiii*
Acknowledgments   *xxi*

Introduction: The Rise of RAD Research Methods for Writing Studies: Transcontextual Ways Forward
Tricia Serviss   3

PART 1: DEVELOPING TRANSCONTEXTUAL RESEARCH PROJECTS

INTERCHAPTER 1: What Do We Mean by Transcontextual RAD Research?   25

CHAPTER 1: The Evolution of the Citation Project: Developing a Pilot Study from Local to Translocal
Sandra Jamieson   33

CHAPTER 2: Reports from the LILAC Project: Designing a Translocal Study
Katt Blackwell-Starnes and Janice R. Walker   62

POINTS OF DEPARTURE 1: Replication and the Need to Build on and Expand Local and Pilot Studies   83

PART 2: BUILDING ON TRANSCONTEXTUAL RESEARCH

INTERCHAPTER 2: What Does Design-Based Research Offer as a Tool for RAD Research in Writing Studies?   91

CHAPTER 3: The Things They Carry: Using Design-Based Research in Writing-Teacher Education
Tricia Serviss   102

CHAPTER 4: Storied Research: Using Focus Groups as a Responsive Method
Crystal Benedicks   123

CHAPTER 5: Terms and Perceptions: Using Surveys to Discover Student Beliefs about Research
Kristi Murray Costello   141

POINTS OF DEPARTURE 2: Developing Design-Based Local and Translocal Studies   *162*

PART 3: EXPLORING INFORMATION CONTEXTS

INTERCHAPTER 3: What Does Threshold-Concept Research Offer Writing Studies RAD Research?   *171*

CHAPTER 6: Research and Rhetorical Purpose: Using Genre Analysis to Understand Source Use in Technical and Professional Writing
Lee-Ann Kastman Breuch and Brian N. Larson   182

CHAPTER 7: Asking the Right Questions: Using Interviews to Explore Information-Seeking Behavior
M. Whitney Olsen and Anne R. Diekema   209

CHAPTER 8: Just Read the Assignment: Using Course Documents to Analyze Research Pedagogy
Elizabeth Kleinfeld   227

POINTS OF DEPARTURE 3: Using Existing Research to Think beyond the Local   *245*

Afterword: Teaching Hybridity in Graduate Research Courses
Rebecca Moore Howard   252

About the Authors   *259*
Index   *263*

FIGURES

1.1.	Class blog post from November 2006 showing draft IRB application for a Citation Project precursor	39
1.2.	Extract with citations blocked for coding	49
1.3.	Paper from the three-school study coded using the pilot study method	50
1.4.	Paper from the final study coded using the four-color, boxed-citation method	51
5.1.	Familiarity with college-level research and writing	149
5.2.	Unintentional plagiarism	149
6.1.	Distribution of Move 4 units	195

TABLES

1.1.	Frequency of source integration method in 1,911 student citations	43
1.2.	Type of source integration method occurring at least once per five-page extract from 174 papers	43
2.1.	LILAC Project pilot participant academic demographics	71
3.1.	Author codes (first term)	110
3.2.	External codes (first term)	110
3.3.	Author codes	112
3.4.	External codes	112
3.5.	Author C's, coding of first term	114
3.6.	External coding of Author C's first term	114
3.7.	Author C's coding of second term	115
3.8.	External coding of Author C's, second term	115
6.1.	Rhetorical-move coding scheme	187
6.2.	Coding scheme for subcategories of Move 4, reference to previous research	188
6.3.	Confusion matrix from coding training	190
6.4.	Frequency of coding categories in IMRAD papers	193
6.5.	Overview of IMRAD papers and presence of Move 4 and its subcategories	194
8.1.	Summary of data pool	233

APPENDICES

These appendices may be downloaded from https://upcolorado.com/utah-state-university-press/item/3188-points-of-departure and used or modified for teaching or research purposes with attribution.

1.A	Citation Project: Procedures for Paper Coding	54
1.B	Citation Project: Paper Coding Sheet	56
1.C	Citation Project: Glossary for Paper Coding	57
1.D	Citation Project: FAQs for Source Coding	58
2.A	LILAC Project: Questionnaire	76
2.B	LILAC Project: Participant Instructions	81
3.A	Design-Based Research: Basic Interview Questions (Pre- and Post-Coding)	118
3.B	Design-Based Research: Coding Workshop Schedule and Prompts	119
3.C	Design-Based Research: Self-Guided Coding Sheets (Participant Version)	120
4.A	Academic Honesty Survey Created by Sandra Jamieson, 2008	135
4.B	Wabash College Academic Honesty Survey, 2010	137
4.C	Wabash College Focus Group Questions, 2011	140
5.A	Student Beliefs About Research: 2010 First-Year Writing Research Study	152
5.B	Student Beliefs About Research: 2011 First-Year Writing Research Study	156
6.A	Research and IMRAD Structure: Assignment Description	200
6.B	Final Coding Guide for Holistic Assessment of Student Papers' Conformity with IMRAD Structure	201
6.C	First Draft Coding Guide for Atomistic Assessment of Sentences/Units	201
6.D	Final Coding Guide for Atomistic Assessment of Sentences/Units	202
7.A	Information Seeking Behavior: Interview Guide	223
8.A	Writing from Sources Syllabi Coding Sheet	241
8.B	Writing from Sources Syllabi Coding Definitions	242

FOREWORD

Karen J. Lunsford

Somewhat to my surprise, as I write these words, I realize it has been over a decade since Rich Haswell (2005) published his influential article, "NCTE/CCCC's Recent War on Scholarship." Calling on writing scholars to return to conducting empirical studies, Haswell coined a term to encompass both the qualitative and quantitative research needed—"RAD scholarship," or "replicable, aggregable, and data-driven scholarship." He also implied an agenda for the discipline: to define areas in which our collective research will make a difference. In the decade since then, writing scholars have responded to his call. As the contributors to this collection argue, there has been an uptick in interest in conducting empirical work, as well as in creating the infrastructures and training needed to support that work. Conferences and journals have been established dedicated to empirical study, among them the international Writing Research Across Borders (WRAB) conferences and the *Journal of Writing Research* (2008–present) (*JoWR*).[1] The National Council of Teachers of English (NCTE) and the affiliated Conference on College Composition and Communication (CCCC) have initiated research grants to support both established and emergent researchers. Not least, as Kevin Roozen and I noted in a review of one hundred years of NCTE journals, there has been an expansion of the "scenes of writing," especially in the last decade, that empirical research has addressed (Roozen and Lunsford 2011, 198).

And yet, as this collection points out, whereas the data-driven aspect of Haswell's definition appears to have been embraced, the aggregable and replicable aspects are still being considered, adopted, and adapted. To be sure, the last decade has seen the development of several large-scale, collective projects. For example, the Digital Archive of Literacy Narratives (DALN), spearheaded by Cynthia Selfe, Ben McCorkle, and Michael Harker, provides rich, openly accessible data sets to be analyzed according to different research agendas (Selfe, McCorkle, and Harker n.d.). The archive also provides a resource to be used in graduate programs to prepare emergent scholars to conduct their own studies. Likewise, the Research Exchange Index (REx, organized by Jenn Fishman and Joan Mullin, with many contributors) allows researchers to discover studies in progress, to connect with scholars with similar interests, and to examine the methods being employed (Fishman and Mullin 2006–present). Other projects have taken advantage of existing infrastructures that provide comparable data sets. For instance, Paul Anderson et al. (2008) established the Consortium for the Study of Writing in College, which developed supplemental, writing-specific questions institutions may elect to include in the National Survey of Student Engagement (NSSE).

Projects such as these are supporting the trend of RAD work, especially in terms of communal data collection. However, the replication of studies remains sporadic, and rare are the analyses that aggregate processed data, not just raw data sets. As a result, when writing specialists find themselves needing empirical evidence to build persuasive arguments for certain audiences—for example, arguing to upper administrators about the measurable impacts of class size—the discipline often lacks definitive reports to support its official statements. Despite movements toward RAD research, there appears to have been some delay, a residual reluctance if not an active resistance, in fully embracing it.

Why might this reluctance linger? This collection's impact lies in the dual nature of its answers, both pragmatic and theoretical. Pragmatically speaking, the contributors identify throughout several reasons writing studies has had an on-again, off-again relationship with empirical research, reasons ranging from the historical to the institutional to the personal. Historically, in the United States, writing studies has been housed within English departments. Scholars within these departments frequently have been critical of empiricism in general, and replication and aggregation in particular. Intermittently, English departments have expunged RAD-oriented research in favor of more interpretive approaches. Witness, for example, the disappearance of empirical linguistics research from NCTE journals throughout the 1950s and 1960s as linguistics departments separated from English departments to establish their own research domains (Roozen and Lunsford 2011, 196–97). Similarly, empirical research on business and professional writing has been shunted to separate journals, and writing programs appear to be migrating to stand-alone units. As a stand-alone field now recognized by the National Research Council as an "emerging discipline" and by the federal Classification of Instructional Programs as a category (Phelps and Ackerman 2010), rhetoric and composition/writing studies is still in the process of consolidating its institutional resources and infrastructures for designing and carrying out empirical research. The institutional resource most lacking is funding. The monies typically allocated for single-authored, interpretive research are inadequate for extensive and/or long-term empirical studies, and the contributors to this collection have been wise in finding ways to sustain their projects. Not least, from a personal perspective, researchers transitioning from more interpretive research traditions must remake themselves to adopt RAD methods. They also must question whether their RAD efforts will be rewarded in an institutional home that traditionally has valued originality. As difficult as these pragmatic issues can be, however, they do not entirely account for relative lack of replication and aggregation in writing studies.

Theoretically speaking, the editors respond by proposing a new concept, transcontextual research, or a commitment not just to duplicate methods when replicating them but also to expand and reflect on them. In proposing this concept, I argue, the editors address a fundamental issue at play when researchers hesitate over replication and aggregation: a concern that to conduct empirical work, especially to create measures and codes, is also to create reifications. For my purposes, a *reification* is a word or image or other semiotic sign treated as a given across contexts without pausing to examine the processes by which it has achieved a privileged status as, for instance, a code for other texts. Bruno Latour (1999, see chapter 2, esp. 58–64) illustrates this process when he discusses a case in which scientists compare soil samples to a manual of color codes (the Munsell codes) that provides the labels they should use in describing and assessing those samples. As Latour explains, the color manual is considered a given across different contexts, whether paintings or physical landscapes. None of the scientists in his study question it, consider the processes by which it was first developed, or mention in their final record—a diagram using the color reference numbers—the conversations or debates they have in matching the samples with the provided codes in the manual. In a word, all of these processes are black-boxed.

Ironically, as the editors of this collection suggest in the introduction, black-boxing also has been applied to the words replication and aggregation themselves. What, exactly, does it mean to replicate a study and to aggregate data? Writing researchers have yet to agree. In a cognate field, applied linguistics, Congjun Mu and Paul Kei Matsuda report that although researchers have called for the replication of studies, participants in their survey favor "approximate replication," or the duplication of studies with nonessential differences (Mu and Matsuda 2016). What participants understand as nonessential, however, is open to interpretation. Even in the physical sciences, *replication* and *aggregation* are not simple to define. Jutta Schickore (2011), for example, identifies at least seven forms replication might take. That said, the problem of black-boxing becomes even more acute when we consider the specific processes of constructing measures and codes, as writing researchers by training have a particular sensitivity to the power of using semiotic signs to create labels.

To code means to operationalize words, images, punctuation, and other semiotic signs. Because the everyday definitions of words (to focus on one example) are not precise enough to serve as analytical tools, the codes must be carefully constructed and applied. In RAD research, certain thematic words become operationalized when precise, technical definitions and examples are provided to determine whether or not certain bits of data can be counted as evidence of that theme. In quantitative research (e.g., in surveys), the codified words often appear in the questionnaire's prompts and/or in the multiple-choice options respondents can choose among. In qualitative research, the trend has been to employ grounded-theory techniques to identify emergent themes that then become the mechanisms for analysis. In addition, researchers define the exclusions, or bits of data that may seem close to, but do not precisely fit, the criteria defined by the code. Recognizing that these codified criteria may still contain ambiguities for researchers, there are also research methods for operationalizing the coders: by norming, by discussing responses to increase interrater reliability, and by performing statistical analyses (e.g., Cohen's kappa) to measure that reliability. To operationalize words, then, is to perform a number of activities through which choices and assumptions become entrenched within codes and through which researchers learn to be disciplined.

Nevertheless, these processes tend to receive scant attention within a final report; instead, codes may take on a life of their own, disconnected from the processes that first informed them. For instance, when I reviewed the literature of empirical studies that employed the Toulmin model of argumentation (Lunsford 2002), I found that researchers were taking up his terms (or equivalents) as code words as if they were unequivocally understood across different writing contexts. Some of these studies, for example, assessed student writing according to whether the students' texts contained claims, data (evidence), warrants, rebuttals, and so on. Without difficulty, it seems, researchers could identify which bits of text should be tagged according to Toulmin's terms—and researchers attempting to use computers to parse language were particularly inclined to treat the model as offering unequivocal categories. However, as shown by a close analysis of classroom conversations, a community must engage in complex negotiations to first identify a particular utterance as a claim and then to maintain it as such. Such agreement among a community is often temporary, yet empirical studies have treated Toulmin's terms as immutable and universally applicable.

Fundamentally, I argue, writing researchers resist this tendency toward reifying language even as we are drawn to reifications, especially as we consider replicating studies and aggregating data. Our discipline has given us several warnings against such moves. First, the sociocultural turn has oriented researchers toward language use within specific contexts. We are wary of seeing bits of language as frozen capsules of meaning and of seeing writing conventions as universal. To give one example, Chris Anson et al. (2012) argue strenuously against applying the same generic rubric to writing samples from across a campus, maintaining that assessments should be sensitive to disciplinary conventions. Second, writing scholars are well aware that assumptions black-boxed and codified within category names are never neutral, as researchers of databases and indexes (Bowker and Star 1999) and metaphors (Lakoff 1987) have long and frequently argued. Unfortunately, users may not be alert to the implications categories contain or to the processes by which they achieve and ascribe status. Third, the terms from the Toulmin model of argumentation may appear to be harmless, but I argue that they, and other codes, are not. As feminist studies, critical race theory, and queer theory, among many other perspectives, have all argued, the unquestioned assumptions embedded within codes can have dire consequences for people and artifacts so labeled. To label is to exert power, and the unexamined use of words sustains power regimes.

This larger concern—that empirical methods will be taken out of context and applied in harmful ways—has long been a component of the discipline's reluctance to embrace empirical work. For example, Kevin Roozen and I examined an essay published in 1953 in *College English* that satirized the Flesch readability formula (Roozen and Lunsford 2011, 197). The formula parses a text according to sentence length and word length, and it assigns texts to different levels according to their measured ease of reading. Flesch originally developed the formula for professional writing. In the satire, the formula is humorously applied to literary classics such as a *Paradise Lost, The Legend of Sleepy Hollow,* and work by Boethius with the joke being that of the three, *The Legend* is rated as the most difficult to read. The satire focuses on the absurdity of reducing literary works to raw measurements, with the implication that English departments ought to have nothing to do with such empirical nonsense. Without defending the Flesch readability measures, writing researchers today might point out that the knee-jerk, *reductio ad absurdum* satire rests on misappropriating a method designed for one context to another. However, it is also worth noting the extent to which often unreflexive appropriations of the Flesch measures continue today. They form the basis of the readability measures embedded in word processors, for example, and the Internet is littered with sites that promise to improve writing by providing authors with their texts' Flesch-Kincaid scores (an adaptation that indicates reading difficulty according to grade levels in US schools). In these contexts, the Flesch formula has become an end unto itself, a reification that has replaced other considerations of what constitutes good writing.

Whether they are considered knee-jerk or well founded, these objections to reifications must be addressed if writing researchers are to become more comfortable with all aspects of RAD research. Otherwise, researchers, especially in the United States, will continue to be caught in an institutional and historical binary between the interpretive humanities and not the sciences but scientism. How many writing scholars conducting empirical research, I wonder, have been told they were selling out to positivistic research traditions? To avoid that binary, we need to develop techniques and habits for articulating our methods that highlight our awareness, as researchers, of the nuances and power of operationalized language.

The transcontextual approach proposed and examined in this collection provides an answer by building a bridge between empirical research and other theoretical discussions in writing studies. In particular, it aligns RAD research with North American genre theory. Instead of treating methods and codes as universal givens to be applied across contexts, it treats them, in Catherine Schryer's (1993) phrase describing genres, as "stabilized for now." A skeptic might reply that empirical methods, including codes, are temporary constructions in any case; however, one point of the transcontextual approach is to *emphasize* that empirical methods are operationalized to do specific work under specific, if potentially recurring, circumstances. Given the histories that can be traced in our research literature, as I found by tracking the uptake of the Toulmin model as a set of codes to parse arguments, researchers need this explicit reminder. In short, the transcontextual approach highlights the otherwise black-boxed, hidden processes—and the rhetorical work—we perform to treat methods and codes as stabilized for now, as well as to apply them to new situations.

Specifying this work of stabilization, adaption, and reflection requires the space an edited collection such as this one provides. Although Peter Smagorinsky (2008) has claimed that the methods section of a social science article articulates the epistemological center for a study, descriptions of methods are often the first sections to be cut to meet page limits. Nor do most journals in writing studies, especially those initially based in print culture, offer other opportunities to expand on the methods reported on in an article. Digital journals such as *Kairos* (1996–present) and *Enculturation* (1997–present) do allow more space for reflection. Even so, such an expanded reflection on methods is not routinely included as part of their empirical webtexts. In contrast, publishers of science and social science journals in the last decade have offered authors an online space reserved for expanded appendices associated with an article, sites known as *supplemental folders*. In these supplemental folders, readers may find commentary on the methods employed in the study, including alternatives that were tried and speculations about further applications for them. One of the implications of this collection is that researchers in writing studies must continue building the information architectures to support our reflective values in RAD research.

Those values include not only reflecting on methods but also better articulating the tacit processes by which researchers are disciplined. Even the supplemental folders in science journals fail to reflect explicitly on the personnel who conduct the studies, their movements among different projects, and their direct influences on each other. In our discipline, this invisible college has been made more transparent with the introduction of the Writing Studies Tree, which tracks the genealogies of academic advisors and their students (Miller, Licastro, Perl, et al. 2012–present). The current collection takes a further step by illustrating in detail how researchers develop new projects from the established projects and personnel that influenced them.

Thus, much is to be learned from this collection, and I urge readers to take the title, *Points of Departure*, seriously. The collection serves as a starting point for future RAD research by discussing projects currently underway in the field, projects that may provide inspiration. More important, the collection models how writing studies researchers may avoid reifying their methods and codes, and thus it models how to forestall the historical fear and distrust of empirical work in a discipline that values the power of language. May it inform and forward the next generation of collective research projects in our field.

Note
1. Both supported by the International Society for the Advancement of Writing Research, http://www.isawr.org.

References

Anderson, Paul, Chris Anson, Chuck Paine, and Bob Gonyea. 2008. "Partnership for the Study of Writing in College." Consortium for the Study of Writing in College. http://comppile.org/wpa+nsse/.

Anson, Chris, Deanna Dannels, Pamela Flash, and Amy Housley Gaffney. 2012. "Big Rubrics and Weird Genres: The Futility of Using Generic Assessment Tools across Diverse Instructional Contexts." *Journal of Writing Assessment* 5 (1). http://www.journalofwritingassessment.org/article.php?article=57.

Bowker, Geoffrey C., and Susan Leigh Star. 1999. *Sorting Things Out: Classification and Its Consequences.* Cambridge, MA: MIT Press.

Enculturation: A Journal of Rhetoric, Writing, and Culture. 1997–present. http://enculturation.net.

Fishman, Jennifer, and Joan Mullin. 2006–present. *REx: Research Exchange Index.* http://researchexchange.colostate.edu/.

Haswell, Richard H. 2005. "NCTE/CCCC's Recent War on Scholarship." *Written Communication* 22 (2): 198–223. http://dx.doi.org/10.1177/0741088305275367.

Journal of Writing Research. 2008–present. http://www.jowr.org/.

Kairos: A Journal of Rhetoric, Technology, and Pedagogy. 1996–present. http://kairos.technorhetoric.net.

Lakoff, George. 1987. *Women, Fire, and Dangerous Things: What Categories Reveal about the Mind.* Chicago, IL: University of Chicago Press. http://dx.doi.org/10.7208/chicago/9780226471013.001.0001.

Latour, Bruno. 1999. *Pandora's Hope: Essays on the Reality of Science Studies.* Cambridge, MA: Harvard University Press.

Lunsford, Karen J. 2002. "Contextualizing Toulmin's Model in the Writing Classroom: A Case Study." *Written Communication* 19 (1): 109–74. http://dx.doi.org/10.1177/0741088302019001005.

Miller, Ben, et al. 2012–present. *Writing Studies Tree.* http://writingstudiestree.org/live/.

Mu, Congjun, and Paul Kei Matsuda. 2016. "Replication in L2 Writing Research: *Journal of Second Language Writing* Authors' Perceptions." *TESOL Quarterly* 50 (1): 201–19. http://dx.doi.org/10.1002/tesq.284.

Phelps, Louise Wetherbee, and John M. Ackerman. 2010. "Making the Case for Disciplinarity in Rhetoric, Composition, and Writing Studies: The Visibility Project." *College Composition and Communication* 62 (1): 180–215.

Roozen, Kevin, and Karen J. Lunsford. 2011. "'One Story of Many to Be Told': Following Empirical Studies of College and Adult Writing through One Hundred Years of NCTE Journals." *RTE: Research in the Teaching of English* 46 (2): 193–209.

Schickore, Jutta. 2011. "What Does History Matter to the Philosophy of Science? The Concept of Replication and the Methodology of Experiments." *Journal of the Philosophy of History* 5 (3): 513–32. http://dx.doi.org/10.1163/187226311X599934.

Schryer, Catherine F. 1993. "Records as Genre." *Written Communication* 10 (2): 200–34. http://dx.doi.org/10.1177/0741088393010002003.

Selfe, Cynthia L., Ben McCorkle, and Michael Harker. n.d. DALN: Digital Archive of Literacy Narratives. Accessed June 29, 2016. http://daln.osu.edu/.

Smagorinsky, Peter. 2008. "The Method Section as Conceptual Epicenter in Constructing Social Science Research Reports." *Written Communication* 25 (3): 389–411. http://dx.doi.org/10.1177/0741088308317815.

ACKNOWLEDGMENTS

A generous community of researchers helped this collection emerge as a publication. The initial idea bubbled up in conversations with Rebecca Moore Howard and Kelly Kinney as we discussed the fascinating research Citation Project contributors were doing at their institutions and reporting on at national conferences. Those who participated in the sixteen-campus study were working hard in response to the initial data; many were acquiring new methodological skills and learning valuable lessons about both writing studies research methods and ways to support student source use in the process. Additional scholars were also drawing on and in some cases replicating the research. After hearing about such work at a CCCC convention we realized it was time to collect it to share with a larger audience. Interest in The Citation Project often went beyond findings to the research methods that produced them, so we determined to place an equal emphasis on developing, revising, and replicating research and solicited chapters from contributors who were willing to share their research process in addition to its product. We brought our manuscript to Michael Spooner, who, not surprisingly, made the project vastly better and supported us with the right questions and confidence in the project.

The book would not be in your hands if it were not for the tireless work of the team at Utah State University Press, particularly Michael Spooner, aided by Kami Day, Laura Furney, Kylie Haggen, Daniel Pratt, Charlotte Steinhardt, and Beth Svinarich, who collectively brought this collection to fruition. The scholars included in this collection are the heart of the matter and we are indebted to their willingness to share their research processes and to earnestly reconsider our work together. Like us, they are grateful to friends and colleagues who read drafts and provided feedback as the chapters developed. Rebecca Moore Howard, Louise Wetherbee Phelps, and Norbert Elliot provided generous responses to—and support of—this collection.

Our title, "Points of Departure," is taken from Charles Cooper and Lee Odell's *Research on Composing: Points of Departure and Evaluating*

Writing as a conscious recognition that research in our young field stands on the shoulders of and builds on the work of others, some of whom are no longer with us. We are all indebted to the scholars of writing studies broadly defined who developed the research questions, methods, and responses that have shaped our field. The Citation Project was our jumping off point for this collection and, as we indicate in chapter 1, would not exist in its current form without the generosity of time and intellectual energy of many people. We are grateful to them all, and to Trish's colleagues at Santa Clara University and Sandra's at Drew University. In addition, Trish thanks Tamika Carey, Tanya Rodrigue, Laurie Gries, Laura Davies, Julia Voss, Sreela Sarkar, Margaret Lucero, and, most importantly, Claudia Serviss for their intellectual energy and love; Sandra is grateful for Walter Jacobsohn's wise feedback and support as we editor`s skyped and emailed our way through vacations, sabbaticals, and sunny weekends.

POINTS OF DEPARTURE

Introduction

THE RISE OF RAD RESEARCH METHODS FOR WRITING STUDIES
Transcontextual Ways Forward

Tricia Serviss

Today's research in composition, taken as a whole, may be compared to chemical research as it emerged from the period of alchemy: some terms are being defined usefully, a number of procedures are being refined, but the field as a whole is laced with dreams, prejudices, and makeshift operations. Not enough investigators are really informing themselves about the procedures and results of previous research before embarking on their own. Too few of them conduct pilot experiments and validate their measuring instruments before undertaking an investigation. Too many seem to be bent more on obtaining an advanced degree or another publication than on making a genuine contribution to knowledge. . . . And far too few of those who have conducted an initial piece of research follow it with further exploration or replicate the investigations of others. Composition research, then, is not highly developed. If researchers wish to give it strength and depth, they must reexamine critically the structure and techniques of their studies.
       —Richard Braddock, Richard Lloyd-Jones, and
       Lowell Schoer, *Research in Written Composition*, 1963

Braddock et al. proceeded by summarizing existing research and by identifying five exemplary comparison-group research studies. By contrast, contributors to this volume review very little research except insofar as it helps explain the new lines of inquiry being developed in their chapters. Further, when authors in this volume describe anticipated or ongoing research studies, they are not concerned with illustrating conventional methodologies. Rather, their intent is to suggest what seem like useful ways we might begin to lift ourselves out of our ignorance.
       —Charles R. Cooper and Lee Odell, *Research on
       Composing: Points of Departure*, 1978

DOI: 10.7330/9781607326250.c000b

INTRODUCTION: REPLICATION, TRANSPARENCY, AND THE SEARCH FOR METHOD

Investment in data-driven research and the writing-education reforms it might allow dominated conversations about research methods and methodology in the first decade of the twenty-first century. Chris Anson argued at the Council of Writing Program Administrators 2006 conference, and in print two years later (Anson 2008), that the field of writing studies needed to attend to data-driven research if we hoped to reach audiences beyond ourselves, referencing what Rich Haswell (2005) calls "RAD," or "replicable, aggregable, data-driven research." In addition to speaking to those outside the discipline, such data also challenges some of our own assumptions about student writing, expanding theories about how writing works and pushing us to find better pedagogies and therefore productive relationships with our students. Data-driven research, as Haswell (2005), Charles Bazerman (2008), and others have demonstrated, can move our discipline in more effective and informed directions, but for too long we neglected such research, to our detriment, as Haswell (2005) and Anson (2006) contend. Yet what seems apparent now is that these conversations also exposed a further desire to reprioritize research methods themselves; calls for data-driven research (what we are generally calling *RAD research* in this collection) are also calls to fortify our methodological practices so different genres of research become plausible options for scholars in our field.

The interest in coding methods and RAD research at recent conferences, most notably the Conference on College Composition and Communication (CCCC), suggests a significant ongoing shift in writing studies research. We are turning quite explicitly toward research methods themselves as crucial sites of inquiry and as acquisitions necessary for the field's health and expansion. Too much research still focuses exclusively on the originality of the research site and on the results, with only a brief discussion of research methods and little critical reflection about them. This kind of imbalance makes it difficult to replicate existing studies, both because the methods are not sufficiently clear (as Karen Lunsford [2013] observed) and because our field still does not value replication as much as originality, a predicament that leaves us where Richard Braddock, Richard Lloyd-Jones, and Lowell Schoer found us in 1963. It is, of course, important that innovative research be defined by the originality of its site and the uniqueness of its approach; however, this collection argues that the design, transparency, and potential expansion of the research via presentation of methods is equally important. The call to replicate research in writing studies is most fruitfully a call to develop our research findings together rather than striving to do alone what none have done before.

Emerging graduate student-scholars and experienced researchers in writing studies alike are hungry for greater transparency and accessibility to research methods so they may replicate and directly respond to other research; too often what we find is a discussion of methods that describes what was done but is not detailed enough to allow replication or adaptation of that method by other researchers. This lack of detail occurs with good reason, perhaps, because, too often, to present methods—including the initial failures and adjustments that mark the development of pilot studies—is to invite critique rather than the refinement and revision Braddock, Lloyd-Jones, and Schoer (1963) present as part of the process healthy research communities engage in together. At the same time, the need for "original" research as part of one's professional credentialing causes many to fear (often correctly) that replication of other research will be perceived as less important work. In the field of writing studies, questions have too often been perceived as resolved once one study has been published, however provisional the results. But the calls to research arms issued by Anson, Haswell, and others throughout our disciplinary history are too important to ignore. Those calls have propelled us to develop a collection of chapters that describe research mostly in the form of the pilot as Braddock, Lloyd-Jones, and Schoer (1963) imagine it. The authors in this collection make their methods visible to allow for adjustments; they present and discuss them in detail to encourage refinement and reproduction.

Points of Departure works to capture *how* research happens in particular instances, concretizing processes of research design and the pivotal role of the pilot study by focusing on research methods—practices, mechanisms, strategies, artifacts, lessons learned—rather than solely highlighting research findings. In this way, the collection hopes to challenge and inspire readers to create the kinds of research called for by Anson (2006), Haswell (2005), Bazerman (2008), and Lunsford (2013). The collection also calls on readers to explore research methods and build on the work of other important edited collections in this conversation including those by Cooper and Odell (1978), Lauer and Asher (1988), Kirsch and Sullivan (1992), Smith (1999), Smagorinsky (2006), McKee and DeVoss (2007), Kirsch and Rohan (2008), Ramsey et al. (2010), Schell and Rawson (2010), Nickoson and Sheridan (2012), and Powell and Takayoshi (2012). This collection issues these challenges not from the standpoint of sanitized final research but from within what Adam Banks (2015) calls the "funkiness" of evolving research methods.

The chapters in this collection also present findings, in most cases provisional results at the end of a pilot project. Like the research methods, the findings are also in process, subject to revision and reproduction over time. Each chapter in *Points of Departure* presents initial research using a different method, but all are concerned in some way with the same question: how can we understand and better teach source-based writing? Many, but not all, of the research projects presented are derived from, complementary to, or expand on the work of the Citation Project (see chapter 1). But in addition to their originality, the chapters present their research so other projects may build on or from it. Authors featured in *Points of Departure* represent their research methods as transparently as possible, describing how the methods worked in practice. Contributors also imagine how such initial pilot studies might be revised and advanced into more substantial, more robust research projects in the future. Researchers in this collection work to expose the processes of research design and development rather bravely, inviting readers into the recursive worlds researchers must navigate as they establish research projects sound enough to extend beyond initial iterations.

It is our hope that presenting methods and findings in this way will

1. inspire a more nuanced conceptualization of research *as a process* that can develop only with methodological transparency; a process that depends on pilot studies, reflection and revision of method; and one that ideally leads to expanded transcontextual studies building on and strengthening initial studies;

2. generate discussion about how we talk about research methods in writing studies, making such conversation more holistic—including the failures and revisions—and more productive, offering points of departure for richer understandings of research and refined research methods;

3. invite readers to use these preliminary studies to deepen our understandings of student literacies, launching additional and expanded research projects that reproduce key aspects of these local studies transcontextually based on revised methods where necessary.

A BRIEF HISTORY OF METHOD IN WRITING STUDIES
Recurrent Calls to Methodological Transparency

Calls to conduct particular kinds of empirical research are not new or novel in writing studies but rather a kind of recursive tension that cycles through our disciplinary consciousness with regularity. The development of the modern field of writing and rhetorical studies can be understood as a tale of methodological evolution. Founding documents—reports on the first Conference on College Composition and Communication (CCCC), the first issues of *College Composition and Communication* (*CCC*), and research surveys like Braddock, Lloyd-Jones, and Schoer's (1963) *Research in Written Composition* and Cooper and Odell's (1978) *Research on Composing: Points of Departure*—recount worries about our formation as a research community. Debates about research methods are central to these worries. The earliest *CCC* articles (Gerber 1950; Wells 1950) describe efforts to aggregate "known" research and best teaching practices in surveys and what Gerber calls "friendly correspondence" across institutions (Gerber 1950, 12). The blooming infrastructure of CCCC in particular is reportedly driven by a desire to compile existing and facilitate further research all at once. Research methods are quite secondary to the accumulation of knowledge itself in these earliest disciplinary moments. Throughout the 1950s, *CCC* articles embody a perpetual call to gather and document common, accepted knowledge, to create an organization to regulate and distribute such knowledge and therefore a discipline.

By the 1960s, *CCC* authors refine this stance toward research, moving from calls to aggregate existing knowledge toward the articulation of particular research agendas and questions. Robert Wright (1960) reports research prompts deemed "most pressing" by a CCCC subcommittee on research in composition, calling on *CCC* to begin publishing articles that present "research" in both design and findings as well as articles focused on pedagogical practices. Wright's call to prioritize research-driven discourse about writing typifies the first two decades of *CCC* articles, yet divergent voices also challenged this disciplinary trajectory. Taylor Culbert (1961) cautions compositionists about such research agendas, arguing that they—we—are ill prepared to conduct research of the kind being proposed. Compositionists, Culbert argues, are humanists who ought to stick to humanistic inquiry. In the paradigm generated by cross talk in these early *CCC* issues, authors argue that we don't have training in scientific methods and so ought to embrace humanistic inquiry. Yet humanistic inquiry is not attached to any particular research methods; as a result, a number of gaps have opened between research and disciplinary knowledge, research and resulting best practices, and research findings and research methods. What we know as a disciplinary community does not rest in clear relationship to research traditions or methods. This invisibility of research traditions and methods became an important affordance for the field's development in many ways, encouraging scholars to discover research traditions best suited for their particular questions. The invisibility of research design and methods also, however, weakened—and continues to weaken—the coherence and therefore integrity of writing and rhetorical studies.

The roots of such angst about research methodologies and disciplinary identity are deep, and the field repeatedly addresses this weakness. The publication of *Research in Written Composition* in 1963 was the culmination of the work of the CCCC's Committee on the State of Knowledge about Composition, promising a cache of research dealing with "actual writing" and using "scientific method" to control experimentation and textual analysis. Braddock, Lloyd-Jones, and Schoer disclose their own research methods (they start with 1,000 bibliographic citations and narrow it down to the 485 "best scientific" composition studies, half of which are unpublished) and in so doing reveal their own attitudes; they prioritize what they deem to be empirical research even while suspicious of it. The report is crucially important in two ways. First, it moves conversations from compilation of research to *generation* of research in writing studies; second, it calls on the field to return to methodological training, emphasizing the utility of designing pilot studies that are refined, through peer review, into more substantial studies. *Research in Written Composition* is often noted as a research charter for the discipline as it distinguishes particular *sites* of study for consideration; Braddock, Lloyd-Jones, and Schoer's calls to methodological training are less celebrated. In fact, Braddock, Lloyd-Jones, and Schoer's (1963) research report highlights two pressing claims that *Points of Departure* contends are still ongoing concerns:

1. Researchers are not methodologically prepared to undertake pressing research questions in predictable ways.
2. Researchers are not collectively invested in arriving at transcontextual findings that might be accumulated and meaningfully connected to other research on a broad scale.

Yet the move from compilation of knowledge toward investigation and systematic generation of new, sound research with transparent research methods launched from the report. And it motivates this collection.

Conceptualizations of research practices, methods, and methodologies are greatly altered by the rise of varied research itself in writing studies scholarship of the 1970s and 1980s. Charles Cooper and Lee Odell's 1978 *Research on Composing: Points of Departure* is a second major compilation of research "knowledges" in writing and rhetorical studies. Cooper and Odell's collection brings together contemporaneous research findings just as Braddock, Lloyd-Jones, and Schoer's did in 1963; Cooper and Odell argue in their introduction that research must come to be treated as explicitly tentative (xiv). The book looks forward to the invention of new inquiry (in place of empirical research), new questions, and new procedures to replace a simple cataloguing of what we already know. Cooper and Odell (1978) refocus Braddock, Lloyd-Jones, and Schoer's (1963) dreams of disciplinary knowledge, embodied in that historic moment by inquiry-based works of Jane Emig (1982), Sondra Perl (1980), and Mina Shaughnessy (1979).

By the time histories of our field emerged in the late 1980s (Berlin 1987; North 1987), the work of Emig, Perl, and Shaughnessy represented a movement toward inquiry-driven empirical research within writing studies. These early histories work toward solidifying research practices and debates into a few basic binary oppositions, grouping the individual work of scholars like Emig, Perl, and Shaughnessy together into, in North's telling, an era of "postivistic certainty" (North 1987, 204) and, in Berlin's history, an era of research defined by a scholar's ideological stance. The era between 1960 and 1975 is therefore explained in our disciplinary histories as a time of either methodological madness that, North claims, made us disciplinarily fragile with our eight isolated methodological communities, or ideologically problematic via Berlin's description of various rhetorical influences on our research questions, methods, designs, and findings, most famously transactional rhetorics.

The founding of the Research Network Forum (RNF) as an additional preconference event at CCCC in 1988 emerged as a potential remedy for the fracturing effects of such divergent research communities within writing studies. In his statement upon the founding of RNF, Bazerman (1989) suggests that researchers are isolated from one another largely through ideological differences rather than methodological ones; the solution implied is the transparent sharing of research practices, problems, and solutions through activities like the RNF itself. Geisler and Jarratt (1989) point out RNF's purpose as discouraging silencing "evaluations" of one another's scholarship in favor of learning about *how* we work as researchers. While not named explicitly, it seems that RNF was imagined as a place to encourage research transparency, a place to share methods and refine research projects together. RNF was charted to host these conversations, highlighting points of intersection of these communities related to our ultimate shared purposes of student empowerment, the pairing of research and pedagogical practice, and community formation among compositions (Geisler and Jarratt 1989, 291).

The field journeyed on from those founding RNF moments of research-method transparency and debate. The same 1988 CCCC conference also showcased the first Octalog, a panel made of rhetorical historians declaring methodological positions as ideological expressions (Octalog 1988). Panelists insisted upon the dialectic nature of historical research (Berlin 1987) just as they called for the recovery of lost voices (Jarratt in Octalog 1988). These official institutional efforts captured a movement in our disciplinary conversations about research that highlighted methodology and perhaps unintentionally dwarfed consideration of methods and practices. Yet at the same time, researchers like Gail Hawisher (1989) took inventory of ongoing research projects and made recommendations that continue to circulate in the field today. Hawisher (1989) challenged us to build new research in relationship to previous studies, plan for several studies to pursue research questions, and take a longitudinal approach to our research. These calls and efforts culminated in the methodologically driven debates about research as ideological framework that dominated the field in the 1990s.

Throughout the 1990s, articles in composition journals contested the role of empiricism (Charney 1996; 1997) and paid renewed attention to expanding the sites of our research (Cintron 1998; Gere 1994). Debates about our research identity throughout this era orbited around conversations about methodological stances rather than the practices of our methods (Berkenkotter 1991). Yet Rose and Weiser's 1999 *The Writing Program Administrator as Researcher* includes chapters focused primarily upon the methods and processes required to be successful writing program administrators (see Harris; Martin; Liggett; Weiser; Rose; Anson and Brown; Peeples; and Phelps in their collection), arguing that the methods and skills of research are necessary for writing programs to thrive and even continue to exist. *Composing Research: A Contextualist Paradigm for Rhetoric and Composition* (Johanek 2000) articulates worries about the future of writing and rhetorical studies if we do not intervene more actively in the teaching of our research to new scholars—and the methodological training of those new scholars. Most significantly for the efforts of this collection, Cindy Johanek calls for a shift in our methodological discussions, suggesting that "instead of arguing . . . about *which* research method or *which* epistemological stance is sensitive to context, we must ask instead: In what context does that sort of argument make sense?" (90). Thus, conversations about *what*, *how*, and *where* in writing studies research opened expansive thinking about these modes and processes of research as the twentieth century ended (see also Barton 2000; Cushman 1999; Flinders and Eisner 1994; Kirsch 1992; Newkirk 1991).

At the start of the twenty-first century, these conversations shifted, prompted by changes in the North American academy. Calls to renew the rigor of peer review in scholarly journals across disciplines, and for greater explication of writing studies' relationship to English studies and other humanities, proliferated. By the latter half of that first decade, these conversations bloomed to include discussions of research sites in an evolving educational landscape (Smagorinsky 2006), a globalizing world (Hesford 2006), and digital networks (McKee and DeVoss 2007) and collided with what *Points of Departure* contends is an explicit, strategic return to research methods (Anson 2008; Bazerman 2008; Haswell 2005; Howard 2014; Lunsford 2013). This wave swelled into our current decade as conference workshops, panels, collections, and articles focused on method abounded (Fleckenstein et al. 2008; Howard 2014; Mackiewicz et al. 2014; Mueller 2012; Nickoson and Sheridan 2012; Powell and Takayoshi 2012; Ramsey et al. 2010; Royster and Kirsch 2012; Schell and Rawson 2010; Serviss and Jamieson 2014; and many others). These conversations invigorated discussions of method, providing additional ways to think about our research sites, our research questions, our analyses of our research, and efforts to bring coherence to the expanse of writing studies.

At the same moment the discipline was reawakening to the possibilities of replicable and reproducible (RAD) research in writing studies, two different writing-research handbooks emerged—most notably Charles Bazerman's (2008) *Handbook of Research on Writing* and Charles MacArthur, Steve Graham, and Jill Fitzgerald's (2006) *Handbook of Writing Research*. Both texts are provocative guides to writing research past and future, compiling research traditions through categorization of research sites (historically in the classroom, in the workplace, etc.) and depicting methodological traditions through examples of research premised upon those methodological traditions. MacArthur, Graham, and Fitzgerald's 2006 *Handbook* brings together experts from across categories including writing assessment, histories of writing, and the cognitive development of child writers. Their collection offers an extremely useful overview of research in those areas, particularly for new researchers. Published two years later, *Handbook of Research on Writing* (Bazerman 2008) pursues a similar purpose; it is also organized according to different areas of inquiry (writing in society, writing in school, etc.). These research collections are both crucially important in that they collect research about writing, just as Braddock, Lloyd-Jones, and Schoer attempted to do with *Research in Written Composition* in 1963. What all these endeavors are missing, however, is the kind of in-depth transparency of methods necessary for the development of international and interdisciplinary writing studies RAD research. While the handbooks offer wonderful summaries of research projects and their findings, what the collections aren't purposed to do is make that research—the activities, methods, and processes of research—transparent or reproducible.

These handbooks highlight the relationships between disciplinary knowledge and our historically opaque research methods. They celebrate research findings and data analysis across different research sites, helping research communities recognize coherence across sites of research and design research projects and questions as intentionally *transcontextual*.[1] The handbooks are *an invitation* to join ongoing research conversations more than a methodological guide instrumental in the development of RAD research in writing studies. These handbooks illustrate the great potential for the refinement and innovative development of research methods that allow for the proliferation of RAD research projects in writing studies. Presenting research methods transparently along with findings helps researchers not only reproduce research and test theories about how writing works but also to connect research sites, questions, and projects more meaningfully, advancing what and how we think about writing.

Primed for conversations about research methods and methodologies across different research traditions, numerous crucially important books followed (see Kirsch and Rohan's 2008 *Beyond the Archives: Research as a Lived Process*; McKee and DeVoss's 2007 *Digital Writing Research: Technologies, Methodologies, and Ethical Issues*; McKee and Porter's 2009 *The Ethics of Internet Research: A Rhetorical, Case-Based Process*; Ramsey et al.'s 2010 *Working in the Archives: Practical Research Methods for Rhetoric and Composition*). Eileen Schell and K. J. Rawson's 2010 *Rhetorica in Motion* captures the *processes* of feminist research as the development and use of methodologies and methods. Katrina Powell and Pamela Takayoshi's 2012 *Practicing Research in Writing Studies* offers what they call "theories of research," presenting methodological approaches such as grounded theory as well as powerful reflections about the pressing issues of research, particularly qualitative research. Lee Nickoson and Mary Sheridan's 2012 *Writing Studies in Practice: Methods and Methodologies* makes a tremendous contribution to this ongoing conversation, pursuing fundamental, emerging questions about what we still want to discover about writing and multiple promising ways forward. This proliferation suggests we are committed to fortifying our methods and methodological training as a discipline. *Points of Departure* celebrates and contributes to this commitment, highlighting that while we acknowledge RAD as one of many useful tools, it involves a significant, promising, and relatively unexplored set of traditions that contributors to this collection explore and expand. Directing our attention to shared and fully transparent research methods within RAD traditions *as well as* attending to our research sites and findings helps us not only to fortify individual research projects' findings (through reproducibility and replication with similar results) but also to refine and innovate additional research tools that afford new transcontextual research projects and understandings.

WAYS FORWARD: TRANSPARENT RESEARCH DESIGN AND METHODS AS POINTS OF DEPARTURE

Research methods and research sites are most compelling when considered together, a sentiment that echoes across nearly every methodological text surveyed above. These conversations suggest a need for research findings that can deepen our understanding across different locations of writing; they also suggest a need for research *methods* that are flexible and applicable across contexts. For writing studies to truly flourish, *Points of Departure* argues, we need research to become more accountable via reproducibility, but we also need research designs that go beyond replication.

One way to achieve this is to work within and across gaps in our research that appear via our seemingly unrelated sites, our disparate research designs, or our unfamiliar methods and tools. By expecting, including, and then prioritizing discussions of research methods, sharing actual research mechanisms alongside findings in our scholarship, we not only allow for potential reproduction of research, we also encourage individual research projects to live beyond their original incarnation and evolve. It is precisely this kind of inclusion and prioritization of research methods, positioned as a crucial part of our pursuit and delivery of scholarship in our presentations and publications such as this collection, that allows for the intentional and strategic expansion of writing studies.

In addition to reporting mature findings, writing studies scholars need ways to report issues of design, methods, and piloting research. We need more than an abstract goal of producing dynamic research that illuminates discrete literate activities if we are to design, pilot, reproduce, refine, and expand meaningful research projects, and we need more explicit direction than research guides or published research findings in isolation can present. It is not sufficient to read the results of a study and be inspired to replicate it. If the research in our field is to continue to evolve, this collection contends, we must develop deeper knowledge of not only our research methods but also of the reiterative research processes that build those methods. Methodological finesse and expert execution must be accompanied by an investment in better understanding, navigating, and sharing our own research processes, opening our research to not only review but, more important, to collaborative refinement. While research findings clearly and dramatically play a role in catalyzing this process, one dynamic way forward is to make the *methods and practices* of writing research as central as the findings reported from the research. Transparent representation and integration of our research methods into our analyses and publication of our findings is important, allowing for potential reproducibility and development. Without such transparency, the expansion and advancement of writing studies will be stunted and staled, a sentiment that echoes across so many of our texts (Braddock, Lloyd-Jones, and Schoer 1963; Cooper and Odell 1978; Lauer and Asher 1988; and more). Such transparency means exploring the struggles and failures that precede completed projects, minimizing the mysterious, unknown spaces between method and findings, the gap containing what Lunsford (2013) calls the "hidden" aspects of research.

As suggested earlier, this still undefined terrain represents one of the main struggles of writing studies as it stretches to expand into transnational, translocal, and transcontextual inquiries: how do researchers learn to navigate the messy spaces between learning about research processes and producing research themselves? There are currently several significant venues that strive to help writing studies researchers move through these questions and work through the complexities, modifications, and false starts that characterize the process of designing and conducting robust research projects. Most notable are the annual Dartmouth Seminar and the annual preconvention Research Network Forum, Qualitative Research Network Forum, and numerous workshops held each year at the CCCC. These meetings of scholars focus upon *how we conduct research*, and as such they allow researchers to share methods, seek out methodological preparation, and receive research-design advice from seasoned researchers. Yet we need even more access and infrastructure as we introduce and bring a vast network of research methods into maturity in writing studies. *Points of Departure* is designed with such infrastructure considerations in mind.

This collection takes the potential of transparent, refined, and potentially reproducible research in writing studies seriously, presenting pilot studies across research sites that study how students use sources, sharing research methods as transparently as possible to invite further development and transcontextual thinking about these individual yet linked projects. In these ways, this collection inserts itself into ongoing conversations focused on research methods as a crucial disciplinary tool, taking up the same challenges issued by the founders of RNF and seeking to respond directly to Braddock, Lloyd-Jones, and Schoer's (1963) direct critique and the many other indirect critiques of research. It responds to the need for ecumenical research about writing, research that expands and values work across contexts, research sites, research communities, and research methodologies. Calls to ecumenical approaches to research, what several scholars call the *little narratives of writing* (Brandt and Clinton 2002; Daniell and Mortensen 2007; Hesford 2006), might even be considered part of the constitution of the interdisciplinary and transnational formation of writing studies as we struggle to include many perspectives, questions, and strategies involved with the infinite questions we ask about writing itself: How do we write? How do we write with sources? How do we write with sources in an information-saturated, digital, networked world? This collection is a response to some of those questions and the little narratives behind them.

THE EMERGENCE OF THIS COLLECTION

Points of Departure emerged as researchers involved in the Citation Project (citationproject.net), a national study of undergraduate student source use, discussed our desire to understand how students engage with source material more deeply (Howard, Serviss, and Rodrigue 2010; Jamieson 2013). Many of the contributors to this collection were involved in initial Citation Project data collection and coding; involvement in the Citation Project led authors to develop research projects and methods that pursued the questions we shared as a research community: How can we best study how students incorporate cited source material? And, how can we go about studying people writing with sources across contexts with different kinds of tools, purposes, and audiences in ways that help us recognize transcontextual significance and meaning? As Sandra and I collected submissions and imagined the collection, we became driven by two particular questions about our research methods and processes.

1. How can we represent and engage with research still in formation within RAD research traditions, reporting provisional findings with the transparency necessary for replication?
2. How do we develop research methods and processes that are simultaneously robust and open for further development and revision as researchers learn more about their data and context?

Points of Departure addresses these big questions. All the chapters contribute to our evolving understandings of source-based writing.

Contributors also took these framing questions seriously, sharing not only their initial findings but also offering up their research methods and mechanisms in accompanying appendices; this collection is organized to invite readers into ongoing research projects in which readers and researchers can explore methods and processes together.

Explicitly focusing on research methods and processes allows us to share, exchange, and expand what and how we know about writing. As contributors share the foundations of their research studies in this collection, often in the form of pilot studies, they operationalize their research methods and designs, a key step in the development of research that we cannot only replicate but that we can also build atop previous research. Transparent operationalization of method traditionally allows research communities to *reproduce* and *replicate* the studies of their peers and therefore understand and explore research findings more fully. This tradition of transparency and reproducibility is a great asset for research communities, allowing teams of researchers to produce related data, compare results, and move from studying situated, single, discrete sites of literate activity to studying practices as situated activities across several sites, becoming what Brandt and Clinton (2002) call "translocal" research. Deeply invested in understanding the situatedness of literacy practices, Brandt and Clinton (2002) "theorize the transcontextulaized and transcontextualizing potentials of literacy—particularly its ability to travel, integrate, and endure" (337), challenging us to think about literacy practices as *more than local* practices. "What appears to be a local event," they write, "can also be a far-flung tendril in a much more elaborate vine" (347). While they use the term *transcontextual* to describe an orientation they want literacy studies scholars to adopt, the idea of transcontextuality itself reverberates loudly (and fittingly) beyond this context. Brandt and Clinton (2002) conclude that "we need . . . more complicated analytical frames—a 'continual progression of inquiry' (Latour 1993, 121) at sites of reading, writing, and print that can follow the threads of networks both into and out of local context and other contexts" (347–48).

Points of Departure is built on this foundation of transcontextuality, applying Brandt and Clinton's argument that practices are always *both local and beyond the local* for RAD research in writing studies. Our research projects, designed and implemented within a local site and its context, must adopt Bruno Latour's "continual progression of inquiry" that *is* a transcontextual research orientation. If transcontextual literacies are literacies simultaneously local and networked (making them translocal), so transcontextual writing studies research is local and networked at the same time. In other words, if we want to develop transcontextual research methods necessary for the establishment of RAD projects in writing studies, we need research methods designed with a local context in mind but also accounting for networked, translocal research contexts beyond its origins. We can use transcontextual research methods to develop transcontextual research about source-based writing, in this instance, to advance our theoretical understandings of source use in the many simultaneous contexts in which it happens. Transcontextual understandings about how source use happens can result, then, in the development of translocal praxis and paradigms that propel our knowledges and strategies forward. Transcontextual research methods and findings can expand our accumulated knowledge about writing itself. The promise of research maturity this orientation might bring is powerful and important to harness as writing studies expands.

ORGANIZATION OF THE COLLECTION

Points of Departure: Rethinking Student Source Use and Writing Studies Research Methods is designed to invite readers into the research processes of the contributors and to inspire readers to consider developing projects that contribute to our knowledges about source-based writing in eclectic, transcontextual ways. To achieve these goals, we have divided the eight chapters featured here into three thematic parts framed by prefatory essays, which introduce methods of research at work in the chapters, and by reflective points of departure that close each part, discussing how the studies might be developed or expanded for further research.

Part 1, "Developing Transcontextual Research Projects," explores how two research projects about student research and source-based writing developed to extend beyond one locality with RAD values and goals in mind. The interchapter "What Do We Mean by Transcontextual RAD Research?" begins this section, recognizing the value of transcontextual research orientations in fostering the productive and strategic expansion of writing studies even further. In the first chapter, "The Evolution of the Citation Project: Developing a Pilot Study from Local to Translocal," Sandra Jamieson recounts the methodological history of the Citation Project, historicizing the development of methods necessary to expand the project to multiple sites. Following that, Katt Blackwell-Starnes and Janice R. Walker's "Reports from the LILAC Project: Designing a Translocal Study" narrates the evolution of the pilot LILAC (Learning Information Literacy across the Curriculum) study of undergraduate students' information-seeking behaviors in preparation for a multisite, national study. Blackwell-Starnes and Walker describe how they used Camtasia software to capture think-aloud protocols and screen shots of students' search strategies and how they designed and circulated reflective questionnaires, forming a data set they analyzed using open-coding strategies. A brief reflection on the research questions and methods in part 1, "Points of Departure: Replication and the Need to Build on and Expand Local and Pilot Studies," concludes part 1, describing challenges and presenting strategies for creating scalable pilot studies from local research.

Part 2, "Building on Transcontextual Research," begins with the interchapter "What Does Design-Based Research Offer as a Tool for RAD Research in Writing Studies?," which introduces design-based research orientations as tools for conducting transcontextual RAD research that simultaneously inquires into and intervenes in student learning. Following that, in "The Things They Carry: Using Design-Based Research in Writing-Teacher Education," Tricia Serviss presents a pilot study of graduate-student writing that used citation context analysis as a tool to help novice writing teachers better understand their own academic writing. Drawing on coding methods of the Citation Project to both learn about and intervene in the formation of graduate students as writers and teachers, Serviss describes initial coding results alongside excerpts of individual interviews with participants. Crystal Benedicks's "Storied Research: Using Focus Groups as a Responsive Method" tells the story of three kinds of research-based pedagogical interventions: the initial participation of an SLAC in the Citation Project, the development of a student-survey mechanism to provide coded contextual analysis, and the evolution of both faculty and undergraduate focus groups designed to reshape institutional plagiarism policies. A student survey is also used in the next chapter, "Terms and Perceptions: Using Surveys to Discover Student Beliefs about Research," in which Kristi Murray Costello presents a pilot study of undergraduate student attitudes and conceptualizations of source use. Costello describes the refinement of a student survey to both learn about and influence student understanding of research practices. As with part 1, each chapter ends with an appendix (also available at https://upcolorado.com/utah-state-university-press/item/3188-points-of-departure), providing readers with citation analysis coding glossaries and sheets, writing prompts, and interview prompts (Serviss); student surveys and focus-group prompts (Benedicks); and survey materials and protocols (Costello). The reflective "Points of Departure: Developing Design-Based Local and Translocal Studies" concludes part 2 by emphasizing what we learn about RAD processes and methods in writing studies from Serviss's, Costello's, and Benedicks's pilot studies, outlining the promise of design-based research orientations and prompting readers to imagine possibilities to develop those pilots further.

Part 3, "Exploring Information Contexts," explores the relationships between research-project design and threshold concepts in writing studies, beginning with an interchapter that considers the question "What Does Threshold-Concept Research Offer Writing Studies RAD Research?" The chapters that follow demonstrate different transcontextual RAD research methods that collectively reveal the multiple ways threshold concepts can advance or block student researching and writing. The first chapter, "Research and Rhetorical Purpose: Using Genre Analysis to Understand Source Use in Technical and Professional Writing," presents a pilot study inspired by programmatic assessment and a desire to understand the ways students use sources in papers for technical and professional communication courses. Authors Lee-Ann Kastman Breuch and Brian N. Larson coded technical and professional communications papers using the IMRAD schema developed by John Swales to help them understand the rhetorical purposes for which students used sources and the conceptual understanding that use revealed. The question of what students understand about the selection of sources is also taken up by M. Whitney Olsen and Anne Diekema in "Asking the Right Questions: Using Interviews to Explore Information-Seeking Behavior." They describe the interviews they developed across two sites to extend their understanding of students' online information-seeking behavior, building on previous research focused on information seeking in general and revealing the need for structured engagement with librarians and research expectations. In the final chapter in this section, "Just Read the Assignment: Using Course Documents to Analyze Research Pedagogy," Elizabeth Kleinfeld explores why students do not articulate their information-seeking and source-use strategies in the ways we expect. Her transcontextual, multisite research replicates and extends aspects of previous rhetorical studies of course documents, noting the principles and concepts instructors fail to explain and challenging us to rethink the way we frame our assignments and explanations. The final reflective section that ends section 3, "Using Existing Research to Think Beyond the Local," synthesizes these chapters and offers points of departure for researchers who wish to take up and modify the research or research methods discussed in these chapters. The research described by Breuch and Larson, Olsen and Diekema, and Kleinfeld all drew on and extended research by others, demonstrating the model of RAD research as a process of refinement and sharing in addition to the need for the kind of replication that allows us to make comparisons and generalizations. Appendices accompanying these chapters include coding protocols and artifacts (Breuch and Larson); interview artifacts (Olsen and Diekema); and a coding sheet and explanation (Kleinfeld).

The collection ends with a final afterword, "Teaching Hybridity in Graduate Research Courses," by Rebecca Moore Howard, which discusses the state of methodological training in contemporary doctoral programs, focusing on the graduate education of emerging scholars as researchers posed to depart from and charter the future of RAD research in writing studies.

Note

1. *Transcontextual* is a term discussed more fully in interchapter 1, "What Do We Mean by Transcontextual RAD Research?"

References

Anson, Chris M. 2006. "The Intelligent Design of Writing Programs: Reliance on Belief or a Future of Evidence?" Paper presented at the Council of Writing Program Administrators Annual Conference, Chattanooga, TN.

Anson, Chris M. 2008. "The Intelligent Design of Writing Programs: Reliance on Belief or a Future of Evidence?" *WPA: Writing Program Administration* 32 (1): 11–38.

Banks, Adam. 2015. "Ain't No Walls Behind the Sky, Baby! Funk, Flight, Freedom." Chair's address at the Conference on College Composition and Communication, Tampa, FL.

Barton, Ellen. 2000. "More Methodological Matters: Against Negative Argumentation." *College Composition and Communication* 51 (3): 399–416. http://dx.doi.org/10.2307/358742.

Bazerman, Charles. 1989. "What Are We Doing as a Research Community? Introduction." *Rhetoric Review* 7 (2): 223–24. http://dx.doi.org/10.1080/07350198909388856.

Bazerman, Charles, ed. 2008. *Handbook of Research on Writing: History, Society, School, Individual, Text*. New York: Taylor and Francis.

Berkenkotter, Carol. 1991. "Paradigm Debates, Turf Wars, and the Conduct of Sociocognitive Inquiry in Composition." *College Composition and Communication* 42 (2): 151–69. http://dx.doi.org/10.2307/358196.

Berlin, James. 1987. *Rhetoric and Reality: Writing Instruction in American Colleges, 1900–1985*. Carbondale: Southern Illinois University Press.

Braddock, Richard, Richard Lloyd-Jones, and Lowell Schoer. 1963. *Research in Written Composition*. Champaign, IL: NCTE.

Brandt, Deborah, and Katie Clinton. 2002. "Limiting the Local: Expanding Perspectives on Literacy as a Social Practice." *Journal of Literacy Research* 34 (3): 337–56. http://dx.doi.org/10.1207/s15548430jlr3403_4.

Charney, Davida. 1996. "Empiricism Is Not a Four-Letter Word." *College Composition and Communication* 47 (4): 567–93. http://dx.doi.org/10.2307/358602.

Charney, Davida. 1997. "Paradigm and Punish." *College Composition and Communication* 48 (4): 562–65. http://dx.doi.org/10.2307/358459.

Cintron, Ralph. 1998. *Angels' Town: Chero Ways, Gang Life, and Rhetorics of the Everyday.* New York: Beacon.
Cooper, Charles, and Lee Odell. 1978. *Research on Composing: Points of Departure.* Carbondale, IL: NCTE.
Culbert, Taylor. 1961. "Methodology in Research in Composition." *College Composition and Communication* 12 (1): 39–42. http://dx.doi.org/10.2307/354310.
Cushman, Ellen. 1999. "The Public Intellectual, Service Learning, and Activist Research." *College English* 61 (3): 328–36. http://dx.doi.org/10.2307/379072.
Daniell, Beth, and Peter Mortensen. 2007. *Women and Literacy: Local and Global Inquiries for a New Century.* Mahwah, NJ: Routledge.
Emig, Janet. 1982. "Inquiry Paradigms and Writing." *College Composition and Communication* 33 (1): 64–75. http://dx.doi.org/10.2307/357845.
Fleckenstein, Kristie S., Clay Spinuzzi, Rebecca J. Rickly, and Carole Clark Papper. 2008. "The Importance of Harmony: An Ecological Metaphor for Writing Research." *College Composition and Communication* 60 (2): 388–419.
Flinders, David J., and Elliot W. Eisner. 1994. "Educational Criticism as a Form of Qualitative Inquiry." *Research in the Teaching of English* 28 (1): 5–21.
Geisler, Cheryl, and Susan Jarratt. 1989. "The Research Network 1988: Impressions from the Floor." *Rhetoric Review* 7 (2): 289–93. http://dx.doi.org/10.1080/07350198909388862.
Gerber, John. 1950. "The Conference on College Composition and Communication." *College Composition and Communication* 1 (1): 12.
Gere, Anne Ruggles. 1994. "Kitchen Tables and Rented Rooms: The Extracurriculum of Composition." *College Composition and Communication* 45 (1): 75–92. http://dx.doi.org/10.2307/358588.
Haswell, Richard H. 2005. "NCTE/CCCC's Recent War on Scholarship." *Written Communication* 22 (2): 198–223. http://dx.doi.org/10.1177/0741088305275367.
Hawisher, Gail. 1989. "Research and Recommendations for Computers and Composition." In *Critical Perspectives on Computers and Composition Instruction*, edited by Gail Hawisher and Cindy Selfe, 44–69. New York: Teachers College Press.
Hesford, Wendy. 2006. "Global Turns and Cautions in Rhetoric and Composition Studies." *PMLA* 121 (3): 787–801. http://dx.doi.org/10.1632/003081206X142887.
Howard, Rebecca Moore. 2014. "Why This Humanist Codes." *Research in the Teaching of English* 49 (1): 75–81.
Howard, Rebecca Moore, Tricia C. Serviss, and Tanya K. Rodrigue. 2010. "Writing from Sources, Writing from Sentences." *Writing & Pedagogy* 2 (2): 177–92. http://dx.doi.org/10.1558/wap.v2i2.177.
Jamieson, Sandra. 2013. "Reading and Engaging Sources: What Students' Use of Sources Reveals about Advanced Reading Skills." *Across the Disciplines* 10 (4). https://wac.colostate.edu/atd/reading/jamieson.cfm
Johanek, Cindy. 2000. *Composing Research: A Contextualist Paradigm for Rhetoric and Composition.* Logan: Utah State University Press.
Kirsch, Gesa. 1992. "Methodological Pluralism." In *Methods and Methodology in Composition Research*, edited by Gesa Kirsch and Patricia Sullivan, 247–69. Carbondale: Southern Illinois University Press.
Kirsch, Gesa, and Liz Rohan. 2008. *Beyond the Archives: Research as a Lived Process.* Carbondale: Southern Illinois University Press.
Kirsch, Gesa, and Patricia Sullivan. 1992. *Methods and Methodology in Composition Research.* Carbondale: Southern Illinois University Press.
Latour, Bruno. 1993. *We Have Never Been Modern.* Cambridge, MA: Harvard University Press.
Lauer, Janice, and William Asher. 1988. *Composition Research: Empirical Designs.* New York: Oxford University Press.

Lunsford, Karen. 2013. "Replicating Codes: What Does This Mean for Writing Studies?" Paper presented at the Conference on College Composition and Communication, Las Vegas, NV.

MacArthur, Charles A., Steve Graham, and Jill Fitzgerald, eds. 2006. *Handbook of Writing Research*. New York: Guilford.

Mackiewicz, Jo, Karen Lunsford, Rebecca Rickly, and Jason Swarts. 2014. "Collecting, Analyzing, and Talking about Data." Paper presented at the Conference on College Composition and Communication, Indianapolis, IN.

McKee, Heidi, and Danielle DeVoss. 2007. *Digital Writing Research: Technologies, Methodologies, and Ethical Issues*. New York: Hampton.

McKee, Heidi, and James E. Porter. 2009. *The Ethics of Internet Research: A Rhetorical, Case-Based Process*. New York: Peter Lang.

Mueller, Derek. 2012. "Grasping Rhetoric and Composition by Its Long Tail: What Graphs Can Tell Us about the Field's Changing Shape." *College Composition and Communication* 64 (1): 195–223.

Newkirk, Thomas. 1991. "The Politics of Composition Research: The Conspiracy Against Experience." In *The Politic of Writing Instruction: Postsecondary*, edited by John Trimbur and Richard Bullock, 119–35. Portsmouth, NH: Boynton.

Nickoson, Lee, and Mary Sheridan. 2012. *Writing Studies Research in Practices: Methods and Methodologies*. Carbondale: Southern Illinois University Press.

North, Stephen. 1987. *The Making of Knowledge in Composition: Portrait of an Emerging Field*. Upper Montclair, NJ: Boynton/Cook.

Octalog. 1988. "The Politics of Historiography." *Rhetoric Review* 7 (1): 5–49. http://dx.doi.org/10.1080/07350198809388839.

Perl, Sondra. 1980. "Understanding Composing." *College Composition and Communication* 31 (4): 363–69. http://dx.doi.org/10.2307/356586.

Powell, Katrina, and Pamela Takayoshi. 2012. *Practicing Research in Writing Studies: Reflexive and Responsible Research*. New York: Hampton.

Ramsey, Alexis, Wendy Sharer, Barbara L'Eplattenier, and Lisa Mastrangelo. 2010. *Working in the Archives: Practical Research Methods for Rhetoric and Composition*. Carbondale: Southern Illinois University Press.

Rose, Shirley, and Irwin Weiser. 1999. *The Writing Program Administrator as Researcher: Inquiry in Action and Reflection*. New York: Heinemann.

Royster, Jacqueline Jones, and Gesa E. Kirsch. 2012. *Feminist Rhetorical Practices: New Horizons for Rhetoric, Composition, and Literacy Studies*. Carbondale: Southern Illinois University Press.

Schell, Eileen, and K. J. Rawson. 2010. *Rhetorica in Motion: Feminist Rhetorical Methods and Methodologies*. Pittsburgh, PA: University of Pittsburgh Press.

Serviss, Tricia, and Sandra Jamieson. 2014. "The Citation Project: Understanding Undergraduate and Graduate Students' Source Choices and Uses." Symposia at the Writing Research Across Borders International Conference (International Society for the Advancement of Writing Research), Paris.

Shaughnessy, Mina. 1979. *Errors and Expectations: A Guide for the Teacher of Basic Writing*. Oxford: Oxford University Press.

Smagorinsky, Peter. 2006. *Research on Composition: Multiple Perspectives on Two Decades of Change*. New York: Teachers College Press.

Smith, Linda Tuhiwai. 1999. *Decolonizing Methodologies: Research and Indigenous Peoples*. New York: Zed Books.

Wells, Edith. 1950. "College Publications of Freshman Writing." *College Composition and Communication* 1 (1): 3–11. http://dx.doi.org/10.2307/355660.

Wright, Robert L. 1960. "Research in Composition/Communication." *College Composition and Communication* 11 (3): 170–72. http://dx.doi.org/10.2307/355579.

PART 1

Developing Transcontextual Research Projects

Interchapter 1
WHAT DO WE MEAN BY TRANSCONTEXTUAL RAD RESEARCH?

> *One of the most powerful motives of quantitative researchers is the desire to publish representations of the real world that can be challenged . . . [and therefore] to publish quantitative research takes, among other things, courage.*
> —Richard H. Haswell (2012, 191–92)

Many researchers in writing studies resist quantitative research because they feel unprepared in statistical methods or lack the time required to learn and then conduct such research. This worry is hardly new, though. It has been repeatedly articulated by those struggling to develop research methods since the earliest days of our national conferences and journals (see Serviss, introduction to this collection). Members of our discipline, particularly WPAs, often employ qualitative or quantitative research, or a combination of the two, in response to local institutional need, but when those local questions are answered, they move on to the next issue. Sometimes they share their findings through conference presentations or publications in the same way compositionists have traditionally shared locally based ethnographic or text-based research; however, too often all they do is write and file a final report. Frequently, they do not share their results more widely. The (re)turn to quantitative research in recent years has brought with it the renewed hope that such research will be shared—and shared in a way that helps us answer more global questions about writers, writing, and our work between and beyond local, singular sites.

Such RAD-conceived research is developed with other contexts and applications in mind, expecting replication and expansion. For this to work, it is crucial that we share methods to invite others into the inquiry and thereby generate the refinement that comes with reproduction and expansion of a study. Instead of researchers sharing a brief description of methods to frame their findings, RAD researchers share methods for an additional reason: for replication and expansion. Making methods transparent, however, often takes courage because of reasonable fears that the method will be challenged and the results questioned as readers dismiss the project entirely rather than considering the larger, ongoing goal and suggesting ways to revise the method accordingly. These fears are all too familiar to many students, but as they prepare to submit drafts we, their supportive writing teachers, encourage them to trust readers to be active participants in the writing process, to be co-inquirers who recognize that thinking evolves through constructive feedback. In this collection, we editors argue that RAD research in writing studies should be treated the same way; sharing research methods ought not be small acts of courage but part of a shared effort to understand student writing better and challenge unhelpful assumptions that can emerge from limited observation and formulaic expectations.

Conceptualizing RAD research this ways means pilot studies are not just spaces to "try out a gamut of dimensions with a few participants or texts in order to trim hypotheses and variables," as Richard Haswell (2012, 194) puts it. Instead, they are opportunities for research to emerge—along with the refinement of methods and initial analysis of provisional data that are in turn generative of additional research. That sharing can take the form of publication, as did Howard, Serviss, and Rodrigue's (2010) study of patchwriting (see Jamieson's discussion of the evolution of that pilot study in chapter 1 of this collection), or conference presentations and workshops like those used by the LILAC Project to refine their study (see Blackwell-Starnes and Walker's description in chapter 2). Both these research projects evolved from other studies they revised and replicated; however, it isn't just this replication that makes these studies significant as RAD projects. Equally important is the acknowledgment of the processes of method refinement across sites and time. This premise—that research is a process as much as writing is a process—challenges part of the RAD paradigm. For example, advocating for RAD research, Haswell recommends newer researchers start by replicating existing studies because the "design and statistical procedures are already established" (194). We resist that stance in this collection, arguing that the relationship between researcher and design must remain dynamic and responsive in writing studies RAD-oriented research. The emergent stances adopted during pilot studies ought to continue. (A pilot study inherits the etymology of the word *pilot* that includes pilots as leaders of expeditions, piloting a vessel through dangerous terrain, as well as pilots as experimental trails designed to be revised and refined. Pilots are complicated and crucial—not just objects to deploy but processes that teach us about research itself.)

Committing to a responsive approach means approaching all research as recursive and contextual processes. Engaged researchers may even find themselves recoding data beyond the typical pilot phase (as shown in chapters 1 and 2). Such an approach generates more reliable findings and also opens the possibility of further adaptations, apparent in the various research projects extending Citation Project research (see chapters 3–5). It is within this paradigm of mindful research that we call not just for replicable, aggregable, data-driven studies but also for studies that adopt transcontextual research approaches presented in this collection.

DEFINING TRANSCONTEXTUAL RAD RESEARCH

Within the context of their article, *Limits of the Local: Expanding Perspectives on Literacy as a Social Practice*, Brandt and Clinton (2002) ask literacy-studies scholars to revise their studies of literacy as social practices happening translocally across and within several contexts simultaneously, accounting for a transcontextual sense of literacy. We editors extend their paradigm of transcontextual literacy studies in this collection, suggesting that this idea of trancontextuality is not just applicable to local literacy studies but is also a valuable way to think about writing studies research itself. We extend Deborah Brandt and Katie Clinton's call to transcontextuality and argue that researchers should apply this idea of trancontextuality not only to our thinking about how writing happens but also to our research projects and findings. A transcontextual orientation toward research asks scholars to imagine not only literacy practices as transcontextual but also research studies themselves, including individual studies. We contend that locally situated writing studies research continues to be valuable for local problem solving, and sharing it *beyond the local* origins of the project is equally valuable; presuming that research is useful beyond local contexts creates generative connectivity that dissolves isolationist tendencies across research contexts, fostering the expansion and strengthening of our cumulative understandings of writing while also remaining mindful of contextually specific differences.

The term *transcontextual*, as Brandt and Clinton (2002) use it, refers to the "limits of the local" and the importance of studying socially situated literacy practices with an understanding that literacies are both local and beyond the local. In other words, literacies happen translocally. Transcontextual literacy practices, they argue, ought to be an anticipated premise in studies of literacies; we argue that the same translocal understanding must be anticipated in the study of source-based writing. Research parameters must be extended to account for *not only* the local but also for the networked and expansive ways source-based writing is developed and practiced. Brandt and Clinton's (2002) approach to literacy studies as the study of transcontextual literacy practices has been embraced in literacy and writing studies quite widely. Many in the field now expect writing studies researchers to account for the translocality of writing practices across different communities, genres, spaces, tools, purposes, occasions, time, and multidimensional contexts. We celebrate this orientation as we ask, what can this transcontextual approach *afford* us as researchers investigating source-based writing?

Transcontextuality, taken from Brandt and Clinton's conceptualization of literacy practices, invites writing studies scholars to value individual research studies as part of ongoing, connected inquiries about writing even when the contexts and sites of research appear initially unrelated. In this context, RAD research in writing studies ought to be continuously evolving rather than simply being reproduced and verified via replication. We describe the research in this collection as *transcontextually oriented* because contributors share their methods in great detail as well as some findings, acknowledging the local context of their research while also imagining its potential value and contribution beyond their local context. We highlight the *transcontextual value* of the research in this collection by (1) presenting studies in relationship to one another and (2) offering their methods as useful not only to the locality that prompted them but as part of Bruno Latour's (1993) "continual progression of inquiry" that transcontextual research enables.

The research projects described and discussed in chapters 1 and 2 became *transcontextually oriented* when their methods and research processes were designed or redesigned to maintain their integrity as they travel beyond original sites. In this transcontextual paradigm, research is designed and presented as emerging from specific places, problems, and needs while also emphasizing that these contextually specific studies exist in dynamic relationships with other research projects and methods in the past, present, and future. A transcontextual research orientation accounts for the local origins of research while also expecting some unanticipated applications and relationships to emerge from a site-specific inquiry. Transcontextually oriented RAD research, then, is research designed to allow for yet-unknown relationships among seemingly unrelated or disparate research questions, designs, methods, and sites to thrive. As a kind of RAD research, transcontextual projects embrace transparency and explication of research processes specifically so others can synthesize, connect, or mobilize them to develop theories about writing; yet those research projects themselves may typically be imagined as discrete and original because of their local contexts.

In this way, transcontextual research can compel us to move from mere replication toward loftier goals for our research as networked and translocally influential *by design and transparent presentation*. To create research traditions and communities that work transcontextually we must embrace two premises.

1. Research is a set of processes that are recursive and reiterative; like writing, research is never *finished*. Acknowledging, circulating, and appreciating such developing research is an important part of RAD research traditions.

2. Research emerging from failure, refined by disciplinary conversation, and documented through its adolescent development is *as valuable* as research presented only after maturation. In fact, a transcontextual orientation urges researchers to imagine *all research* as in the midst of awkward adolescence, sets of working methods that help us study and theorize about how writing happens.

RETHINKING RAD RESEARCH THROUGH THE TRANSCONTEXTUAL

Our understanding of translocal and transcontextual methods dovetails with traditional notions of RAD research, which has, at its heart, the ideas that data can be collected from more than one site using the same method and that as a result of replicating the method, researchers can compare aggregated findings across contexts. A transcontextual orientation expands RAD by valuing the findings of those local sites in and of themselves in addition to their importance as part of a larger data set. Chapter 1 shows what happened when Citation Project researchers applied a revised version of the method developed locally by Howard, Serviss, and Rodrigue (2010) to student research papers from sixteen institutions. The data from the single-site study revealed a total lack of summary, yet when the method was refined and developed into a transcontextual study, the researchers found some summary in the collected student writing (Jamieson and Howard 2013). This discovery led to the revision of some initial conclusions drawn by Howard, Serviss, and Rodrigue (2010) while also confirming that study's larger conclusion that when working with sources, students write from the sentences in the source. The most revealing way to study student source use was studying that activity across a wide range of intentionally disparate contexts—institutional contexts, regional contexts—brought together by the commitments of researchers to explore and connect those local data sets and analyses in synthetic ways.

We see a similar connection between local data and research contexts at play in chapter 2, which describes a research project exploring the sources students select and use. The Citation Project also coded sources in a separate study (Jamieson 2017) and, like the LILAC Group, took the same local study by McClure and Clink (2008) as a point of departure. The Citation Project replicated the coding categories to address other questions about source use (Jamieson 2017), and chapter 2 explains how the LILAC Group took up the same research question and expanded it to ask what students do when they are seeking sources and what they think they are doing. As they developed research questions, LILAC researchers also drew on findings from transcontextual research by Project Information Literacy (PIL), as did the research described in chapters 4 and 5 of this collection. This development of research within the context of a dynamic web of relationships between isolated local studies and already translocal and transcontextual research exemplifies the kind of transcontextual RAD research we are proposing.

Unlike the Citation Project, the researchers in the LILAC Group developed an initial pilot study at a single institution but with an eye to both the translocal forces at work and ways the project could be expanded to other institutions. The chapter leaves those researchers in the process of making refinements to and expanding on their project but also concludes by suggesting other research that could "spin off" from the initial study. As researchers attend to the multiple and intersecting literacies always already embedded in a research site, these kinds of networks and new directions for research emerge. Chapter 2 provides a narrative of the work of the LILAC Group, showing how it expanded from other research and making it possible for others to join, replicate, or revise the methods it shares. It also demonstrates the rich possibilities opened up by transcontextual RAD research.

The kind of transcontextual RAD orientation we propose in this collection, illustrated by chapters 1 and 2, positions the shared results and methods of local and pilot studies not as reports of finite truth but as points of departure for further and perpetually ongoing research. We call on researchers who publish valuable local (qualitative and quantitative) studies to share their research processes and methods with this transcontextual orientation in mind, allowing others to treat local pilot studies translocally while also refining them toward reproducibility and expansion. Understanding emergent local research and pilot studies in this way, as part of a process that makes space for deeper and broader understanding, means that sharing possibly imperfect initial studies ought not require bravery but should be celebrated as part of a process that is itself the sustenance of writing studies research.

References

Brandt, Deborah, and Katie Clinton. 2002. "Limiting the Local: Expanding Perspectives on Literacy as a Social Practice." *Journal of Literacy Research* 34 (3): 337–56. http://dx.doi.org/10.1207/s15548430jlr3403_4.

Haswell, Richard H. 2012. "Quantitive Methods in Composition Studies: An Introduction to Their Functionality." In *Writing Studies Research in Practice: Methods and Methodologies*, edited by Lee Nickoson and Mary P. Sheridan, 185–96. Carbondale: Southern Illinois University Press.

Howard, Rebecca Moore, Tricia C. Serviss, and Tanya K. Rodrigue. 2010. "Writing from Sources, Writing from Sentences." *Writing & Pedagogy* 2 (2): 177–92. http://dx.doi.org/10.1558/wap.v2i2.177.

Jamieson, Sandra. 2017. "What the Citation Project Tells Us About Information Literacy in College Composition." In *Information Literacy: Research and Collaboration across Disciplines*, edited by Barbara D'Angelo, Sandra Jamieson, Barry Maid, and Janice R. Walker, 117–41. Perspectives on Writing Series. Fort Collins, CO: WAC Clearing House and University Press of Colorado.

Jamieson, Sandra, and Rebecca Moore Howard. 2013. "Sentence-Mining: Uncovering the Amount of Reading and Reading Comprehension in College Writers' Researched Writing." In *The New Digital Scholar: Exploring and Enriching the Research and Writing Practices of NextGen Students*, edited by Randall McClure and James Purdy, 109–32. Medford, NJ: Information Today.

Latour, Brian. 1993. *We Have Never Been Modern*. Cambridge, MA: Harvard University Press.

McClure, Randall, and Kellian Clink. 2008. "How Do You Know That? An Investigation of Student Research Practices in the Digital Age." *Libraries and the Academy* 9 (1): 115–32. http://dx.doi.org/10.1353/pla.0.0033.

Chapter 1

THE EVOLUTION OF THE CITATION PROJECT
Developing a Pilot Study from Local to Translocal

Sandra Jamieson

ABSTRACT

The historical narrative in this chapter traces the evolution of the Citation Project from its origins in a graduate seminar to the publication of pilot data (Howard, Serviss, and Rodrigue 2010) and the development of a transcontextual, multisite research project with internationally reported and replicated data. Based on interviews with principal and participating researchers and coders, analysis of research and coding notebooks, two blogs and various shared Google Docs, and e-mails as well as shared personal experiences, this chapter offers a historical account of methodological development that reveals the complexity and messiness of multisite research as well as the necessary adjustments that allow pilot research to be scaled to multisite projects. By being willing to expose not only their methods but also the false starts, challenges, and lessons they learned, Citation Project researchers hope to ease the transition to data-driven research and thereby increase the frequency of information-based policies and pedagogies.

INTRODUCTION

This chapter provides an antidote to the (necessarily) highly systematized accounts of research processes to which new researchers frequently turn, accounts that in users' minds too easily become ideals to be achieved and standards by which to measure their work. Books such as Johnny Saldaña's (2013), Stefan Titscher et al.'s (2000), and John Creswell's (2014) are invaluable procedural guides for conducting

DOI: 10.7330/9781607326250.c001

research—and highly recommended—but while they do acknowledge the unruliness of qualitative research, they nevertheless present a linear, cleaned-up version of the process that can leave new researchers at a loss when their own work is stalled. Along with recent calls for writing studies researchers to share their methods and research design (Lunsford 2013), there is also a need for transparency in our field's research narratives. The reality of research, especially data-driven research, is that it is often a very messy, start-and-stop, revise-and-start-over process marked by frustration at many points along the way, as Rebecca Moore Howard and I noted in a keynote to the CCCC Research Network Forum (Howard and Jamieson 2012). Those of us trained in literary or rhetorical research methods are generally ill prepared for the challenges and time-consuming nature of data-driven research, and because it has not been a staple of our field until very recently, many of us lack mentors who can help. Similarly, most of us are unused to working collaboratively on research and writing, something probably essential for larger-scale research as our colleagues in the social and natural sciences learned long ago. There are many things to consider before beginning a RAD research project; this chapter presents some of those factors in hopes of encouraging other such endeavors.

Collaborative RAD research is infinitely more rewarding than anyone imagines, though, and, as the other chapters in this book reveal, has the potential to lead to the kinds of changes in pedagogies, policies, and practices many of us desire. I believe research narratives that are honest about failures and setbacks, coupled with the methods and design of the final research projects they engendered, will help researchers—experienced and prospective alike—imagine and plan large-scale research projects of their own. I hope narratives like this one will also help my fellow researchers work through the inevitable messiness and rethinking that brings such projects to successful completion.

The research project that is the focus of this chapter is the Citation Project, specifically a study of eight hundred pages of researched writing produced by 174 students enrolled in first-year writing courses at sixteen US colleges and universities. Researchers coded both the kinds of sources selected and the ways students incorporated information from those sources into their papers (summary, paraphrase, quotation, patchwriting, or copying). They also coded the kinds of sources used, including type, length, and reading difficulty.

The methods and findings of the Citation project sixteen-school study have been described elsewhere (Jamieson 2013; Jamieson and Howard 2013), and documents from that research are included in the appendix to this chapter.[1] My purpose here is not to describe those methods per se or discuss the findings (although I will mention them by way of comparison) but to narrate the evolution of the project's procedures and coding methods over a considerable time and through a series of messy drafts that ultimately allowed the collection and analysis of transcontextual RAD data on a broad scale. Using information from interviews with founding researchers (principal and participating researchers and coders), analysis of research and coding notebooks, two blogs, and various shared Google Docs and e-mails, in addition to personal experience, I will describe the various challenges encountered as the research moved from a series of questions generated in a graduate seminar to a single-institution study, then to a three-school study conducted after I became one of the two principal researchers, and thence to the sixteen-school study whose data I reported above. By sharing not only their methods but also the false starts, challenges, and lessons they learned, Citation Project researchers hope to ease the transition to data-driven research and thereby increase the frequency of information-based policies and pedagogies.

While there are things we all wish we knew before we started this research, what is more useful to future researchers is what we learned in the process and the ways it led us to refine our research and develop methods we can share with others who are conducting their own citation context research or replicating the sixteen-school study.

CITATION PROJECT ORIGINS

It is instructive to trace the development of large-scale research like this to the various points of origin, both to give credit to the many people involved and to emphasize the importance of ideological and theoretical frameworks that necessarily shape research. Going back to the original motives and influences can help researchers when they become blocked, reminding them of the reasons they are doing what they are doing and how many problems they have already overcome—which is why the kind of record keeping that led to this chapter is so important.

Origin Stories
Everything has an origin story; the Citation Project has two.

Narrative 1: The Linear Narrative
Rebecca Moore Howard first became interested in student source use in the mid-1980s, coining the term *patchwriting* in 1993 when she described

her analysis of writing by students in one of her classes (Howard 1993). A decade later, Diane Pecorari set out to empirically test Howard's claims in the writing of second-language graduate students (Pecorari 2003). These two articles helped shape a doctoral seminar in curriculum design focused on authorship studies at Syracuse University in the fall of 2006, from which developed a small class project that experimented with textual coding and then developed into an actual pilot study at a single institution. The results of that study were published in 2010 (Howard, Serviss, and Rodrigue).

I joined the project in 2008. While Serviss and Rodrigue turned their attention to other projects, Howard and I expanded the single-institution pilot study to three institutions (a liberal arts college, a private research university, and a state university). We brought in contributing researchers to help test the citation-analysis methods and code the papers, and we described our findings in a presentation entitled "The Citation Project Three-School Study" at the Conference on College Composition and Communication (Benedicks et al. 2010; Jamieson 2010).

After that three-school study came a plan to collect and code papers from ten colleges and universities that would represent a wide geographic distribution and institutional variety. Ultimately, 174 papers from sixteen institutions were collected and coded and the initial data from all sixteen was presented at the CCCC conference two years later (Jamieson 2012). Although Citation Project researchers generally refer to the initial single-institution study as the pilot study in that it developed the general coding categories used to code source use throughout the expansion of the project, the coding procedures and terminology continued to be refined in the process of conducting the study of papers from three quite different institutions, and those papers were ultimately recoded using the final criteria developed for the sixteen-school study. New research is now being conducted by scholars involved in that initial study, and new projects are developing in the United States and abroad, necessitating more fine tuning of methods to accommodate different citation styles. In 2012, principal researchers Rebecca Moore Howard and Sandra Jamieson were joined by Tricia Serviss, a co-researcher for the single-school pilot study and coauthor of this collection. Serviss and I are also working with Angela Feekery to revise and repeat the study across universities in her native New Zealand.

Narrative 2: Theoretical Underpinnings

There is also a second origin story. This one concerns not the Citation Project research per se but the theoretical and methodological frameworks that made it not only possible for Howard and I to imagine doing such research but impossible for us not to do so. And the origin story here is the moment when we were confronted by the realization that our field needs data-driven research and we needed to do it. This realization led me to take a statistics class at my institution and therefore to be able to talk about the language of statistical analysis when I read a draft in progress of the article "Writing from Sources" (Howard, Serviss, and Rodrigue 2010); it also led me ultimately to become a principal researcher with the Citation Project.

The realization about the importance of data-driven research came as we listened to Chris Anson's keynote presentation at the 2006 conference of the Council of Writing Program Administrators (Anson 2006; 2008). In that keynote, Anson argued that the shared assumptions of writing studies researchers and practitioners make it relatively easy to make a case for change others would endorse. Outside our own field, though, those shared assumptions do not necessarily prevail, and the *ethos* of the person making the argument is a much less powerful piece of evidence than it is within our field. Anson contended that if writing program administrators are to persuade cross-curricular colleagues, higher administration, fund-granting foundations, legislators, and the like to do or change anything, those WPAs need data-based evidence. Statistics, he specified, are the gold standard of universal evidence.

Rebecca Moore Howard and I were sitting side by side in the audience in Chattanooga when he delivered that keynote, and we spent the remainder of the conference talking about its possible implications for our own work. We two had been coauthors since 1993, when we began *The Bedford Guide to Teaching Writing in the Disciplines* (Howard and Jamieson 1995), and we shared scholarly and pedagogical interests. This collaborative history is important because it allowed us to work through the inevitable disagreements and setbacks as we developed and worked on the Citation Project. However, what has really motivated us through this work and continues to motivate us as we write and speak about the data and expand the project is the idea that statistical and transcontextual evidence can bring change in ways anecdotal evidence cannot (see Howard 2011, 2014). Before Howard published her data about the students in her class in 1993, other scholars had published individual case studies highlighting the challenges experienced by developmental writers as they try to incorporate sources (Hull and Rose 1989 and 1990, for example) and try to build papers from those sources (Kantz 1990; Kennedy 1985), but the *numbers* provided in Howard's 1993 article had resonance and, of course, she also named the phenomenon.

Once named and defined, patchwriting could be identified as such and measured, and scholars could begin the process of establishing it as a separate category from plagiarism (Jamieson 2016). The frequency with which the 2010 article describing Howard, Serviss, and Rodrigue's initial study is cited speaks to a larger thirst for data-driven findings. It is the need for more data that motivated Howard and me because we both want to see the pedagogical and policy changes Anson argues, and we agree, only data can bring.

DESIGNING CITATION CONTEXT RESEARCH

Howard shared a copy of Anson's keynote with students in her doctoral seminar in fall 2006 along with the recommendations of the CCCC Caucus on Intellectual Property. In response, the students—Sarah Etlinger, Tanya Rodrigue, Tricia Serviss, Zosha Stuckey, and Terri White—set about exploring how such data-driven research could be used to investigate authorship issues (the topic of the class). They focused on how to study what undergraduates do with the sources they use in their college papers and collectively designed (and named) the research project described in the class blog (Figure 1.1) and drafted information for an IRB application.

The "pre-determined units of analysis" (Figure 1.1) were those developed by Diane Pecorari (2003)—transparent and opaque source use—to test Howard's hypotheses from ten years earlier (Howard 1993). Working with nonnative speakers of English, Pecorari took ten randomly selected pages from portions of seventeen draft dissertations and collected an additional ten pages from each of eight published PhD theses. Samples were "divided into passages of varying length, the passage boundaries being determined by the source use" (Pecorari 2003, 322), allowing her to compare each passage with the source from which it drew. She coded source use as *transparent* or *opaque*. If one could tell where a source was used (ideally where it began and ended), the citation was transparent; where it was difficult to separate the source from the student prose, the material was coded as opaque. Working from this same method of citation context analysis, the seminar participants set out to replicate Pecorari's research by coding five student papers from their own institution. While no coded material was preserved, the blog contains discussions of individual sections and the struggles the researchers experienced as they tried to code ("CCR732F06" 2006). Without definition, the codes were difficult to consistently apply and the coders simply couldn't find consensus. By

> ## Project Grande v. 2.0 – Operation Writer Freedom!
>
> *How do students use sources in their academic writing? Why do students use sources in their academic writing? How do students draw on sources for information? How do students understand the purpose and ethical use of sources in academic writing?*
>
> These questions stem from the recommendations of the CCC -Intellectual Property Caucus to compositionists, urging their involvement in "leadership roles...educating their institutions about the limitations of [plagiarism detection services] and conduct[ing] more empirical research to understand better how these technological services affect student's writing and the educational environment." In the spirit of their counsel we have designed a study of student texts which will allow us to examine undergraduates' composition choices as they relate to and complicate ideas of source use and plagiarism. Our project - *Operation Writer Freedom* - will be initiated in the Spring of 2007 at Syracuse University as a pilot study with the projected intention of developing into a national endeavor on a variety of campuses. Ultimately, our goal is to answer CCCC-IP's call for responsible research which will help promote productive pedagogy and aid in a better comprehension of student work when engaging sources.
>
> *The Process of Operation Writer Freedom*
>
> * We will ask willing instructors to distribute release forms to students, allowing us, through IRB, to use undergraduate texts for this study.
>
> * We will collect course syllabi and text submissions from participating 205 pupils.
>
> * Students will electronically submit their papers to a centralized digital location at the same time as they submit finished work to instructors.
>
> * *Operation Writer Freedom* team members will code these texts using pre-determined units of analysis, carry out a trial comparison of the texts utilizing diverse textual analyses' methods, store the texts, and process the data in order to learn more about student source use.

Figure 1.1. Class blog post from November 2006 showing draft IRB application for a Citation Project precursor

the time they had tried to code three papers, they had rejected the terms *transparent* and *opaque* as insufficient. They also concluded that to understand how the sources were being used, one would need to read every cited source, something they had been unable to do and, they worried, an unsustainable method. So here in this early modification of both coding method and practice are two important realizations that helped shape Citation Project research: *all cited sources must be read by coders; all coding categories must be clearly defined.*

The goal defined in this blog post—to develop "responsible research which will help promote productive pedagogy and aid in a better comprehension of student work when engaging sources"—remains the goal of the Citation Project today, and the process they describe can also be traced in current methods. Ultimately, although the class did not complete the research they designed, Citation Project research did follow the trajectory described in Figure 1.1 and "develop[ed] into a national endeavor on a variety of campuses." The process of moving from initial idea to action was not the smooth linear process many people imagine when they set out to do research—or when they hear single-point origin stores. Many theoretical discussions, microstudies, revisions, and collaborations go into the design and execution of successful transcontextual research, and frequently people leave and others join along the way. Such fluidity is alien to writing studies research but common in other fields where transcontextual research is the norm.

FROM DESIGN TO PILOT STUDY

The conclusion of the seminar participants that researchers needed to move from overly narrow coding categories to broader and more focused categories is typical in the development of coding projects (Saldaña 2013, 11). It is not surprising, then, that at the conclusion of the semester when Howard, Serviss, and Rodrigue decided to revise the initial ideas explored in the seminar into a pilot study, their first step was to work on coding categories. The three researchers spent a semester designing coding categories, developing the research plan, securing IRB clearance at their institution, and gathering student papers produced in a required research-writing course. In this first pilot phase, Howard, Serviss, and Rodrigue coded eighteen student papers that had been submitted for a grade in fifteen sections of a composition course at a private, not-for-profit university with an RU/H Carnegie basic classification (Howard, Serviss, and Rodrigue 2010).

To do this, they still drew on Pecorari's citation-analysis methods, but they coded incidences of copying, quotation, paraphrase, patchwriting, and summary—focusing on explicit textual moves rather than reader perception of opacity and transparency. The three researchers had spent months developing methods of analyzing students' source use in the papers so they might reach consensus about their results, and a key aspect of that was articulating clear definitions of each coding category. They defined *summary* as "restating and compressing the main points of a paragraph or more of text in fresh language and reducing the summarized passage by at least 50 percent" (Howard, Serviss, and Rodrigue, 2010,181), and they found no instances of it in any of the papers they coded, even with summary referring to a source passage as brief as a paragraph. Instead, the coding revealed a great deal of *patchwriting*, which they defined in the pilot as "reproducing source language with some words deleted or added, some grammatical structures altered, or some synonyms used" (181). In fact, patchwriting was found in sixteen of the eighteen papers (182), or 89 percent. In this pilot phase, researchers coded for presence or absence of textual behaviors, not for frequency. That approach was to change as the research expanded. The definitions of the key terms evolved as well.

Howard's 1986 introduction to the phenomenon of patchwriting reports that nine of the twenty-six first-year college students in her general education course—34 percent—patchwrote at least once in their papers (Howard 1993, 237). In Pecorari's study of seventeen nonnative speakers of English enrolled in graduate programs at UK universities, sixteen of the seventeen—94 percent—"had one or more passages in their writing samples in which 50 percent or more of the words came from their sources without being indicated as quotation" (Pecorari 2003, 325). Pecorari's data are in line with the 89 percent finding by Howard, Serviss, and Rodrigue (2010, 182). Their study, then, shed light on how many first-year students might be patchwriting in their researched papers, expanding the focus of earlier studies (Hull and Rose 1989 and 1990, for example) beyond "developmental writers" to the general student population. With patchwriting widely reviled among college instructors and described as academic dishonesty in many college plagiarism policies and textbooks, it was important to know that sixteen out of eighteen students included some of it in the researched papers they wrote for their college composition class. The research followed Howard's (1993) interpretation of patchwriting as an example of "a summary technique characteristic of writers in difficulty, or writers in relatively early stages of cognitive development" (Howard 1993, 237). Rather than an act of academic dishonesty, patchwriting was "a healthy effort to gain membership in a new culture" (236) by doing what David Bartholomae (1986) had called "trying on the discourse" of that culture (6), an interpretation that has now become widespread.

This pilot study offered the first data from general first-year composition classes, and it contributed additional evidence to support the increasingly inarguable claim that most school writers—perhaps at all levels, perhaps in all classes—patchwrite sometimes as they work from sources. All three studies (Howard 1993; Howard, Serviss, and Rodrigue 2010; and Pecorari 2003) involved naturalistic data produced by school writers. With Miguel Roig's experimental research revealing that 22 percent of psychology professors patchwrote when trying to summarize a difficult text from outside their field (Roig 2001, 315) and 68 percent of students did so when asked to reproduce the ideas in one single paragraph (Roig 1999, 976), it was plausible to assert that patchwriting is commonplace in writing from sources and therefore requires a pedagogical rather than a punitive response.

WHY REPLICATE THE STUDY?

The other major finding of the study—that students work from sentences in the source rather than extended passages (Howard, Serviss, and Rodrigue 2010, 186)—has held true through all subsequent studies. Similarly, while the national study found patchwriting in only 52 percent of the coded extracts, the finding that it is a common phenomenon that occurs with much greater frequency than previously believed was confirmed. For many writing studies researchers, this confirmation might suggest it was unnecessary to do any additional research after the first study; however, it took replication in the national study to confirm the findings of the pilot. Without that replication, the pilot was just another single-school study and it was impossible to know whether the findings were broadly representative of student source-use practices or simply a result of the local institutional context of the student writers studied. For data to have traction, it must be representative and therefore transcontextual, as Anson (2006) proclaimed and the course blog post noted (Figure 1.1).

RAD Research: The Relationship between Pilot and Sixteen-School Study Findings
While the full findings of the sixteen-school study are available elsewhere (CitationProject.net; Jamieson and Howard 2013), it is useful to include two sets of data here for comparison. The first (table 1.1) shows the frequency with which each kind of source-integration method occurred within the 1,911 citations. The second (table 1.2) shows how many coded extracts included at least one incidence of each form of source integration.

While the pilot study found no summary, the sixteen-school study found that 6 percent of the citations were summary (table 1.1) but that 41 percent of the papers included at least one instance of summary (table 1.2). This finding suggests not so much that students need to learn how to summarize, as the pilot concluded, but that they need to learn how to summarize more frequently, digesting ideas and incorporating them into papers instead of working from sentences in the source. Similarly, the smaller percent of coded extracts that include at least one instance of patchwriting—89 percent in the pilot and 52 percent in the national study (table 1.2)—is further complicated by the fact that 78 percent of the coded extracts include at least one incidence of paraphrase and all but three of the extracts that include patchwriting also include at least one instance of paraphrase.

Table 1.1. Frequency of source integration method in 1,911 student citations

Predominant Use of Source Material within the Citation	Frequency	Percent	Cumulative Percent
Copying cited but not marked as quotation	83	4.34	4.34
Copying cited and marked as quotation	793	41.50	45.84
Patchwriting	306	16.01	61.85
Paraphrasing	609	31.87	93.72
Summarizing	120	6.28	100.00
Total	1,911	100.00	

Table 1.2. Type of source-integration method occurring at least once per five-page extract from 174 papers

	Frequency			Percent		
	Occurs at least once	Does not occur	Total	Occurs at least once	Does not occur	Total
Copying not marked as quotation	33	141	174	18.97	81.03	100
Copying marked as quotation	159	15	174	91.38	8.62	100
Patchwriting	91	83	174	52.30	47.70	100
Paraphrasing	135	39	174	77.59	22.41	100
Summarizing	71	103	174	40.80	59.20	100

These data reinforce the finding of the pilot study that the phenomenon of patchwriting is more frequent than we think but also strengthen the case that cited patchwriting is simply poor writing in need of revision. Coded extracts reveal students slipping from paraphrase to patchwriting and then back to paraphrase—often using the same source (see Figure 1.3)—indicating they were probably unaware they had misused the source. These data, then, suggest not that we must rush to purchase plagiarism-detection software (PDS) but that we must teach students how to revise patchwriting into paraphrase or summary.

By building on the methods and goals of the initial conceptualization of the study in a doctoral seminar and then replicating key aspects of the pilot research, the full study was able to confirm the basic findings of the earlier work, but it also deepened our understanding of the ways writers incorporate source material into their prose. In addition, the sixteen-school study expanded the research to include analysis of the sources themselves, replicating the categories used in single-site studies by Carlson (2006) and McClure and Clink (2009) and allowing researchers to trace correlations between source type and source use and to explore sources and information-literacy skills more deeply (see Jamieson 2017).

FROM PILOT STUDY TO TRANSCONTEXTUAL RESEARCH

As Serviss and Rodrigue turned their attention to their dissertation projects, Howard and I set about developing a method to extend the research beyond the single institution, as the class blog had proposed (Figure 1.1).

Developing Coding Categories

The first step, as it had been for Howard, Serviss, and Rodrigue, was to explore what features should—and could—be coded. At first the coding sheet became more and more complicated as we listed more and more questions we would like to be able to answer. My research notebook reminds me that by the end of a meeting in June 2008, there were six categories, each subdivided into at least two subcategories. If that coding sheet had been used, researchers would have been coding naturalistically produced text for sixteen separate features of source integration, some that included embedded subcategories such as "misrepresents what the source is saying on a denotative level or attributes something to the source that it doesn't actually say" and "copies from a source, makes copying errors, marks it as a quotation, and cites the source." The papers were to be coded electronically, with coding sheets assigning a different color to each of the sixteen categories. Coders were to highlight each category with one of these colors. When they had coded the paper, they were to total the number of times they had marked each of the sixteen categories and enter those totals into the form, giving a frequency count for each.

Part of the reason for this added complexity was my arrival on the scene having not participated in the previous studies. Howard, Serviss, and Rodrigue had spent months developing their coding categories, but it is common to revisit categories when a new researcher joins the team. I had not yet coded and had no idea how impossible my enthusiasm for data would be. We got increasingly excited about the many things our data set could reveal about student source engagement and so developed more and more increasingly complex categories. Finally, we realized that less is more and we did not need to code everything at once, a lesson we consider essential for code-based research. We began reducing and ultimately returned to the five categories of the pilot study (copying but not marked as quotation, copying marked as quotation, summary, paraphrase, and patchwriting). The sources selected and used were coded separately by a separate team of coders who combined the data into the final SPSS document (see Jamieson 2017).

While Howard, Serviss, and Rodrigue had done their own coding, expanding the project also meant expanding the number of people who would code the papers and bringing in coders unfamiliar with the project and the long conversations about categories and definitions. As training began, we realized the importance of category descriptions. On a research trip to the United States in 2009, experienced coder and plagiarism researcher Wendy Sutherland-Smith took part in a two-day coding session of papers from one of the first three institutions. The coding categories had already been streamlined somewhat by then, but still the coders struggled to apply them to the papers, and Sutherland-Smith gently suggested that the problem was the categories themselves. She was right.

The category causing the problem was *patchwriting*, a word that carries negative connotations for many people. We began with Howard's 1993 definition ("copying from a source text and then deleting some words, altering grammatical structures, or plugging in one-for-one synonym substitutes," 233). That definition had changed pedagogy and policies and led to other scholarship; however, we soon found that a *definition* of patchwriting was not necessarily helpful to coders who came to the task with their own well-established definitions of patchwriting as plagiarism. The use of language in coding terms that has negative associations predisposes coders who identify an instance of that feature in the *text* to view the *author* of that text negatively (as *unethical* in this case) and so to transfer that negative predisposition back to the remainder of the paper they are coding. This phenomenon, in which an association with one feature produces a similar association with the whole, is known in psychology as the *halo effect* (Nisbett and Wilson 1977; Thorndike 1920). Once the association is made, coders are not only more inclined to find examples of the negative feature but also to actively look for it. Terms and phrases like *copying, deleting, altering,* and *plugging in one-for-one synonym substitutes* suggest patchwriting is a deliberate attempt to conceal borrowing and implicitly prompt coders to assess the intention of the author rather than simply describing what they see in the text. This increases the likelihood of miscoding. In early coding sessions in particular, once they had identified a few incidences of patchwriting, coders often identified quite clear examples of paraphrase as patchwriting further into the paper. Understanding the halo effect led us to suspect that once they had identified an incidence of patchwriting, coders were inclined to think of the author of the paper as "a patchwriter" and as a result to be on the lookout for more examples and to see them where they weren't.

We also found a second cause of miscoding. This one was connected to the quality of the student prose in general and our tendency to associate patchwriting and plagiarism with weak writers. When a paper is deemed to be well written overall, patchwriting tends to be initially coded as paraphrase, or even summary; when the overall prose, organization, or grammar of the paper is weak, paraphrase is frequently coded as patchwriting. This, too, is an example of the halo effect, and it may also explain why faculty more typically find patchwriting in the work of weak writers but not in that of stronger writers despite the Citation Project's finding that more than 50 percent of all writers in the sample patchwrote at least once.

Coders needed a *description* that would focus attention on what they saw in the text and so help them agree upon where they saw instances of patchwriting and how they could distinguish it from paraphrase or copying. But they also needed a description of patchwriting that forced them to ignore the connotations of the word and placed the *text* in the subject position rather than the writer. We were reminded by those who have studied the halo effect that a category must help coders "report the evidence, not a rating" (Thorndike 1920, 29). By the time we led a preconvention workshop at the 2010 CCCC, we were using a description of patchwriting in which a passage of text is described as "restating a phrase, clause, or one or more sentences while staying close to the language of the source" (Benedicks et al. 2010). This description neither speculates on nor insinuates why or how the students stayed close to the language of the source; it just describes the fact that they do. And it is sufficiently reliable to allow us to achieve acceptable levels of interrater reliability. Coders were instructed to use this definition and remain descriptive in their coding of all features; coders ought to ask *what is happening in the text in front of me? How is the source material being incorporated?*

Responding to Economies of Scale
What to Code
We had already collected papers from two schools in addition to the institution in the pilot study, and in fall 2009 and spring 2010, we collected papers from thirteen more institutions. It quickly became apparent that

with institutions contributing papers whose lengths varied considerably, data from some of those schools would skew our results. After consulting with several statisticians, we decided to code the same number of pages from each of ten papers from each institution. We selected pages 2–6 because there is less source use on the first page of researched papers and because most of the student papers sent to us were at least seven pages long. This decision to code partial papers allowed us to compare institutions without having to adjust for sample size, and an assessment of patterns within the entire sample would give us the desired "snapshot" of methods of source integration across contexts. *This was the second of several revisions that made it possible for us to move from a small study at one institution to a large study drawing on different sites, one that ultimately allowed us to code eight hundred pages of student prose.*

In January 2010, we began to analyze ten papers from those two additional institutions and to recode ten randomly selected papers from the pilot institution. At that point, we were coding every sentence of entire papers, an extremely laborious process even with only ten papers from each institution. Other aspects of our method were also still evolving as we worked with these papers, and in many ways the three-school study functioned as a more advanced pilot for the sixteen-school study (indeed, once the coding methods and categories were finally settled, we had to recode the paper extracts from those first three institutions). When we began this stage of the research, coders identified source blocks as they read, and when they found material that appeared to come from a source, they read the source and coded how it was used. If the material did not appear to come from the source cited, they searched all the sources in the Works Cited list (a process made easier because the sources had been saved as searchable PDF documents, but still long and arduous). Sometimes they found that the wrong source had been cited, so they coded the type of source integration and noted on the coding sheet and in the margin that the wrong source had been cited. While it was agreed that only material from cited sources would be coded, we composition instructors have been so heavily inscribed by an ideology of "seek out all plagiarism" that it was sometimes too difficult for coders to ignore uncited material that appeared "obviously" to have been drawn from a source. My research notebook describes a memorable coding session at which two of the coders spent several hours each on an exhaustive (and unsuccessful) web search for material they believed to have been plagiarized—even though our coding guidelines clearly excluded such searches from the process.

What Not to Code

That detour—and the need to avoid others like it if coding was to be completed on any reasonable schedule—led to a third important procedural revision, one that more than any other made it possible to scale up the research from a localized pilot to a multisite, multicoder study and that also shaped the way we described the process. My research notebook records the decision this way: "The Citation Project is concerned with the ways students USE material from the sources they cite. If material is not cited, we ignore it. If it is incorrectly cited, we mark it as such and then move on." The notebook heading for this decision is "No Hunting," with this additional observation in red ink: "*This research is not about [catching] plagiarism; it is about what happens when students use sources that they cite.*" We revised our method to prevent plagiarism hunting and focus coders' attention on the text the student cites as coming from a source. Before coders begin coding a paper, the researcher responsible for finding the sources marks up the paper, drawing a box around material indicated as cited and noting the alpha-numeric code assigned to the cited source (see Figure 1.2). The coders then *only* code what is in those boxes. If the source cannot be found, or if it is the wrong source, the box is not coded, but the coder marks *source not found* or *incorrect source cited* in the margin of the paper and on the coding sheet (see the coding guidelines in Appendix 1.A).

The Need for Systemization

The fourth and final significant change came as we tried to recode paper extracts following the previous procedural revisions. Coders had been following the method used by Howard, Serviss, and Rodrigue in the pilot study: highlighting material from the source with whatever color highlighter came to hand and then writing in the margin what they found (see Figure 1.3). With many more coders, this process became confusing at best. Each coder had an individual style of marking up the paper, making it often impossible for a second or third reader to understand how specific coding decisions had been reached, and sometimes even what those decisions were. Ultimately, the solution drew on the long-abandoned idea of sixteen colors for sixteen categories: each different method of source integration (paraphrase, summary, patchwriting, and quotation) was to be highlighted with a predetermined color (green, pink, yellow, and blue, respectively). In order to facilitate the new color-coding system, we provided coders with highlighter pens adorned with stickers indicating the color categories and later a multicolored marker

The Evolution of the Citation Project   49

④ S0402 Cont.
> theorists, the classics was not only a vast resource of universal ideas, but there was encouragement in the fact that Classic writers themselves advocated imitation as the best means of developing style, expression, and taste" (Buelow).

⑤ S0401
> In Penelope Alfrey's article, she describes that in literature and in the visual arts, from the Renaissance onwards, an abundant amount of models encouraged artists to engage in copying or imitation. Then there came the distinction between copying and imitation. Imitation has to have generalization to some degree, for this allows the imitator to move around and add things as they desire. Copying is defined as a mechanistic form of reproduction. Through copying an apprentice learned the necessary techniques and skills required of an assistant in a studio. Copying was also a commonly accepted practice as a means of reproduction. The practices of artists and designers, until the early 20th century, relied heavily on copying.

However, predictability, the thing people were used to getting, became offset by the unpredictable. Unpredictability became what people wanted, but unpredictability was seen as an asset that signified genius and therefore it was not an asset everyone had. From then on it was not good enough to just copy and imitate. They were expected to invent.

⑥ S0401
> Alfrey believes that copying is integral to creativity, "With no opportunity to plagiarize, the imagination appears to suffer" (Alfrey). Historical evidence shows that

standards are greatly determined by precedents, the things that have come before.

Figure 1.2. Extract with citations blocked for coding. Material not boxed is not coded.

with a label. Coders would also note in the margin what they had found and the page in the source from which it was drawn and transfer this information to coding sheets (see Appendix 1.B), allowing the principal researchers to double check and recode paper extracts easily, as the samples in Figures 1.3 and 1.4 demonstrate.

Over the life of the research, we relied on many coders (who are named on our website, CitatonProject.net), and our training procedures became more effective each time we ran training and group coding sessions. Eventually, each paper was read by two coders who coded the paper individually and then created one reconciled coding sheet (see Jamieson and Howard 2013). If agreement could not be reached, one of the principal researchers stepped in and recoded. We

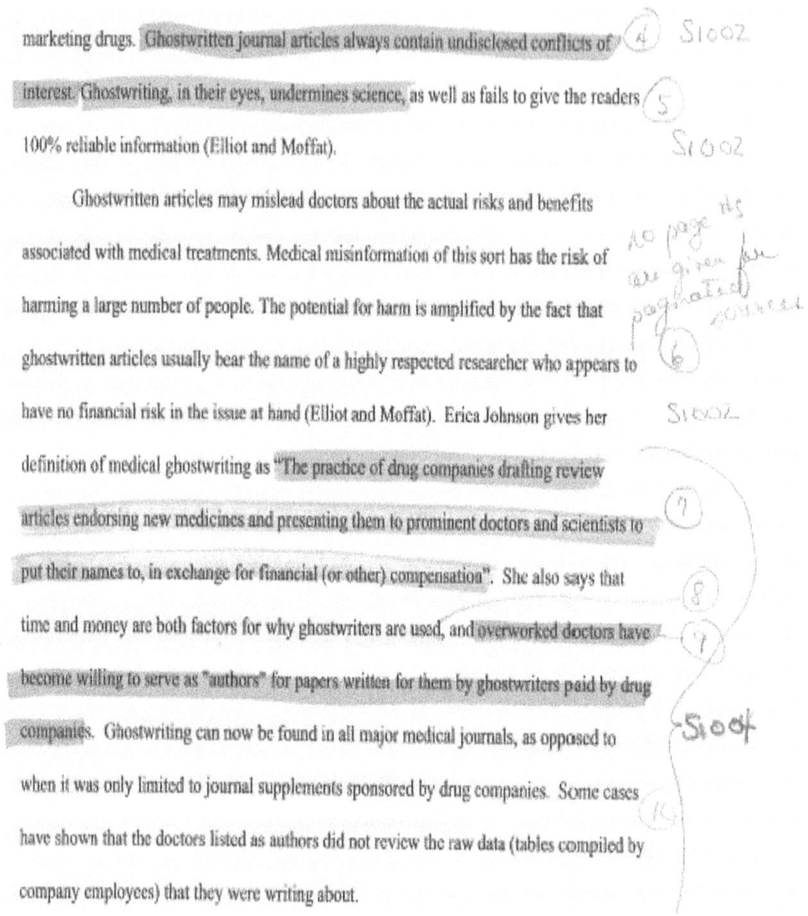

> marketing drugs. Ghostwritten journal articles always contain undisclosed conflicts of
> interest. Ghostwriting, in their eyes, undermines science, as well as fails to give the readers
> 100% reliable information (Elliot and Moffat).
>
> Ghostwritten articles may mislead doctors about the actual risks and benefits associated with medical treatments. Medical misinformation of this sort has the risk of harming a large number of people. The potential for harm is amplified by the fact that ghostwritten articles usually bear the name of a highly respected researcher who appears to have no financial risk in the issue at hand (Elliot and Moffat). Erica Johnson gives her definition of medical ghostwriting as "The practice of drug companies drafting review articles endorsing new medicines and presenting them to prominent doctors and scientists to put their names to, in exchange for financial (or other) compensation". She also says that time and money are both factors for why ghostwriters are used, and overworked doctors have become willing to serve as "authors" for papers written for them by ghostwriters paid by drug companies. Ghostwriting can now be found in all major medical journals, as opposed to when it was only limited to journal supplements sponsored by drug companies. Some cases have shown that the doctors listed as authors did not review the raw data (tables compiled by company employees) that they were writing about.

Figure 1.3. Paper from the three-school study coded using the pilot-study method. See color versions of this coding at CitationProject.net/codingexamples/.

also randomly recoded about 10 percent of the paper extracts to ensure continuity. Initially this method was used only to calibrate coders at the beginning of each session, after which they would code alone; however, we soon realized double coding and discussion led to much more accurate coding, so that is how the papers were coded.

Refining Methods

Working with multiple coders and a large sample, then, led to five significant changes to our method as we transitioned from pilot to trans-contextual research.

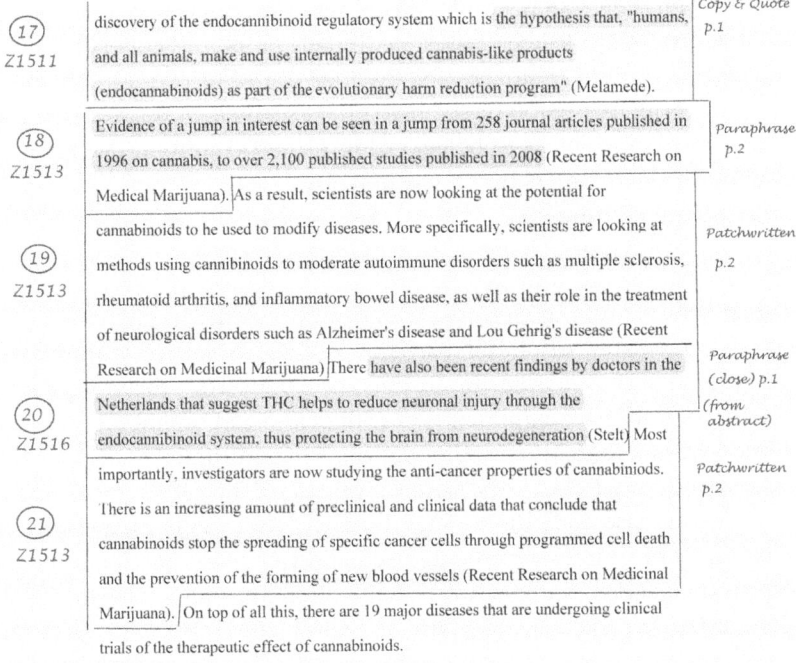

Figure 1.4. Paper from the final study coded using the four-color, boxed-citation method. See color versions of this coding at CitationProject.net/codingexamples/.

- We developed text-focused coding definitions.
- We decided to code only pages 2–6.
- We moved to coding only text in marked citation blocks.
- We asked coders to use predetermined color-coded highlighting.
- We always employed double coding, discussion, and then reconciling coding sheets.

The team successfully recoded paper extracts from the first three schools using this revised method. Had we not made these changes, it is unlikely the research would have been completed. While these modifications reduced much of the complexity initially imagined, these simplifications made it possible to code for one thing and to code a paper in about an hour. With two coders per paper, followed by a conversation, the process was still time-consuming; however, the five or more hours it was taking each person to code a paper in the pilot study simply was not scalable for 174 papers.

As we continued random recoding, we realized some coders were sometimes wildly inaccurate in their coding, and on closer examination, we determined this to be the case when they were knowingly coding papers from their own institution. Although the papers were anonymous and not from any of their classes, we initially employed coders from the submitting institution at least for the first round of coding, but sometimes for both. A version of the halo effect seemed to be in play again: coders were more likely to be generous in their coding of patchwriting as paraphrase in papers they knew to be from their own institutions. So came a sixth adjustment.

- *We agreed coders should never knowingly code papers from their own institution.*

This means we encourage those who would conduct local citation context—or probably any other partially or fully subjective research—to pair with at least one other institution and code each other's papers.

Although we had simplified how coders assessed the method of integration of source material, we found ourselves intrigued by the sources themselves. I had also been working on information-literacy issues, so we agreed to also code the sources, both to gain a deeper knowledge of what kinds of sources were being used and to expand the many single-site studies whose findings were dominating the field (Carlson 2006; Davis 2002; Jenkins 2002; McClure and Clink 2009). We paid a separate set of coders to mark up the papers as described above, find the sources cited in the five pages selected and make PDF copies of them, and then add to a spreadsheet information about the source using a slight modification of categories developed by Carlson (2006) and McClure and Clink (2009). These source coders also ran each cited source through a program that assessed textual difficulty level using Flesch reading-ease and Flesch-Kincaid grade-level analysis (Flesh.app). With source information added to the spreadsheet for each citation, we were able to look for more nuanced correlations about how students incorporate material from different kinds of sources (books, journal articles, websites) and sources with different lengths and different difficulty levels (allowing us to test Roig's claims that writers more frequently patchwrite from difficult sources). By having different coders working on different parts of the project, we avoided confusion and developed richer data (see Jamieson 2017 for a discussion of the kinds of sources selected).

CONCLUSION

As I noted at the beginning of this chapter, data-driven research, and especially transcontextual research, is infinitely more rewarding than anyone who has not done it can imagine. Once we are able to identify which phenomena are the products of good teaching and support and which are national trends that do not significantly vary by institution type, we are in a position to develop pedagogies and fair policies that are likely to achieve our goals. I am hardly the first to bemoan the fact that so many pedagogies, beliefs, and educational policies are based on anecdote or flat-out false beliefs, and I enthusiastically support those who set out to change that situation—including all the contributors to this collection. But as Howard and I have observed in every presentation we have given, and as many authors in this collection also assert, data alone is not sufficient to allow us to understand what is happening when students write from sources. The selection and use of sources is not a simple, linear process, as the new *Framework for Information Literacy for Higher Education* (Association of College and Research Libraries 2015) acknowledges and the Lilac Project is exploring (Starnes and Walker, this volume). We need to know more than simply the frequency with which students do things if we are to understand those actions and respond usefully.

Citation Project research has always had two parts: data analysis and textual analysis (see Howard 2012, 2014; Jamieson 2014; Serviss 2014; Serviss, this volume). The more we have worked with the papers in the Citation Project corpus, the more we have come to realize that this mixed-methods research is essential. The statistical data allows us to plan and execute follow-up research not guided by "something I observed in my class this semester" but by the frequencies and correlations we see in the data. Analysis of papers that move from paraphrase to patchwriting and back, like that shown in Figure 1.4, and those that alternate between quotation and patchwriting with little paraphrase seems to be suggesting there is in fact more than one kind of patchwriting (Jamieson 2014). While the data pointed me to this possibility, it will take close analysis of the papers themselves to discover whether it is true. This research method—using big data to shape close reading—is one we propose for writing studies as the field moves forward, but as I noted at the beginning of this chapter, it is not one that comes easy to all writing studies scholars. I hope that by sharing both the artifacts and the stories of our research, we can help others design—and complete—their own transcontextual projects, moving through the messiness of research design without losing an understanding of the nuance of the text, or what Adam Banks (2015) calls the "messiness of all discourse."

Note

1. These materials are also available on the Citation Project website (citationproject .net), which also requests that in order to avoid confusion between the initial study

and subsequent work, research conducted using these resources should indicate where it replicates Citation Project methods but be called *citation context research*, not Citation Project research (Jamieson and Howard 2013)

APPENDIX 1.A

These appendices may be downloaded from https://upcolorado.com/utah-state-university-press/item/3188-points-of-departure and used or modified for teaching or research purposes with attribution.

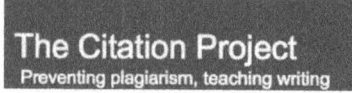

The Citation Project
Preventing plagiarism, teaching writing

Procedures for Paper coding

PRECODING STEPS

1. Enter your name, today's date, and the paper number in the upper right-hand corner of the Paper Coding Sheet.

2. Enter your name and today's date in the upper right-hand corner of the paper.

3. Note that each source has a number (e.g.: Z0102). Also note that each boxed citation in the paper is numbered in the margin and that number is accompanied by the source number to which the citation refers (e.g.: Z0102). We only code the material inside the boxed areas.

4. On each source, you will find the page number in the upper right-hand corner starting with page 1. Do not use the source's internal pagination in your coding. If the source begins with an abstract generated by the database or with a title page and is otherwise blank, that is numbered as 0 – for example the first page of Z0108.

5. Before you begin coding the paper, review "Glossary for Paper Coding" and "FAQs for Paper Coding."

CODING STEPS

6. To code the paper, read the first boxed area of text and then read the corresponding source and identify the passage to which the citation refers. If the cited material does not appear in the source, do not try to code the material. Simply make a note in the margin and on the coding sheet and move to the next boxed section.

7. Following the definitions on the "Glossary for Paper Coding," highlight all source uses within the box:
   pink for summary;
   green for paraphrase;
   yellow for patchwriting;
   blue for copying.
   Highlight only cited material inside the boxes.

   Note misunderstood or misquoted sources, or other issues of potential concern and or interest, in the margin and in the comment section on the coding sheet.

The Citation Project: http://citationproject.net

Sandra Jamieson & Rebecca Moore Howard. August 2011
This work is licensed under a Creative Commons Attribution-Noncommercial-Share Alike 3.0 Unported License, which may be viewed at <http://creativecommons.org/licenses/by-nc-sa/3.0/>

Procedures for Paper coding, *continued*

8. In the second column on the "Paper Coding Sheet," enter the page in the paper where the citation appears. If the citation spans more than one page, enter only the number of the first page (where the boxed area to be coded begins).

9. In the third column of the "Paper Coding Sheet," enter the code of the source used (e.g.: Z0102). The code is written by the boxed area on the paper, and on the first page of the source document itself).

10. In the fourth column of the "Paper Coding Sheet," enter the page number in the source from which the student was working. Use the page numbers written at the top of the PDF, even if this is not the page number cited by the student). If the citation refers to multiple pages in the source or the material spans several pages, enter only the number of the first page used.

11. If there is **only one** type of source use in the boxed area, leave the fifth column of the "Paper Coding Sheet" blank, and write a 1 in one of the last five columns of the "Paper Coding Sheet." (In the case of copying, be sure to check the correct column, depending on whether it was marked as a quotation or not.)

12. If there is **more than one** type of source use in the boxed area, write a 1 in the fifth column of the "Paper Coding Sheet" and determine which type of source use dominates—whichever type has the most words highlighted. Write a 1 in one of the last five columns of the "Paper Coding Sheet."

13. Repeat steps 6-12 for each box of text.

POSTCODING STEPS

14. When you and your coding partner have finished coding the student paper, go through and reconcile. Fill out a new "Paper Coding Sheet" with your agreed-upon codes. In the upper right-hand corner of the new "Paper Coding Sheet," enter both your names, today's date, and the paper number.

APPENDIX 1.B

CITATION PROJECT PAPER CODING SHEET
Phase II

Paper Code (e.g.: B01): _____
Coder Name: _____
Coding Date: _____

Citation #	Fill out these 3 columns			Mark if relevant	Mark an X in one, and only one, of these five columns					
	Page in the paper	Source used (source #)	Page in source	More than one type of source use in the citation	Copying not marked as quotation	Copying marked as quotation	Patchwriting	Paraphrasing	Summarizing	coder notes (optional)
1										
2										
3										
4										
5										
6										
7										
8										
9										
10										
11										
12										
13										
14										
15										
16										
17										
18										
19										
20										

Sandra Jamieson + Rebecca Moore Howard. 2011
This work is licensed under a Creative Commons Attribution-Noncommercial-Share Alike 3.0 Unported License, which maybe viewed at <http://creativecommons.org/licenses/by-nc-sa/3.0/>

APPENDIX 1.C

Glossary for Paper coding

Accurate synonym
Accurate synonyms are those that do not contradict or change the meaning of the source.

Citation
A signpost embedded in one text and pointing to another. The signpost can come in one or more of the following forms:
1. A signal phrase: *Lincoln charges the living to continue the fight waged by the dead.*
2. A parenthetical citation: *The living must continue the fight waged by the dead (Lincoln).*
3. A footnote or endnote: *The living must continue the fight waged by the dead.*[2]

Coding
Analyzing and classifying textual features – in this case, how a paper is using its cited source.

Copying not marked as quotation
Reproducing material into a stand-alone sentence, even if it makes minor errors in transcription.

Documentation
Bibliographic inmformation for works that are cited in the paper. This is usually a list of "References" or "Works Cited" at the end of the paper, but in Chicago style the documentation may appear in footnotes.

Ellipses
Used to signal deletions from a passage copied from a source, e.g., "Now we are . . . testing whether that nation or any nation so conceived and so dedicated can long endure."

Keywords
Non-exchangable labels for major concepts. They are "non-exchangable" in that they have no synonyms; they are terms that the source has coined; or they are such standard labels that using a synonym would cause confusion. When used in a source, words and phrases such as *the Middle Ages, fundamentalism, the White House,* and *deconstruction*, for example, would appropriately be replicated in a paraphrase or summary of that source. What constitutes a keyword is a matter of interpretation rather than rule; hence each coder will have to make these decisions and should make them conservatively: when you are coding and can't decide whether something is a keyword, it isn't.

Paper
The student text that you are coding.

APPENDIX 1.D

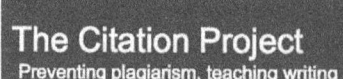

FAQs for source coding

What if the paper attributes something to a source but it isn't in that source?
Don't code it; remove that citation from the numbered list, and renumber the citations that follow it.

What if a paper is paraphrasing sentences from different parts of a source and putting those paraphrases together?
It isn't summary; it's paraphrase.

What if the paper is copying from a source, but with small changes?
— If the changes seem to be typos (transcription errors), code the passage as copying.
— If the changes seem to be deliberate variations, code it as patchwriting.

What if a paper copies subheadings and turns them into a list or sentences?
That's patchwriting, unless quotation marks are used.

How do I code graphics, film, and images?
Because this project is restricted to textual sources, you should not code moving images such as video and film. Do make a note, though, that the paper contains them. Still graphics such as photographs, tables, charts, and graphs should be coded just as any other text. If the paper is generating its own graphics from data elsewhere, you should decide whether the paper is paraphrasing or summarizing. When a paper copies graphics from a source, that is a quotation. Remember to check to see whether the paper cites the source *from which it got the graphics*.

How do I code different uses of a single source *within* a single citation?
Even if more than one type of source use (e.g., copying and paraphrasing) occurs within a single citation, the citation is classified as a single source use. Check the column "More than one type of source use on the citation." Then count the number of words in each source use in the citation and classify the source use according to which source use is greatest (use the coder notes column to make a note of what else is going on in the citation for future study).

What if the paper is misinterpreting its source?
There's no coding category for this, but it would be helpful if you were to note it in the margin of the paper and in the coder notes column on the coding sheet to aid future studies.

What if one source cites another and the student represents it as if the citing source said it?
We're not coding for this, but we would nevertheless like a note about it. Make a note in the margin and the coder notes column, and then code the type of source use.

References

Anson, Chris M. 2006. "The Intelligent Design of Writing Programs: Reliance on Belief or a Future of Evidence." Plenary address at the annual conference of the Council of Writing Program Administrators, Chattanooga, TN.

Anson, Chris M. 2008. "The Intelligent Design of Writing Programs: Reliance on Belief or a Future of Evidence?" *WPA: Writing Program Administration* 31 (3): 11–38.

Association of College and Research Libraries. 2015. "Framework for Information Literacy for Higher Education." http://www.ala.org/acrl/standards/ilframework.

Banks, Adam. 2015. "Funk, Flight, and Freedom." Chair's address at the Conference on College Composition and Communication, Tampa, FL.

Bartholomae, David. 1986. "Inventing the University." *Journal of Basic Writing* 5 (1): 4–23. First published in 1985 by Guilford in *When a Writer Can't Write: Studies in Writer's Block and Other Composing Process Problems*.

Benedicks, Crystal, Kristi Murray Costello, Rebecca Moore Howard, Sandra Jamieson, Kelly Kinney, Tanya Rodrigue, and Tricia Serviss. 2010. "Understanding Students' Use of Sources through Collaborative Research." Half-day workshop presented at the Conference on College Composition and Communication, Louisville, KY.

Carlson, Jake. 2006. "An Examination of Undergraduate Student Citation Behavior." *Journal of Academic Librarianship* 32 (1): 14–22. http://dx.doi.org/10.1016/j.acalib.2005.10.001.

Creswell, John W. 2014. *Research Design: Qualitative, Quantitative, and Mixed Methods Approaches*. 4th ed. Thousand Oaks, CA: SAGE.

Davis, Philip M. 2002. "The Effect of the Web on Undergraduate Citation Behavior: A 2000 Update." *College & Research Libraries* 63 (1): 53–60. http://dx.doi.org/10.5860/crl.63.1.53.

Howard, Rebecca Moore. 1993. "A Plagiarism Pentimento." *Journal of Teaching Writing* 11 (2): 233–46.

Howard, Rebecca Moore. 2011. "The Background: Why We Need Data-Driven Research to Understand Plagiarism." Paper presented at the Conference on College Composition and Communication, Atlanta, GA.

Howard, Rebecca Moore. 2012. "Rhetorical Consequences of Students' Source Choices." Paper presented at the Conference on College Composition and Communication, Saint Louis, MO.

Howard, Rebecca Moore. 2014. "Why This Humanist Codes." *Research in the Teaching of English* 49 (1): 75–81.

Howard, Rebecca Moore, and Sandra Jamieson. 1995. *The Bedford Guide to Teaching Writing in the Disciplines*. Boston, MA: Bedford Books.

Howard, Rebecca Moore, and Sandra Jamieson. 2012. "Take a Deep Breath and Jump: Doing Data-Driven Research When You Aren't Trained in Data-Driven Methods." Plenary address at the Annual Meeting of the Research Network Forum, Convention of the Conference on College Composition and Communication, Saint Louis, MO.

Howard, Rebecca Moore, Tricia Serviss, and Tanya K. Rodrigue. 2010. "Writing from Sources, Writing from Sentences." *Writing & Pedagogy* 2 (2): 177–92. http://dx.doi.org/10.1558/wap.v2i2.177.

Hull, Glynda, and Mike Rose. 1989. "Rethinking Remediation: Toward a Social-Cognitive Understanding of Problematic Reading and Writing." *Written Communication* 6 (2): 139–54. http://dx.doi.org/10.1177/0741088389006002001.

Hull, Glynda, and Mike Rose. 1990. "'This Wooden Shack Place': The Logic of Unconventional Reading." *College Composition and Communication* 41 (3): 287–98. http://dx.doi.org/10.2307/357656.

Jamieson, Sandra. 2010. "Understanding Students' Use of Sources through Collaborative Research." Paper presented at the Georgia International Conference on Information Literacy, Savanna, GA.

Jamieson, Sandra. 2012. "Students' Source Choices: A Statistical and Rhetorical Analysis of Researched Papers from Sixteen Institutions." Paper presented at the Conference on College Composition and Communication, Saint Louis, MO.

Jamieson, Sandra. 2013. "Reading and Engaging Sources: What Students' Use of Sources Reveals about Advanced Reading Skills." Special issue, *Across the Disciplines* 10 (4). http://wac.colostate.edu/atd/reading/jamieson.cfm.

Jamieson, Sandra. 2014. "Understanding Undergraduate and Graduate Students' Source Choices and Uses." Symposia at the Writing Research Across Borders International Conference (International Society for the Advancement of Writing Research), Paris.

Jamieson, Sandra. 2016. "Is It Plagiarism or Patchwriting? Toward a Nuanced Definition." In *The Handbook of Academic Integrity*, edited by Tracey Bretag, 503–18. Springer. http://dx.doi.org/10.1007/978-981-287-098-8_68.

Jamieson, Sandra. 2017. "What the Citation Project Tells Us about Information Literacy in College Composition." In *Information Literacy: Research and Collaboration across Disciplines*, edited by Barbara D'Angelo, Sandra Jamieson, Barry Maid, and Janice R. Walker, 117–41. Perspectives in Writing Series. Fort Collins, CO: WAC Clearing House and University Press of Colorado.

Jamieson, Sandra, and Rebecca Moore Howard. 2013. "Sentence-Mining: Uncovering the Amount of Reading and Reading Comprehension in College Writers' Researched Writing." In *The New Digital Scholar: Exploring and Enriching the Research and Writing Practices of NextGen Students*, edited by Randall McClure and James Purdy, 109–32. Medford, NJ: Information Today.

Jenkins, Paul O. 2002. "They're Not Just Using Web Sites: A Citation Study of 116 Student Papers." *College & Research Libraries News* 63 (3): 164.

Kantz, Margaret. 1990. "Helping Students Use Textual Sources Persuasively." *College English* 52 (1): 74–91. http://dx.doi.org/10.2307/377413.

Kennedy, Mary Lynch. 1985. "The Composing Process of College Students Writing from Sources." *Written Communication* 2 (4): 434–56. http://dx.doi.org/10.1177/0741088385002004006.

Lunsford, Karen. 2013. "Replicating Codes: What Does This Mean for Writing Studies?" Paper presented at the Conference on College Composition and Communication, Las Vegas, NV.

McClure, Randall, and Killian Clink. 2009. "How Do You Know That? An Investigation of Student Research Practices in the Digital Age." *Portal: Libraries and the Academy* 9 (1): 115–32. http://dx.doi.org/10.1353/pla.0.0033.

Nisbett, Richard E., and Timothy D. Wilson. 1977. "The Halo Effect: Evidence for Unconscious Alteration of Judgments." *Journal of Personality and Social Psychology* 35 (4): 250–56. http://dx.doi.org/10.1037/0022-3514.35.4.250.

Pecorari, Diane. 2003. "Good and Original: Plagiarism and Patchwriting in Academic Second-Language Writing." *Journal of Second Language Writing* 12 (4): 317–45. http://dx.doi.org/10.1016/j.jslw.2003.08.004.

Roig, Miguel. 1999. "When College Students' Attempts at Paraphrasing Become Instances of Plagiarism." *Psychological Reports* 84 (3): 973–82. http://dx.doi.org/10.2466/pr0.1999.84.3.973.

Roig, Miguel. 2001. "Plagiarism and Paraphrasing Criteria of College and University Professors." *Ethics & Behavior* 11 (3): 307–23. http://dx.doi.org/10.1207/S15327019EB1103_8.

Saldaña, Johnny. 2013. *The Coding Manual for Qualitative Researchers*. 2nd ed. Los Angeles, CA: SAGE.

Serviss, Tricia. 2014. "Understanding Graduate Students' Source Choices and Uses." Paper presented at the Conference on College Composition and Communication, Indianapolis, IN.

Thorndike, Edward L. 1920. "A Constant Error in Psychological Rating." *Journal of Applied Psychology* 4 (1): 25–29. http://dx.doi.org/10.1037/h0071663.

Titscher, Stefan, Michael Meyer, Ruth Wodak, and Eva Vetter. 2000. *Methods of Text and Discourse Analysis*. Thousand Oaks, CA: SAGE.

Chapter 2

REPORTS FROM THE LILAC PROJECT
Designing a Translocal Study

Katt Blackwell-Starnes and Janice R. Walker

ABSTRACT

In this chapter, we describe how we used screen-capture software to understand student information-seeking behaviors in order to suggest pedagogical and curricular strategies for teachers, librarians, and others tasked with helping students develop essential research strategies. We used the pilot study to design a larger, ongoing, multi-institutional study, collaborating with other researchers to enhance the methodology and data analysis. Reflections on the methodology and findings emphasize the strengths and weaknesses of the research as well as pointing to ways in which the LILAC (Learning Information Literacy cross the Curriculum) Project could be expanded through multi-institutional studies and additional projects.

INTRODUCTION

In the foreword to *The New Digital Scholar*, Alison J. Head and Michael B. Eisenberg note that "one of the paradoxes of the digital age is that while finding information and answers may be easy, making sense and using all that information is not" (Head and Eisenberg 2013, xi). In that same volume, Barry M. Maid and Barbara J. D'Angelo suggest ways instructors can "think about which pedagogical strategies all of us need to employ in order to develop an [information-literacy]-based curriculum that is relevant in the digital age" (Maid and D'Angelo 2013, 310–11). In this chapter, we discuss a small pilot study of student information-seeking behaviors looking at gaps in students' information-seeking skills in order to suggest pedagogical and curricular strategies for teachers, librarians, and others tasked with helping students develop essential research strategies. We used the pilot study to design a larger, ongoing, multi-institutional study, collaborating with other researchers to enhance the methodology and data analysis. Reflections on the methodology and findings emphasize the strengths and weaknesses of the research as well as point to ways in which the LILAC (Learning Information Literacy cross the Curriculum) Project study could be expanded through multi-institutional studies and additional projects.

FRAMEWORK

Most academics agree that "writing from sources is a staple of academic inquiry" (Howard, Serviss, and Rodrigue 2010, 178). However, the Citation Project's multisite study of students' use of academic sources (Jamieson and Howard 2013) supports the hypothesis of the initial pilot study that many students appear to be "quote mining" the first page or two of sources instead of actually reading them (Howard, Serviss, and Rodrigue 2010, 186). Jamieson and Howard's findings also describe the types of sources students are using, with 24 percent of sources cited being scholarly, peer-reviewed journal articles and an unsurprising 25 percent being "Web-based sources" (Jamieson and Howard 2011). One single-institution study also found a majority of student citations to be from online sources (Barratt et al. 2009), and another single-institution study showed almost half (or 48 percent) of sources to be from web sources (McClure and Clink 2009). The Citation Project results from the same institution where the LILAC Project pilot study took place revealed 34 percent of citations in first-year student papers in 2011 were from the Internet, 14 percent from journals, and only 3.5 percent from books.

Project Information Literacy (PIL), a large study of the information-seeking behaviors of young adults across a broad range of institutions, found that 77 percent of students spent between one and five hours on research (Head 2008, 435), with students often "struggl[ing] with limiting the scope of a research topic and dealing with the inevitable information overload that accompanies new forms of digital media" (433). However, like so many of the studies conducted of student research practices, PIL used a questionnaire-based approach. Thus, the results may show more about what students think they do—or what they want teachers to think they do—than about what they actually do when tasked with finding sources for a scholarly project. The LILAC Project study, thus, attempts to capture not only what students think they do but also what they actually do when conducting research for an academic project.

METHOD

The LILAC Project is a study of student information-seeking behaviors that attempts to discover what students are doing when they conduct research and, even more important, why they are making the choices they do. We conducted the IRB-approved LILAC pilot study (n = 15) at a midsize, research-extensive university in the southeast United States in the spring of 2012. The study consisted of two components: a research session during which subjects demonstrated a portion of their research process and a questionnaire about information-literacy knowledge, perceptions, and instruction (Appendix 2.A). Most of the study participants were first-year students (n = 10), with one sophomore, one junior, two seniors, and one master's student also participating. All students reported English as their first language. Subjects consisted of eight females and seven males between the ages of eighteen and twenty-three. In addition, subjects represented a variety of major fields, including music, education, finance, psychology, and writing, with one student undeclared.

The first component of the LILAC Project pilot study attempted to determine what students are taking away from current classroom and library-based instruction by capturing subjects' actual research behaviors in brief, ten-minute videos. Each subject began the session with a topic for a paper assigned for a course, a topic they were exploring for course-related research, or a topic chosen from a list of suggestions we provided (see Appendix 2.B). Our only stipulation was that subjects begin their video narrative by telling us what their topic would be and what class it might be for (e.g., a subject might be researching global warming for an English class). Subjects conducted research for their selected topic using a research-aloud protocol (or RAP) in which they narrated what they were doing and why they were making the choices they did as they worked; these videos were captured using Camtasia Studio screen-capture software. At least one of the principal investigators (PIs) took extensive handwritten notes of subjects' narrations as they were being recorded in which she particularly noted behaviors she believed should be coded. PIs then viewed representative videos together, along with these notes and the preliminary coding document we had previously prepared, to determine whether the behaviors we observed in the videos and the a priori coding document aligned.

The second component asked subjects to complete a questionnaire detailing what they had been taught about research, when and where they were taught these skills, and what they believed they knew about conducting scholarly academic research. The questionnaire inquired about subjects' information-literacy instruction in high school and college, including specific information on where and how they were taught (e.g., lecture, hands-on workshop, directed reading(s), etc.) and what specific skills were covered. In addition, the questionnaire asked subjects to rate their research abilities and answer a series of questions about information literacy so we could better understand their comprehension and perception of these important skills. Questionnaires were then hand tabulated and analyzed to determine trends in subjects' perceived knowledge.

DISCUSSION OF METHOD

The pilot study provided us an opportunity to test and improve our methodology prior to launching the LILAC Project as a larger, multi-institutional study. The pilot study confirmed our belief in the strength of our methodology while revealing where further tweaks to the method would strengthen confidence in our findings.

During and after the pilot study, we made slight alterations to the ordering of the two components (the questionnaire and the RAP session), to the questionnaire, and to the length of the RAP video captures. Based on feedback from workshops and conference presentations with librarians, teachers, and other researchers, we refined the questions we were asking and reordered the questions to allow greater alignment with behaviors captured in the videos. We further refined the video coding sheets, ensuring that our coding adequately reflected subjects' information-seeking behaviors, both those we could see on the subjects' computer screens and those narrated by subjects. Important to note is that what subjects are actually doing in the captures is not always what subjects say they are doing, so our coding needed to allow for such discrepancies. We also expanded the length of the RAP video captures to fifteen minutes to allow us to capture more information from subjects.

Ordering

The first ten subjects completed their RAP sessions immediately after reading the informed consent form and signing the video release. After the RAP session, the subjects completed the questionnaire. We opted to reorder the questionnaire and the RAP session for the last five subjects. We reordered the two components because we were uncertain whether completing the RAP session prior to the questionnaire would skew subjects' responses to the questionnaire or vice versa. However, results from the final five subjects showed the completion order had no discernible effect on the questionnaire data or on the behaviors captured in the RAP sessions. For the full LILAC study, our IRB[1] allowed us to eschew the signed informed consent document and video release and instead include a passive informed consent document as the first page of the Qualtrics questionnaire since it was determined that this study posed minimal risk and there was no need to collect identifying information from subjects. We opted, therefore, to begin sessions for the full LILAC study with the questionnaire, then follow with the RAP video captures. Since the RAP video captures were anonymous, the IRB further allowed these to be posted to YouTube for purposes of research, teaching, and publication or presentation without requiring subjects' to sign a release assigning any intellectual property rights to the videos.

Questionnaire

Following the pilot study, we redesigned both the content and delivery of the questionnaire. Questions were reordered or reworded for clarity and to align better with behaviors captured in the RAP videos. Pilot-study subjects completed paper questionnaires, which can cause various marking issues. Participants may change an answer but not completely erase or mark through the erroneous mark, or stray marks may be misinterpreted as an answer when responses are tabulated. Questionnaire results were then manually entered into a spreadsheet to allow for analysis. This manual entry also allowed for the introduction of errors. Following the pilot study, therefore, we elected to use Qualtrics online-survey software to host the questionnaire, thus eliminating mistakes possible in hand-tabulated questionnaire data and allowing for easier analysis and reporting of data.

We also reviewed drafts of the questionnaire at LILAC Project workshops held at the Georgia International Conference on Information Literacy, which brought together K–20 cross-disciplinary faculty and librarians. These reviews helped us fine-tune the questionnaire as we prepared to develop the full LILAC Project study. A graduate research assistant also helped order the questions to ensure ease of tabulating results and alignment with coded behaviors in the RAP video captures (see Appendix 2.A).

RAP Instruction Sheet

Subject instruction sheets for the RAP video sessions (Appendix 2.B) included a brief overview of the process, including stressing the importance of subjects' narrative input; suggested ideas for topics for research; and some suggested prompts for subjects to use when narrating (e.g., "The first place I look for information is . . ."). Pilot-study subjects were able to select topics from a variety of sources: topics they were currently working on for a class, topics they had researched for previous classes, topics of their own choosing, or topics selected from the list we provided. We would have preferred to capture subjects working on actual course projects; however, some subjects either had not yet been assigned a research project in their classes or had already completed one. In addition, many subjects claimed they had never had to conduct research for a class project prior to participating in our study, either in college-level classes or in high school. Of course, the majority of our subjects were first-year students, so it is entirely feasible they had not yet been assigned research for a college course-related paper or project at the time of the study.

The variety of topic-selection methods provides a glimpse into the variety of ways students may conduct research for different types of assignments and at different points in their research process. A subject choosing a topic from our list of broad topic areas might use the RAP research session to focus the topic by conducting background research, for example, while a student working with a self-selected course topic might not need the same background information, depending on familiarity with the topic. While not within the scope of the current study, knowing more about how subjects select their RAP session topics could assist in better understanding how students conduct research at various points in the research process.

RAP Session Length

For the pilot study, we set the length of RAP sessions at ten minutes. However, after viewing the RAP videos in conjunction with the questionnaire results, we opted to extend the length of the captures to fifteen minutes. This extension allowed more time for subjects to conduct research without expending too much time. Sessions generally took a total of thirty minutes each, with a few minutes for explaining the project to subjects and going over the informed consent document and subject instructions; subjects then completed the questionnaire and the fifteen-minute RAP session. While lengthier sessions might be possible, asking subjects to give us more time might not be feasible, and certainly coding lengthier sessions would be more time consuming.

After viewing the fifteen ten-minute videos collected during the pilot study as well as over one hundred fifteen-minute RAP videos captured so far from the multi-institutional study, we believe the extra time is warranted in order to allow subjects to fully demonstrate and narrate their information-seeking behaviors but that additional time beyond the fifteen minutes might provide only repetition of behaviors already captured.

It should also be noted that some subjects elected to stop before the end of the ten- or fifteen-minute capture. Many of the subjects who opted to stop early said they had found all the sources they needed (or all the sources they were required to include). At this juncture, only a few subjects have opted to end the session before the timer runs out, so further study might include interviewing subjects to determine whether ending the session early is significant in any way. That is, while not within the purview of this study, it would be interesting to try to determine how much time students actually spend doing research for their academic projects.

Video Coding and Time on Task

We used the pilot study to begin thinking about how to analyze information captured in the videos. First, as Brigid Barron and Randi A. Engle note, to be effective, research videos should be guided by the research questions (Barron and Engle 2007, 24). To this end, we researchers began comparing our research questions, the behaviors captured, the coding sheets, and the questions asked in the survey to ensure alignment. While we considered transcribing both visual and auditory information captured in the RAP video sessions, we ultimately decided against transcription due to the time and complexity of so doing. Further, as Barron and Engle note, such transcripts may not be suited for discovering patterns (24).

We did track subjects' activities throughout their research session, with initial coding taking the form of listing each move made in individual videos and then comparing similarities across videos. We compared both the moves subjects made during their research session and the order in which subjects visited sites throughout their research. In addition, we created lists of search terms used in each video to see whether we could determine trends in the structure and type of search terms used most often. One final aspect of the initial coding looked at time spent on each task in actuality versus clock time in the video[2] and then compared each individual subject's results with the rest of the subjects. Determining time on task provided an accurate portrayal of subjects' research processes, especially in cases in which one subject's clock time on a page lasted for up to two minutes, but a majority of this time was spent on multiple, unsuccessful attempts at highlighting a specific portion of the text to copy and paste into a Word document.

We used the lists we created from viewing individual videos to refine our initial coding sheet, a general list of behaviors captured in the videos. This initial coding sheet helped us determine what subjects were doing in their early research but studying the coding sheets alone did not provide enough detail. For instance, coding for *follows link* from the initial coding sheet did not allow for specificity about which link the student followed without the coder's providing additional commentary to distinguish whether the student selected the sponsored link or the first link in the search results below the sponsored link. Thus, the initial coding sheet highlighted the ambiguity in this coding system and provided a framework for a more detailed coding sheet.

Following the pilot study, we held workshops at conferences that included K–20 cross-disciplinary faculty as well as librarians to ensure our coding would accurately reflect the behaviors captured in the videos. Then we collaborated with our first multi-institutional research partners to develop a revised coding sheet. The revised version provides a more detailed coding system that better aids in identifying subjects' individual moves in their research sessions. As we continue to expand the LILAC Project as a multi-institutional study, we continue to formalize the coding process and contents, bringing together groups of researchers to view the videos, expanding and finessing the coding, and beginning the process of ensuring interrater reliability.[3] Working together to code the videos and refine the coding document improves our interrater reliability by providing more specific items for video coding and allows for greater alignment with questionnaire results. Following the work of the Citation Project, we plan for each video to be double coded, with at least one of the coders from a different institution than the one at which the video is captured.

Thus far, we have hand coded videos, with at least two researchers viewing each video to determine whether identifiable trends exist among subjects. However, for the full study, we plan to use Atlas.ti software to help analyze the coded video data. Atlas.ti is particularly useful for qualitative analysis of unstructured data, such as that found in written texts and visual/graphic, audio, and video files. However, while Atlas.ti should help identify patterns, such as subjects' use of Google as the most prevalent or most-used site in the videos because it will "bubble up" to the top, this software will only produce a "scattershot" of identified behaviors and, hence, may not be useful in capturing the sequence subjects follow, such as consistently using the same search terms, or in identifying mismatches between what subjects say they are doing (captured in subjects' audio RAPs) as opposed to what they are actually doing (as captured by the video). Coding will be a time-consuming process, especially with the large number of RAP video captures we hope to include (N = 1000). And, of course, because it is a mixed-methods study, we still need to determine how well the qualitative data captured by Atlas.ti will relate to the quantitative data captured by the Qualtrics surveys.

FINDINGS

The pilot study included fifteen subjects ranging from first-year undergraduates to graduate-level students. For now, we will consider only the first ten subjects (those who completed the RAP video session prior to completing the questionnaire). The majority of these subjects (eight subjects) were first-year students, with one senior and one graduate student for the remaining subjects. Table 2.1 provides a breakdown of the first ten pilot-study subjects' year of study and academic majors and minors.

Questionnaire results revealed a range of findings regarding subjects' information-literacy education and skills. With reference to general skills, nine subjects reported receiving instruction in high-school English courses, and seven reported further training in college English courses. In relation to online searches, seven reported receiving training in keyword searches and online databases, but only five in web-based searches; four reported having been provided guidance on evaluating these web-based sources. Only two subjects reported receiving instruction in determining the type of source they were working with, yet all subjects felt their abilities to locate and evaluate online sources were well above average. Subjects also reported that the majority of their research involved online search engines. Six of the ten subjects responded with "strongly agree" to the statement about using the Internet for the majority of their research needs; the other four subjects all responded "largely agree" to the statement. We suggest this familiarity with the Internet may represent an overconfidence in online-research abilities.

Subjects' RAP sessions also clearly illustrate the role both Google and *Wikipedia* play in beginning-student research. All undergraduate subjects in the pilot study began with either Google or *Wikipedia*, and eight did not change their search strategy throughout their sessions. One first-year subject mentioned visiting the library for information at the conclusion of his information-seeking session but did not do so during the brief session we captured. Only two undergraduate students explored other online

Table 2.1. LILAC Project pilot participant academic demographics[4]

Name	Year of Study	Major	Minor
Sharon	Master's	Public Administration	N/A
Maria	Freshman	Psychology	N/A
Trevor	Senior	Writing and Linguistics	Journalism
Robert	Freshman	Economics/Finance	Music
Frank	Freshman	Journalism	N/A
Paul	Freshman	History/Political Science	Economics
Jennifer	Freshman	Multimedia Communication	N/A
Laura	Freshman	Sports Management	Business
Michael	Freshman	Computer Science	N/A
Heather	Freshman	Music Education	N/A

options, including Google Books and YouTube, while only one undergraduate subject and the one graduate subject searched the library's online databases. The graduate student also visited Google Scholar.

The RAP sessions show a consistency between where subjects report beginning their research and where they actually begin their research. However, not enough subjects demonstrated the skills reported in their questionnaire responses, so it was difficult to make connections between the questionnaire and video data to determine the extent of the gaps between these perceived research skills and actual research skills used in academic research tasks. That is, since few subjects visited the library website during the RAP video captures, it was not possible to compare subjects' strengths in using the library as reported in the questionnaire with subjects' actual library-search behaviors. As we expand the study, we hope to capture more of these behaviors to address this gap; a spin-off study looking solely at students' use of library resources might also be warranted.

DISCUSSION OF FINDINGS

Findings from the LILAC Project pilot study are not generalizable; however, as we refine and expand the study, we hope to provide a starting point for a better understanding of the connections and disconnections between subjects' perceptions of their academic research skills and their actual behaviors as captured by the RAP video sessions. The questionnaire data allows us to connect our research to other questionnaire studies to determine how our results compare to larger trends, and the pilot study allowed us to recognize ambiguous questions we might consider revising for the larger multi-institutional study. Further comparison of the questionnaire data to the subjects' RAP video sessions offers additional insights that expand our understanding of the questionnaire data. Though the RAP sessions, of course, do not offer a complete portrait of demonstrated student information-literacy skills, they do further our understanding of *how* subjects conduct research while also illustrating areas of ambiguity that possible revisions to the larger study may address. Results from the LILAC Project pilot study, while certainly not generalizable from such a small sample, do allow us to begin ascertaining these trends, and analysis of the results has also allowed us to plan for changes necessary to the methodology as we continue to expand the study to include additional institutions and academic populations.

Questionnaire Data, Large and Small

The pilot-study data does suggest possible trends among our subjects and subjects in other studies. For instance, all ten subjects in the first part of our pilot study indicated they use the Internet for a majority of their research. Alison Head's findings that 88 percent of 358 first-year students and 87 percent of upper-class students surveyed continue to use Google in academic research bears this out (Head 2013, 25). At first glance, more of our subjects reported using Google than those in Head's larger study, which can indicate the need for a larger subject pool, but further analysis of the questions from Head's study, as well as the interview responses in Monica Cólon-Aguirre and Rachel A. Fleming-May's study of *Wikipedia* use among students, illustrates an ambiguity in our questions that can be addressed in future iterations of the study (Cólon-Aguirre and Fleming-May 2012, 394).

For example, the questionnaire term *using online search engines* from our original questionnaire might receive the same response from a student who uses Google to reach a *Wikipedia* page related to their research (a trend among Cólon-Aguirre and Fleming-May's [2012, 394] interviewees), a student who uses Google to reach their university library page, and a student who uses Google to locate sources for their research. Similarly, respondents to Head's question about whether students use Google as an "information resource" (Head 2013, 24) may have also generated ambiguous responses given the vast number of ways students may use Google at various points in the research process. In addition, students using an on-campus connection to conduct research through Google or Google Scholar often can access peer-reviewed sources not available otherwise. In terms of locating information at the start of a research project, there is a significant difference in conducting a quick Google search to locate a *Wikipedia* page (where students can use a single page to gain background information on a topic), using Google to begin searching for specific sources relevant to the research paper, and using Google or Google scholar to access peer-reviewed research. The RAP videos our subjects complete with their questionnaire responses better inform ambiguous responses such as these; however, this leaves questionnaire data ambiguous in itself. Thus, the RAP videos provide more specific information about *how* students perceive their use of Google at the start of a research project was one consideration for questionnaire revisions for the multi-institutional study.

(Only) the First Fifteen Minutes

The pilot study RAP video sessions capture ten minutes of subjects' research activities, and, almost unanimously, these subjects were just beginning their research for a project, which may be a limitation of our study. However, the LILAC Project does not attempt to capture a synoptic view of the research process but rather attempts to identify subjects' research behaviors so pedagogical approaches to teaching information literacy may be revised or expanded as needed to assist students in developing a stronger information-literacy foundation for all research.

One important feature of the RAP sessions is subjects' voice narrations. Not only do these allow us to compare what subjects are actually doing with what they say they are doing—something using questionnaire data alone cannot do—but they also allow us to begin to ascertain why subjects are making the choices they do. For example, a student may avoid *Wikipedia* because teachers have told them it is not a reliable source since "anyone can edit it." However, another subject may opt to use *Wikipedia* anyway since it provides the information they are looking for. One disturbing, though nearly unanimous, reason students give for choosing certain types of sites is that they claim to have been told that .org sites are always reliable while .com sites should be avoided. That is, students are attempting to evaluate the sources they find, but they are often doing so erroneously. One possible reason, of course, is that students are looking for quick answers, which seems to bear out the Citation Project's findings. Another reason, however, may hearken back to what students have been taught—or at least to what students remember or understand from that instruction. Subjects in the pilot study did not often elaborate on these decisions, which means we can only hypothesize from the subjects who were specific about their reasons. This limitation may illustrate a need to ask subjects to participate in a brief interview at the end of their session focusing on specific questions, such as questions about their motivation for *Wikipedia* use or their avoidance of .com sites, and could provide important insight into students' information-literacy knowledge and understanding.

One common finding identified through the pilot study RAP video sessions was that subjects starting with Google and *Wikipedia* are not always searching specifically for sources but rather use these searches as a means of gaining background information on their topic. It was evident to the researchers that, in many of these videos, subjects were actually conducting preliminary research that could be used to help them focus a topic, even though it was not necessarily apparent to the subjects that this was what they were doing. Instead, most subjects simply continued to collect information rather than finding a focus and then conducting further research with that focus in mind. Such an insight helps us identify a process that can assist in the development of new pedagogical approaches; for instance, a better approach might be delaying the library-research workshop until students have a firm understanding of their topic from preliminary research and reading rather than beginning with the research assignment and library skills. Alternatively, introducing research as an ongoing part of the assignment may need to be stressed more. That is, many subjects told us they would begin writing after collecting sufficient sources (either because they thought they had all they needed or because they had the number of sources they were required to include). None of our subjects in the pilot study noted the need to continue research as they write. Further study of students' writing-from-research processes clearly seems to be warranted.

The RAP video artifacts also provide excellent teaching tools. Subjects are not identified by name and the video captures show only the subject's computer screen, thus allowing the ten- to fifteen-minute videos to be viewed without risk of identifying subjects. In addition to the common findings discussed above, some videos contain information that offers opportunities for just-in-time instruction. For instance, one video shows a student copying information from web sources into a Word document without making detailed notations of where she located this information. This portion of the RAP video allows for discussions about the importance of documenting sources from the beginning of research. The videos are long enough to provide a substantial view of an anonymous student's research process but short enough to be viewed and discussed in a single class period. The LILAC Project will be publishing the RAP videos to a publicly accessible YouTube channel, so the videos will be freely available for purposes of teaching, research, or scholarship, following the model of the Digital Archive of Literacy Narratives (DALN) hosted by Cynthia L. Selfe at Ohio State University. Using the RAP videos as discussion starters provides educators with a valuable pedagogical tool for beginning more realistic discussions about students' research processes, whether the educator's institution is associated with the LILAC Project or not.

CONCLUSION

One issue the pilot study identified was the need to expand the LILAC Project in several areas. The pilot study consisted of fifteen students at a single university, but findings, while not generalizable, do seem to agree with other studies that suggest a larger national trend. After completing the pilot study and revising the methodology as discussed in this chapter, we have begun recruiting additional universities to partner with us in collecting data. Expanding the study offers the chance to work with a more diverse subject population—from community colleges to doctoral universities, from rural and urban campuses, and from a variety of geographic areas. Such a diverse participant population will, we hope, eventually allow us to better discover trends within specific universities, specific disciplines, and specific student populations and to report more general findings across institutions, institution types, and geographic and demographic divisions. Among the expanded findings, we hope to see not only where and how students obtain and use essential lifelong information-literacy skills but also to determine whether there are specific markers for the academic time in which students begin to turn more to academic research. Spin-off studies might include future iterations of RAP sessions, for example, by offering instructions to subjects that focus more specifically on other skills. For instance, a revised RAP subject instruction sheet might ask students to conduct research using only library databases so we can establish connections with other areas of questionnaire results and better assess how different levels of students interact with the library databases and how proficient these students are with this type of research. Questionnaires could also be designed to include teaching information or an expanded section targeting more specific research skills, as well as to address questions that could emerge with a more diverse subject population.

We are currently seeking additional partner institutions to join us in collecting data for the LILAC Project. Ultimately, we hope to gather data from as many as one thousand subjects from a variety of institutions. We also encourage spin-off projects, such as one currently being conducted with pre- and in-service teachers at a regional university in the southeastern United States. For researchers considering partnering with us or developing spin-off projects on their own, we have made all the materials for the LILAC Project, including the IRB application—which includes the questionnaire, subject instructions, recruitment flyers, coding instruments, and more—available in a publicly shared Google Drive folder. In addition, we will be publishing RAP videos collected from both the pilot study and the full, multi-institutional study to a public YouTube channel, which we hope will be a useful repository for teaching and research.[5]

Notes

1. The final LILAC IRB, along with our partner and subject instructions, a link to the Qualtrics survey, and revised coding documents can be accessed in our shared Google Drive folder at http://tinyurl.com/mkzzrbo.
2. Discrepancies included such things as page not loading or taking extensive time to load, subjects contemplating search terms, and subjects correcting spelling of search terms after the initial loading of results.
3. See the Citation Project's Information for Participants at http://site.citationproject.net/wp-content/uploads/2011/11/Citation-Project-Information-for-Participants.pdf.
4. All subject names are pseudonyms.
5. For more information on the LILAC Project, contact the authors at jwalker@GeorgiaSouthern.edu or ablackwellst@lamar.edu.

APPENDIX 2.A

These appendices may be downloaded from https://upcolorado.com/utah-state-university-press/item/3188-points-of-departure and used or modified for teaching or research purposes with attribution.

QUESTIONNAIRE

Do NOT write your name anywhere on this questionnaire. The coded number in the upper-right-hand corner will associate the data in this questionnaire with your video, but will NOT be associated with your consent form or any other identifying information.

This questionnaire is part of a research project aimed at studying student information-seeking behaviors. By completing this questionnaire you consent to participate in this research study. We greatly appreciate your cooperation in completing this survey. Please be assured that information collected will be kept confidential and anonymous. You may refuse to answer any question or you may stop at any time with no penalty.

DEMOGRAPHIC INFORMATION:

1. Age:
2. Gender:
3. Major (Program of Study):
4. Minor (if applicable):
5. Is English your first language? Please circle: Yes / No
6. Are you a (check one):
    a. Freshman
    b. Sophomore
    c. Junior
    d. Senior
    e. Graduate Student (Masters level)
    f. Graduate Student (PhD level)
    g. Other (please specify):

QUESTIONNAIRE:

1. In what course(s), if any, were you taught library and/or online research skills? (Check all that apply.)

    English course—high school
    English course—college
    College Orientation
    Other (please specify):
    None (Proceed to Question 4)

2. How was instruction provided? (Check all that apply.)

    Lecture
    Hands-on workshop
    Directed reading (textbook, handout, online tutorial)
    Other (please specify):

3. What research skills (if any) were you taught? (Check all that apply.)

    Using Boolean operators
    Keyword searching
    Subject/Author/Title searches
    Library catalog
    Online library databases
    Web search strategies
    Note taking

Citation practices (e.g. MLA, APA, etc.)
Summarizing information
Paraphrasing information
Integrating information from sources with your own arguments
Using quotations effectively
Avoiding plagiarism
Interlibrary loan
Knowing when information from outside sources is needed
Determining source types (e.g. difference between an edited collection and a single author source)
Evaluating sources (Print)
Evaluating sources (Online)
Evaluating sources (Web)
Conducting interviews
Composing effective surveys and/or questionnaires
Determining the type of information needed
Citing sources in the text
Compiling a Works Cited list following MLA format
Compiling a References or Bibliography list following APA format
Compiling a source list following another style (please specify):
Using a bibliographic generator (EasyBib, BibMe, etc.)
Citing media other than text (for instance, pictures, video, or audio sources)
Other (please specify):

On a scale of 1–10, with 1 being the lowest and 10 being the highest, please rank the following.

1 (Lowest)————————————*10 (Highest)*

4. Your ability to locate books on a given topic in the university library
5. Your ability to locate articles in scholarly journals in print
6. Your ability to locate articles in scholarly journals online
7. Your ability to locate information on a topic online
8. Your ability to evaluate the reliability of online information sources
9. Your ability to evaluate the reliability of print information sources
   Yes or No
10. Have you ever been required to include information from library and/or online research in a paper or project? Yes/No
11. If you answered yes, to question #10, what course or courses was it for?

Please indicate the extent to which you agree with the following statements using a scale of 1 to 5, 1 being "Strongly Disagree" and 5 being "Strongly Agree."*

12. I am a strong writer.
    1 2 3 4 5
14. Writing will be important in my career.
    1 2 3 4 5
15. My library research skills are adequate to my needs.
    1 2 3 4 5
16. My online research skills are adequate to my needs.
    1 2 3 4 5
17. I would like to improve my research skills.
    1 2 3 4 5
18. I have been provided adequate instruction in library and online research skills.
    1 2 3 4 5
19. I do most of my research using online search engines.
    1 2 3 4 5
20. I do most of my research using library resources.
    1 2 3 4 5
21. I know how to cite information obtained from outside sources in my papers.
    1 2 3 4 5
22. I know how to cite quotations in my papers.
    1 2 3 4 5
23. I know how to summarize information.
    1 2 3 4 5
24. I know how to paraphrase information.
    1 2 3 4 5
25. I know how to evaluate the information I find.
    1 2 3 4 5
26. I understand the importance of using and presenting information ethically.
    1 2 3 4 5
27. I understand the difference between summarizing and/or paraphrasing information from sources and plagiarising.
    1 2 3 4 5
28. I understand how to cite multimedia (pictures, audio, and/or video components) that I may include in my papers or projects (online or in print).
    1 2 3 4 5
29. I have been instructed in the basic tenets of copyright legislation and fair use.
    1 2 3 4 5

30. I believe teaching research skills in schools and colleges is a waste of time.
    1 2 3 4 5

31. Research is about finding information to support my opinions.
    1 2 3 4 5

32. If I already know what I want to say, I do not need to locate information on opposing points of view.
    1 2 3 4 5

33. If information is posted on a government Web site (.gov), it is accurate.
    1 2 3 4 5

34. If information is posted on a commercial Web site (.com), it is not credible.
    1 2 3 4 5

35. If information is posted on a news or newspaper Web site, it is accurate.
    1 2 3 4 5

36. If information is posted on an organizational Web site (.org), it is credible.
    1 2 3 4 5

37. Information posted by an educational institution (.edu) is always reliable.
    1 2 3 4 5

38. I understand the difference between primary and secondary sources.
    1 2 3 4 5

39. Once I have located the required number of sources, I do not need to look for more.
    1 2 3 4 5

40. I often use a bibliography generator to automatically format my citations for the Works Cited list.
    1 2 3 4 5

41. I maintain detailed records or notes of my research.
    1 2 3 4 5

42. I sometimes forget where I got information from.
    1 2 3 4 5

43. I understand what a "scholarly peer-reviewed journal" is.
    1 2 3 4 5

44. I usually use the Web for most of my research needs.
    1 2 3 4 5

45. I usually use the library databases for most of my research needs.
    1 2 3 4 5

46. I know how to use Interlibrary Loan (ILL) services.
    1   2   3   4   5
47. I ask the reference librarians at my university library for help when I get stuck (either in person, via email, or "Ask a Librarian" chat services, if available).
    1   2   3   4   5
48. Most of my research is completed at home.
    1   2   3   4   5
50. I often wait until the last minute to do my research and write my papers.
    1   2   3   4   5

Thank you for completing this questionnaire! Please return the questionnaire to the drop box.

* NOTE: no question 13 in original

APPENDIX 2.B

PARTICIPANT INSTRUCTIONS

You need information for a paper you are writing for a class. For this study, we will record a brief 10–15 minute video of your information-seeking (research) behaviors along with your spoken narrative, telling us what you are doing and why. We will not be recording any video of your face, and no personally identifiable information will be included.

There are no "right" or "wrong" answers; we are interested in finding out how students such as you locate information for their academic projects. Please do whatever you would normally do when you need to locate information for papers or projects.

You may choose one of the following topics or one of your own. Please identify your topic at the beginning of your narrative (for examples, "I am writing a paper on X for a class in Y. The first place I would look for information is . . . ").

SUGGESTED TOPICS

1. Global warming/environmental issues
2. Health care/health issues
3. Diversity issues (gender, race, ethnicity, etc.)
4. Historical events/issues
5. Literature/literary research
6. Engineering and/or technical topics

Please let us know when you are ready to begin, and we will start the recording. You may stop at any time, or we will stop you after no longer than 15 minutes.

Thank you for your help with this project!

References

Barratt, Caroline Cason, Kristin Nielsen, Christy Desmet, and Ron Balthazor. 2009. "Collaboration Is Key: Librarians and Composition Instructors Analyze Student Research and Writing." *Libraries and the Academy* 9 (1): 37–56. http://dx.doi.org/10.1353/pla.0.0038.

Barron, Brigid, and Randi A. Engle. 2007. "Analyzing Data Derived from Video Records." In *Guidelines for Video Research in Education: Recommendations from an Expert Panel*, edited by Sharon J. Derry, 24–33. Chicago, IL: Data Research and Development Center, University of Chicago. http://drdc.uchicago.edu/what/video-research-guidelines.pdf.

Cólon-Aguirre, Mónica, and Rachel A. Fleming-May. 2012. "You Just Type in What You Are Looking For: Undergraduates' Use of Library Resources vs. Wikipedia." *Journal of Academic Librarianship* 38 (6): 391–99. http://dx.doi.org/10.1016/j.acalib.2012.09.013.

Head, Alison. 2008. "Information Literacy from the Trenches: How Do Humanities and Social Science Majors Conduct Academic Research?" *College & Research Libraries* 69 (5): 427–46. http://dx.doi.org/10.5860/crl.69.5.427.

Head, Alison J. 2013. "Learning the Ropes: How Freshmen Conduct Course Research Once They Enter College." Project Information Literacy Research Report. Seattle: Information School, University of Washington; http://projectinfolit.org/publications. http://dx.doi.org/10.2139/ssrn.2364080.

Head, Alison J., and Michael B. Eisenberg. 2013. Foreword to *The New Digital Scholar: Exploring and Enriching the Research Practices of NextGen Students*, edited by Randall McClure and James P. Purdy, xi–xiv. Medford, NJ: Information Today.

Howard, Rebecca Moore, Tricia Serviss, and Tanya K. Rodrigue. 2010. "Writing from Sources, Writing from Sentences." *Writing & Pedagogy* 2 (2): 177–92. http://dx.doi.org/10.1558/wap.v2i2.177.

Jamieson, Sandra, and Rebecca Moore Howard. 2011. "Unraveling the Citation Trail." In *Smart Talks*. Project Information Literacy. http://projectinfolit.org/st/howard-jamieson.asp.

Jamieson, Sandra, and Rebecca Moore Howard. 2013. "Sentence-Mining: Uncovering the Amount of Reading and Reading Comprehension in College Writers' Researched Writing." In *The New Digital Scholar: Exploring and Enriching the Research and Writing Practices of NextGen Students*, edited by Randall McClure and James Purdy, 109–32. Medford, NJ: Information Today.

Maid, Barry M., and Barbara J. D'Angelo. 2013. "Teaching Researching in the Digital Age: An Information Literacy Perspective on the New Digital Scholar." In *The New Digital Scholar: Exploring and Enriching the Research Practices of NextGen Students*, edited by Randall McClure and James P. Purdy, 295–312. Medford, NJ: Information Today.

McClure, Randall, and Kellian Clink. 2009. "How Do You Know That? An Investigation of Student Research Practices in the Digital Age." *Libraries and the Academy* 9 (1): 115–32. http://dx.doi.org/10.1353/pla.0.0033.

Points of Departure 1
REPLICATION AND THE NEED TO BUILD ON AND EXPAND LOCAL AND PILOT STUDIES

In August 2015, the Open Science Collaboration (OSC) published the results of a project that attempted to replicate the results of one hundred experimental and correlational studies reported in three top-tier psychology journals in a single year (2008). The collaboration warns that there is no single indicator that can describe replication success, but based on the five different indicators they employed, they report that between 53 and 64 percent of the studies they replicated did not produce the same results as the original. They report that their replication studies used materials provided by the original authors and were reviewed in advance for methodological fidelity. They also report that the experience and expertise of the researchers was not predictive of the replicability of the research. Their report was widely shared in the media and even more so on social media—it even has a *Wikipedia* entry under *replication crisis*—adding to an already simmering concern about the reliability of research data in the sciences and social sciences, especially large-scale RAD research.

In the field of writing studies, the move from small observational studies to larger qualitative, quantitative, and mixed-methods research is often heralded as one that will bring more reliable and thereby generalizable information to help us understand things previously believed based on what Steven North (1987) called "lore." In its call for transcontextual RAD research, *Points of Departure* is designed to facilitate replication of studies and methods. So how do we respond to concerns raised by the OSC research, and how do we continue to make the claims we do about the importance of data-driven research? For one thing, the OSC research provides a cautionary tale about the danger of drawing final conclusions without conducting follow-up research. It reminds us that all findings are provisional and actually strengthens the argument we are making in this collection that researchers must not stop at small or local studies but must explore and reexplore questions both transcontextually and transtemporally as part of the process of increasing understanding. It also reminds us that terms like *replication* are complex, and, as Karen Lunsford puts it (this collection), "The specific processes of constructing measures and codes . . . operationalize words, images, punctuation, and other semiotic signs" (xii). Such operationalizing introduces ambiguity and complicates the process of replication in the way attempted by the OSC researchers.

While concerns like these have, as Lunsford observes (this collection), increased the nervousness about replication within the field of writing studies, the OSC researchers also express concern about the infrequency of replication. They are critical of psychology for "prioritizing novelty over replication" and of journal reviewers and editors who refuse to publish replication research if it confirms the original research because it is "unoriginal"—an experience Citation Project researchers report in the field of writing studies as well. In their conclusion, the OSC notes,

> The claim that "we already know this" belies the uncertainty of scientific evidence. Innovation points out paths that are possible; replication points out paths that are likely; progress relies on both. Replication can increase certainty when findings are reproduced and promote innovation when they are not. This project provides accumulating evidence for many findings in psychological research and suggests that there is still more work to do to verify whether we know what we think we know.

It is our hope that research stemming from chapters in *Points of Departure* will also provide both "accumulating evidence" and opportunities for "still more work."

The story of the one hundred studies does not end in 2015, though. The OSC authors conclude that "even research of exemplary quality may have irreproducible empirical findings because of random or systematic error." Taking them at their word, other researchers replicated the replication and concluded that such error also marred the OSC research (Gilbert et al. 2016). The OSC explains that "direct replication is the attempt to recreate the conditions believed sufficient for obtaining a previously observed finding and is the means of establishing reproducibility of a finding with new data." The challenge is to determine which conditions should be replicated and what impact that will have on the findings. Congjun Mu and Paul Kei Matsuda report that in writing studies, researchers prefer the term "approximate replication" that allows for studies to ignore "nonessential differences" because they recognize this challenge and the impact of local context and language (Mu and Matsuda 2016; see Lunsford, this collection). Similarly, Daniel T. Gilbert et al. (2016) conclude that the OSC researchers should have been more fully conscious of the impact of differences between the original studies and the replications. When the original researchers reviewed the method used to replicate their research prior to OSC's actually conducting it, only 70 percent found the proposed method to replicate their method sufficiently to be reliable. Of the remaining 30 percent, in some cases the context was significantly different. In others, the passage of time or differences in the research sample were the cause of anxiety. Gilbert et al. report that those 30 percent were less likely to be successfully replicated. They also found that when a larger sample was used in the replication than in the original, the results were more likely to be replicated, suggesting that the method was reliable but the small sample size could too easily skew results.

In the first chapter of this collection, Jamieson describes a similar experience in the research conducted by the Citation Project as it moved from a small study to a transcontextual project. While the overall conclusion of the single-school study (Howard, Serviss, and Rodrigue 2010)—that students write from sentences—was replicated in the larger study, the initial finding that students do not include summary was not replicated. Why the difference? The larger sample size was more reliable. If one were to replicate the pilot with the same number of students, it is quite possible the new data would differ for several reasons. First, as with the OSC replications, using a different population allows for all kinds of other differences to have an impact. Gilbert et al. (2016) describe a study initially conducted on students at Stanford that was "replicated" using students in Amsterdam and reported in 2015 to have failed to produce the same results, calling the initial study into question. They report, however, that the same study repeated using other US students produced results similar to the Stanford-study results. The chapters in this section encourage replication in order to explore difference as well as to track similarity. One might replicate research across contexts in order to gain a deeper understanding of local influences, and a different finding would not negate the initial finding but rather expand it and prompt further contextual research. Chapters 1 and 2 emphasize research philosophies that would make differences between cohort groups, especially nationally, an invitation for further local and translocal research rather than an indication that the initial research was flawed, and the significance of this difference cannot be understated.

The OSC researchers remind us that research results that do not replicate the original can lead to productive new research, but we should also be mindful of the larger lesson from Gilbert et al. (2016): replication is a tricky business. Replication of method includes not just the ways data is collected and coded but also how it is analyzed. For example, while the percentage of citations coded as summary in the full Citation Project study is small (6 percent), the sample also reveals that 41 percent (seventy-one of the 174 students) summarized at least once. As appears to have happened in the studies described by the OSC (2015), if researchers report only part of the data, they skew the interpretation, whether intentionally or not. The 6 percent finding tells us summary is infrequent and seems to indicate that few students use summary. Used alone, it sounds the same alarm as the single-site study. In contrast, if only the 41 percent were reported, the initial study might be dismissed as purely a local phenomenon. When both figures are reported, we see that a sizeable number of students in the sample did summarize, but they did not do so with great frequency. This combined finding adds support to the calls for more pedagogical attention to summary writing that followed the pilot study. It also suggests the need for further research to understand how students use sources and the reasons they incorporate the ideas of others as they do. Papers might be coded using the citation context method employed by Citation Project researchers, but then students might be interviewed (see Serviss, this collection), participate in a focus group (see Benedicks, this collection), or be asked to complete a survey (see Costello this collection). Or researchers might code summary with more nuance, exploring whether it is employed to remind readers of the plot, capture the main argument, or briefly reference additional information, for example.

DEPARTURE POINTS: SOME PARTICULAR WAYS FORWARD

Both studies in this section can be used in many different ways as points of departure for other researchers; they are themselves based on replications and revisions of smaller and more local studies. For example, like the Citation Project described in chapter 1, the LILAC Project (chapter 2) collects information about sources selected, and further research could include coding those sources using the categories used by the Citation Project, which were themselves drawn from other, single-site, studies (Carlson 2006; McClure and Clink 2009). Or they could be coded using categories developed for other studies of sources (see Jamieson 2016). The LILAC Project offers the opportunity to deepen our understanding of the reasons students select specific sources and what they expect to get from them. It challenges simplistic assertions about the impact and use of Google, the concept of students as lazy rather than ill informed, and offers the opportunity to design a study using similar screen-capture methods to focus on any one of those topics. Researchers could also develop a study that combines citation context coding of papers with video capture of the process used to find sources for those papers, which would produce rich data for deeper analysis.

Just as local studies can be scaled up to become transcontextual projects, so larger studies can be scaled down to answer local questions, and if the method is replicated closely and the results align with the larger study, useful conclusions can be drawn about the local context. Based on their local data and the ways it aligned with the larger findings, institutions that participated in the Citation Project study of researched writing produced in FYW courses have responded by revising their first-year programs, developing new curricula, and changing plagiarism-prevention programs and policies, among other things. Some writing centers have modified tutor training and practices, other institutions have introduced writing fellows to work with courses assigning researched writing, and several have enriched relationships with libraries and information-literacy programs. Other institutions have replicated the method and made similar adjustments without being part of the larger study. In other words, the very needs that provoke local and unreplicated research are also served by transcontextual projects like these. In fact, the opportunity to compare local data with that of other institutions makes such research more locally powerful. The Citation Project PIs compiled reports for participating institutions, placing their data within the context of the larger findings, but local institutions could do that for themselves—especially if PIs are drawn from multiple campuses.

The two projects described in this section also invite other institutions to join with them. As chapter 2 indicates, the LILAC Project is seeking to expand its database (lilac-group.blogspot.com/2015/06/the-lilac-group-is-still-seeking.html), and the Citation Project is expanding internationally. The Citation Project website (citationproject.net) includes the researchers' methods and the documents that appear in the appendix to chapter 1 and notes that researchers are also willing to work with other scholars who propose related research. On a larger scale, the goal of the LILAC Project is to expand to include new sites of research and to assemble data on the information-literacy practices of one thousand students to produce a public database that can be used to answer other questions than those that drove the initial research. Expansion of the Citation Project offers similar possibilities. As we see from other essays in this collection, though, both of these research projects may also be used as jumping-off points for other research, which may become transcontextual RAD research in its own right. The value is in the transparency of methods that allows other researchers to adapt or replicate research, first in pilot studies and then, after feedback from peers, as larger studies. By sharing the process of moving from idea to research, we hope chapters 1 and 2 will facilitate the kinds of research proposed in this collection and help others avoid the pitfalls of replication that Gilbert et al. (2016) claim occurred in the OSC (2015) study.

References

Carlson, Jake. 2006. "An Examination of Undergraduate Student Citation Behavior." *Journal of Academic Librarianship* 32 (1): 14–22. http://dx.doi.org/10.1016/j.acalib.2005.10.001.

Gilbert, Daniel T., Gary King, Stephen Pettigrew, and Timothy D. Wilson. 2016. "Comment on 'Estimating the Reproducibility of Psychological Science.'" *Science* 351 (6277): 1037. http://dx.doi.org/10.1126/science.aad7243.

Howard, Rebecca Moore, Tricia Serviss, and Tanya K. Rodrigue. 2010. "Writing from Sources, Writing from Sentences." *Writing & Pedagogy* 2 (2): 177–92. http://dx.doi.org/10.1558/wap.v2i2.177.

Jamieson, Sandra. 2016. "What the Citation Project Tells Us about Information Literacy in College Composition." In *Information Literacy: Research and Collaboration across Disciplines*, edited by Barbara D'Angelo, Sandra Jamieson, Barry Maid, and Janice R. Walker, 117–41. Perspectives in Writing Series. Fort Collins, CO: WAC Clearing House and University Press of Colorado.

McClure, Randall, and Killian Clink. 2009. "How Do You Know That? An Investigation of Student Research Practices in the Digital Age." *Portal: Libraries and the Academy* 9 (1): 115–32. http://dx.doi.org/10.1353/pla.0.0033.

Mu, Congjun, and Paul K. Matsuda. 2016. "Replication in L2 Writing Research: Journal of Second Language Writing Authors' Perceptions." *TESOL Quarterly* 50 (1): 201–19.

North, Stephen. 1987. *The Making of Knowledge in Composition: Portrait of an Emerging Field*. Upper Montclair, NJ: Boynton.

Open Science Collaboration. 2015. "Estimating the Reproducibility of Psychological Science." *Science* 349 (6251).

PART 2

Building on Transcontextual Research

Interchapter 2
WHAT DOES DESIGN-BASED RESEARCH OFFER AS A TOOL FOR RAD RESEARCH IN WRITING STUDIES?

One of the great challenges and opportunities of educational research is rectifying predictions about how learning theoretically works with how learning *actually* works in—and across—different contexts. Those of us who study writing and literacy are uniquely aware of these tensions. In fact, writing studies research traditionally inquires into how beautifully divergent and surprising learning can be in practice. Conversations about writing processes in 1960s writing-pedagogy research embody this tension; theoretical understandings of *typical* processes of developing writers became dangerously calcified into *the* writing process quite quickly. What began as inquiry about how writing happens (Cooper 1986; Emig 1971; Flower and Hayes 1981; Hairston 1986; Kostelnick 1989; Murray 1980; Odell 1980; Perl 1980; Selzer 1983; Sommers 1980) was shaped by some readers into the steps of "the writing process" we find in many primary-school classrooms (brainstorm, outline, draft, peer review, revise). We have long recognized that this singular sense of "the writing process" doesn't capture the actual experiences and productive strategies of writers in practice. While many student writers embrace some of these steps in writing a research paper (such as outlining and annotating sources), writing studies scholars agree we need to look beyond the *typified* writing practices frequently reported in school settings in favor of studying the actual ways successful writing works (Pigg 2014; Prior 1998; Sheridan and Rowsell 2010; Shipka 2011; Roozen 2012; and many others). To that end we remain invested in

DOI: 10.7330/9781607326250.c002b

questions like, how do writers in different multilinguistic, intercultural, and multimodal contexts develop and enact writing processes that help them to evolve further? How do we attend to the practices and strategies of individual writers while also learning more about how writing develops with translocal and transcontextual applications in mind?

One way for writing studies to address this tension is central to this edited collection: embracing RAD research designed in anticipation of eventual transcontextual use and discovery (see the introduction and the interchapter "What Do We Mean by Transcontextual Research?" in this collection). We turn to our research methodologies and designs to help us make these productive, generative connections between the local and translocal, the contextual and transcontextual. In some communities, RAD-oriented research is a clear way forward (see the introduction). Yet even within these enthusiastic communities who embrace RAD values, researchers struggle with *how* to systematically and sustainably conduct such studies in ways that honor the many different ways learning can happen.

We aren't alone in this quest for flexible and expansive, yet potentially reproducible, research designs. Many learning scientists are interested in a similar kind of research that observes learning in its natural forms and that works to articulate local findings about learning in helpfully "generalized" ways (Collins, Joseph, and Bielaczyc 2004; Kelly 2004). Our fellow education researchers in the learning sciences also need methodologies that could accommodate the unpredictable places where learning actually happens: not in laboratories or controlled studies, but in the many spaces where we learn—from classrooms to camping trips. Education researchers know learning happens in messy, divergent, and unpredictable ways at times, particularly deep and lasting learning that (hopefully) persists and perhaps even transfers to other contexts. Learning scientists began to confront this issue explicitly with the development of design experiments (Brown 1992; Collins 1992) in the 1990s that evolved into what is now recognized as design-based research methodologies and orientations. This interchapter works to introduce (1) the development of design-based research (DBR) in learning sciences, (2) values and practices of the methodology, and (3) affordances offered to writing studies research like the projects presented in chapters 3, 4, and 5 in part 2.

DESIGN-BASED RESEARCH METHODOLOGY

Learning-science scholar Ann Brown (1992), one of the recognized founders of design-based research (Anderson and Shattuck 2012), sought a flexible research methodology that would bridge theories and practices of learning explicitly. Brown wanted to design pedagogical and curricular interventions that were also intentional research projects meant to test and expand theories about learning. Most important, she needed to find methods and tools to help her understand student learning outside laboratory-like conditions, embracing the dynamic environments of realistic learning spaces (classrooms, dining rooms, etc.) as assets in the research design rather than limitations. Brown struggled to describe the features of such a research methodology as she worked with others to design learning experiments (pedagogical practices, classroom activities, etc.) that were then studied, refined, and retrospectively analyzed across several iterations of that designed learning experience. Allan Collins (1992; Collins, Joseph, and Bielaczyc 2004) contributed to this ongoing conversation, incorporating his interest in what Herbert Simon (1985) called "the design sciences"—fields like architecture, engineering, computer science, robotics, aeronautics, and artificial intelligence—for help and inspiration designing the kind of praxis research Brown was already piloting. Collins (1992) explicitly used Simon's conceptualization of the design sciences as a guiding principle. The foundations of innovation and surprise that defined these design fields brought a culture of surprise and heuristic vitality to education research previously constrained by acontextual theories about learning (design fields also explicitly influence writing studies: see Arola 2010; Carpenter et al. 2015; George 2002; Marback 2009; Müller 2011; Purdy 2014; Wysocki 2005).

In this design culture, researchers gain the affordances of emerging tools, curricula, and pedagogies but also must grapple with the tensions that come with using these inventions in practice. This kind of juncture between *poiesis* (what we might take to mean "making" and "becoming") and *praxis* (most crudely understood as "practicing") is where learning happens and thus where education researchers must dwell. Design-based research orientations count on this productive collision/collaboration between *poiesis*—the emergence of new learning tools for both students and researchers—and *praxis*—practicing with these tools, refining and honing the tools as we go—to propel researchers forward. It is the recursive processes involved with designing, deploying, evaluating, and redesigning research/teaching methods within a collaborative team, the most important criteria of DBR, that allow researchers to move from analyzing one small activity/site to analyzing several. It is the dance of *poiesis* and *praxis* that allows methods and knowledges to be both local and translocal in value from the DBR perspective.

THE VALUES AND GOALS OF DESIGN-BASED RESEARCH (DBR)

Brown's (1992) presentation of DBR is built upon some basic assertions that form the foundation of DBR as a methodological approach.

1. Classrooms and learning environments are messy, bearing little or no resemblance to controlled laboratory-like environments. Methodologies used to study learning therefore must be useful and reliable in "naturalistic" environments learners will typically encounter—like complicated, living cultures in classrooms—rather than laboratory-like conditions researchers would have to manufacture and control for the sake of the research project.

2. Education research ideally contributes to both learning theory and practice; our research design ought to account for both within DBR orientations.

3. When researchers study students and teachers in action, we necessarily alter the situation through our presence and engagement; researchers ought to leverage this interference into strategic interventions in our research design.

4. Research ought to account for—and incorporate—the actors and culture of a local site. Classroom cultures provide useful input for researchers. We ought to value the local context as priceless input, conceptualizing teachers and students as collaborative researchers, imagining the curriculum, technology, and classroom culture as affordances.

5. The *design* (or learning experiment) used within DBR must include a clear intervention that informs practice in this environment. The purpose of design-based research orientations is to improve learning *while also* conducting research.

6. There ought to be clear output in the form of contributions to learning theory as well as tangible *artifacts* useful in that local context but also well beyond it. The "artifacts" (Collins, Joseph, and Bielaczyc 2004) from the study can take many forms: activities, curricular components, policy, concepts, software, and so forth.

7. These artifacts ought to be generalizable, or what we call *transcontextual* in this edited collection. Artifacts must be "able to migrate from our experimental [site] to . . . average [sites]" (Collins, Joseph, and Bielaczyc 2004, 143).

8. DBR often requires a system of methods to collect varied data from different perspectives, accounting for all pieces of a designed environment (ethnography, interviews, textual analysis, video recordings, curriculum mapping, etc.).

9. DBR is a methodology that requires researchers to determine, create, and deploy research methods as part of their *design*.

10. DBR requires that researchers engineer—or design—a learning experience or environment and then study that design in collaboration with the students and teachers learning within it.
11. DBR begins with design and also ends with design. Researchers design learning environments and experiences; while studying how this designed activity impacts student learners, the researchers themselves are learning, leading to revision, refinement, and perhaps even reimagining of the design itself. Thus, redesigning is a key element of DBR because the researchers are themselves impacted by the learning experiment they facilitate.
12. All active participants in a learning experience are influenced and changed by it. DBR increasingly emphasizes the importance of inquiring about how the teachers and researchers designing and participating in a learning intervention are transformed along with participating student learners (see Kali 2016 for her definition of DRTL, or design researchers' transformational learning framework). Adding DRTL frameworks to the DBR tradition investigates the *processes of research* that illuminate how meaningful learning happens. This DRTL approach insists that all the participants in a pedagogical intervention are *learners* who can be transformed by their engagement with the experiment.

From a writing studies perspective, then, DBR methodology merges the best that design sciences and education research have to offer, emphasizing the dynamic nature of educational research that must account for the unpredictable nature of learning while also freeing researchers from limiting ideas that *good* research is designed *completely* and *correctly* from the start. DBR/DRTL orientations imagine that research is designed as a starting point rather than a verifiable, concluding one to be proven. Brown needed a methodology that harnessed the *processes* of research to make that research more comprehensive and more useful. Current practitioners (Anderson 2005; Anderson and Shattuck 2012; Barab and Kirschner 2001; Barab and Squire 2004; Cobb et al. 2003; Collins, Joseph, and Bielaczyc 2004; Dede 2004; Edelson 2002; Herrington et al. 2007; Johnson, Veitch, and Dewiyanti 2015; Kali 2016; Kelly 2004; Mingfong et al. 2010; Strappers 2007) embrace these charges and get to work building networks of complementary methods and delineating the doing of such DBR research.

Educational researchers using DBR methodology confront similar challenges we address in this edited collection. DBR pursues ecological validity in educational research (see Sandoval and Bell 2004 and Schmuckler 2001 for further definition and history of the term; see

Fleckenstein et al. 2008 for discussion of this issue within writing studies) just as budding RAD research communities do within writing studies. Ecological validity is defined differently across research communities, but most typically, ecological validity in educational research means sound, transcontextual research can be realized by matching up the study's design, research methods, and data as closely as possible with the actual learning environment where the same kinds of teaching and learning happen. Ecological validity means research design ought to mirror the community and the tasks it studies, adapted to fit the local context while also preparing for eventual extraction from that context. Thus, we can take useful orientations from DBR research into writing studies.

In writing studies, ecological validity is also a typical ideal in our research design; we study writing as it happens in specific learning environments—writing classrooms, writing programs, writing centers, workplaces, community centers, and more so we can honor and investigate writing in those unique cultures and communities. Ideally, writing studies research design *emerges* from actual ("naturalistic") learning environments, shaped by recurring questions scholars have about those environments. Research questions, DBR methodology suggests, ought to come from teacher-researcher observation and engagement with learners as they confront real problems and challenges because the research is meant to expand learning theories and best learning practices.

Writing studies can use DBR methodology to help us do several key things at once. DBR helps writing studies get even closer to ecological validity in our research design; DBR helps writing studies focus on the *processes* and reiterative nature of research as it emphasizes the constant revision involved with research in naturalistic settings; DBR helps writing studies commit to the goal of research *artifacts*—whether pedagogy, curriculum, policy, concept, or tool—that are extractable, useful in both the research site and beyond it. Most crucially, DBR offers writing studies a methodological framework, complete with values and goals, to guide practitioners designing research mechanisms and refining methods *as they go*. The methodological framework is vast and a bit nebulous, as it requires us to think about our research as simultaneous inquiry and intervention as well as simultaneously local and transcontextual. And— it requires us to design research as learning interventions, determine which of the many research methods in our qualitative and quantitative arsenals are most appropriate, and make peace with research projects as evolving and therefore often imperfect at times. DBR allows research projects to be strengthened by reiterations, by follow-up studies, by redesigned studies without the peril of the research being labeled flawed.

Thus, this collection proposes a heuristic-like checklist for the willing writing studies scholar interested in using DBR.

DESIGN-BASED RESEARCH CHECKLIST FOR WRITING STUDIES

Design-based research methodology is defined by some key features (Barab and Squire 2004) and goals (Design-Based Research Collective 2003). Some ingredients are required to begin the processes of DBR:

- Collaborative research teams, most typically made up of faculty/administrators and students inquiring together. Groups of researchers are important to this methodology because of its qualitative nature, because of the interaction of researchers with their own "designed" experiences, and because of the crucial role of reiteration. Collaboration allows for more complete and helpful reflection.
- A specific—or set of specific—and naturalistic (noncontrolled) environments in which a designed learning experience is set in motion.
- Mixed-method research mechanisms designed to both prompt and capture learning (designing assignments [see Melzer 2003], activities, surveys, interviews, etc. that can both capture and intervene in learning).
- Self-reflective researchers who undertake projects as emergent, modifying their research design and methods as they go to make the research—and the learning experiences it is creating—better.
- Culminating transcontextual research *artifacts* about learning and teaching that are useful beyond the local context from which they arose.

The ultimate outcomes of DBR—theories, practices, and artifacts—are meant to *begin* an ongoing inquiry. The artifacts that come from the project are meant to provide access to other researchers who might take up those artifacts and use them differently, might reassess collected data, might extend the project by collecting additional and new kinds of data, might refine some part of the design and run the experience again. The artifacts, in other words, form bridges between individual research projects, allowing research to be reproduced, reconceived, expanded, adapted, and more. Significantly for the purposes of this collection, DBR approaches allow RAD research to thrive.

DESIGN-BASED RESEARCH IN CHAPTERS 3, 4, AND 5

We offer the three chapters in this section as an invitation for readers to delve into research whose goals and strategies exemplify the core principles of design-based research—observing learning where it most naturalistically occurs for the explicit goal of successful intervention. We hope readers will begin to imagine how the research methods discussed in these chapters might be adapted or revised for other contexts, or how the questions that motivated the research might themselves become the basis for other studies. By understanding design-based research in the local contexts described, other researchers may imagine their own interventions, not exactly replicating these studies but building on and from them as part of the process of transcontextual replication described in the introduction to this collection.

In "The Things They Carry: Using Design-Based Research in Writing-Teacher Education," Tricia Serviss describes this methodology in use with graduate students preparing to become teachers. A pilot study emerged as she tried simultaneously to understand how graduate students use sources and to teach those same graduate students to better understand source use as well. The research methods were themselves pedagogical-design experiments. The pilot study embodies several design-based research approaches: the research is conducted collaboratively, incorporating learners as research participants and peer coders; the research is emergent by design, allowing participants to shape how a variety of mixed methods are mobilized; the research is reiterative, premised upon two rounds of the pilot study to invite refinement and development. Most important, the pilot was designed to have transcontextual value so it could either evolve into a broader study with more participants from different sites or become a teaching artifact useful for graduate education in other spaces.

In "Storied Research: Using Focus Groups as a Responsive Method," Crystal Benedicks presents research about undergraduate source use via a mixed-method approach (using surveys and focus groups) that depends upon the engagement of participants as co-researchers. Benedicks's project extends previously generated research (Jamieson's survey), modifying the designed intervention by including focus groups made of both students and faculty. Benedicks modified existing interventions and revised the approach with additional efforts (focus groups) that would allow for simultaneous investigation and intervention in design-based research style.

The opportunities of reiterative research in this tradition are further exemplified by Kristi Murray Costello in "Terms and Perceptions: Using Surveys to Discover Student Beliefs about Research." She describes not only how surveys were refined across two different phases of data collection but also how key realizations were made about the relationship between the surveys, the populations surveyed, and the composition of the local campus community, shaping the research project into a productive intervention. Like the chapters by Serviss and Benedicks, Costello's chapter describes how a team of collaborative coders worked to refine the survey mechanism, illustrating possibilities for further refinements.

These three chapters turn the abstract goals of design-based research into visible strategies and habits, outlining how these broad notions—like collaborative, reiterative research design—might play out. Like other useful methodological traditions, design-based research invites scholars to develop mixed-method studies, embracing the dynamic nature of research as much as the predictability so many of us seek.

References

Anderson, Terry. 2005. "Design-Based Research and Its Application to a Call Center Innovation in Distance Education." *Canadian Journal of Learning and Technology* 31 (2): 69–84.

Anderson, Terry, and Julie Shattuck. 2012. "Design-Based Research: A Decade of Progress in Education Research?" *Educational Researcher* 41 (1): 16–25. http://dx.doi.org/10.3102/0013189X11428813.

Arola, Kristin L. 2010. "The Design of Web 2.0: The Rise of the Template, the Fall of Design." *Computers and Composition* 27 (1): 4–14. http://dx.doi.org/10.1016/j.compcom.2009.11.004.

Barab, Sasha, and D. Kirschner, eds. 2001. "Guest Editors' Introduction: Rethinking Methodology in the Learning Sciences." *Journal of the Learning Sciences* 10 (1–2): 1–2.

Barab, Sasha, and Kurt Squire. 2004. "Design-Based Research: Putting a Stake in the Ground." *Journal of the Learning Sciences* 13 (1): 1–14. http://dx.doi.org/10.1207/s15327809jls1301_1.

Brown, Ann L. 1992. "Design Experiments: Theoretical and Methodological Challenges in Creating Complex Interventions in Classroom Settings." *Journal of the Learning Sciences* 2 (2): 141–78. http://dx.doi.org/10.1207/s15327809jls0202_2.

Carpenter, Russel, Richard Selfe, Shawn Apostel, and Krisi Apostel, eds. 2015. *Sustainable Learning Spaces: Design, Infrastructure, and Technology*. Logan: Composers and Composition Digital Press/Utah State University Press.

Cobb, Paul, Jere Confrey, Andrea diSessa, Richard Lehrer, and Leona Schauble. 2003. "Design Experiments in Educational Research." *Educational Researcher* 32 (1): 9–13. http://dx.doi.org/10.3102/0013189X032001009.

Collins, Allan. 1992. "Toward a Design Science of Education." In *New Directions in Educational Technology*, edited by Eileen Scanlon and Tim O'Shea, 15–22. New York: Springer. http://dx.doi.org/10.1007/978-3-642-77750-9_2.

Collins, Allan, Diana Joseph, and Katerine Bielaczyc. 2004. "Design Research: Theoretical and Methodological Issues." *Journal of the Learning Sciences* 13 (1): 15–42. http://dx.doi.org/10.1207/s15327809jls1301_2.

Cooper, Marilyn M. 1986. "The Ecology of Writing." *College English* 48 (4): 364–75. http://dx.doi.org/10.2307/377264.

Dede, Chris. 2004. "If Design-Based Research is the Answer, What is the Question? A Commentary on Collins, Joseph, and Bielaczyc; diSessa and Cobb; and Fishman, Marx, Blumenthal, Krajcik, and Soloway in the JLS Special Issue on Design-Based Research." *Journal of the Learning Sciences* 13 (1): 105–14. http://dx.doi.org/10.1207/s15327809jls1301_5.

Design-Based Research Collective. 2003. "Design-Based Research: An Emerging Paradigm for Educational Inquiry." *Educational Researcher* 32 (1): 5–8. http://dx.doi.org/10.3102/0013189X032001005.

Edelson, Daniel C. 2002. "Design Research: What We Learn When We Engage in Design." *Journal of the Learning Sciences* 11 (1): 105–21. http://dx.doi.org/10.1207/S15327809JLS11014.

Emig, Janet. 1971. *The Composing Processes of Twelfth Graders*. Urbana, IL: NCTE.

Fleckenstein, Kristie S., Clay Spinuzzi, Rebecca J. Rickly, and Carole Clark Papper. 2008. "The Importance of Harmony: An Ecological Metaphor for Writing Research." *College Composition and Communication* 60 (2): 388–419.

Flower, Linda, and John R. Hayes. 1981. "A Cognitive Process Theory of Writing." *College Composition and Communication* 32 (4): 365–87. http://dx.doi.org/10.2307/356600.

George, Diana. 2002. "From Analysis to Design: Visual Communication in the Teaching of Writing." *College Composition and Communication* 54 (1): 11–39. http://dx.doi.org/10.2307/1512100.

Hairston, Maxine. 1986. "Different Products, Different Processes: A Theory About Writing." *College Composition and Communication* 37 (4): 442–52. http://dx.doi.org/10.2307/357914.

Herrington, Jan, Susan McKenney, Thomas C. Reeves, and Ron Oliver. 2007. "Design-Based Research and Doctoral Students: Guidelines for Preparing a Dissertation Proposal." In *Proceedings of World Conference on Educational Multimedia, Hypermedia and Telecommunications*, edited by C. Montgomerie and J. Seale, 4089–97. Chesapeake, VA: AACE.

Johnson, Steve, Sarah Veitch, and Silvia Dewiyanti. 2015. "A Framework to Embed Communication Skills Across the Curriculum: A Design-Based Research Approach." *Journal of University Teaching & Learning Practice* 12 (4): 1–14.

Kali, Yael. 2016. "Transformative Learning in Design Research: The Story Behind the Scenes." Keynote address for the International Conference on Learning Sciences, Singapore.

Kelly, Anthony. 2004. "Design Research in Education: Yes, but Is It Methodological?" *Journal of the Learning Sciences* 13 (1): 115–28. http://dx.doi.org/10.1207/s15327809jls1301_6.

Kostelnick, Charles. 1989. "Process Paradigms in Design and Composition: Affinities and Directions." *College Composition and Communication* 40 (3): 267–81. http://dx.doi.org/10.2307/357774.

Marback, Richard. 2009. "Embracing Wicked Problems: The Turn to Design in Composition Studies." *College Composition and Communication* 61 (2): W397–W419.

Melzer, Dan. 2003. "Assignments Across the Curriculum: A Survey of College Writing." *Language and Learning Across the Disciplines* 6 (1): 86–110.

Mingfong, Jan, Yam San, and Ek Ming Tan. 2010. "Unpacking the Design Process in Design-Based Research." Vol. 2 of *Learning in the Disciplines: Proceedings of the 9th International Conference of the Learning*, edited by Kimberly Gomez, Leilah Lyons, and Joshua Radinsky. Chicago, IL: International Society of the Learning Sciences.

Müller, Kjartan. 2011. "Genre in the Design Space." *Computers and Composition* 28 (3): 186–94. http://dx.doi.org/10.1016/j.compcom.2011.07.007.

Murray, Donald M. 1980. "Writing as Process: How Writing Finds Its Own Meaning." In *Eight Approaches to Teaching Composition*, edited by Timothy R. Donovan and Ben W. McClelland, 3–20. Urbana, IL: NCTE.

Odell, Lee. 1980. "The Process of Writing and the Process of Learning." *College Composition and Communication* 31 (1): 42–50. http://dx.doi.org/10.2307/356632.

Perl, Sondra. 1980. "Understanding Composing." *College Composition and Communication* 31 (4): 363–69. http://dx.doi.org/10.2307/356586.

Pigg, Stacey. 2014. "Coordinating Constant Invention: Social Media's Role in Distributed Work." *Technical Communication Quarterly* 23 (2): 69–87. http://dx.doi.org/10.1080/1 0572252.2013.796545.

Prior, Paul. 1998. *Writing/Disciplinarity: A Sociohistoric Account of Literate Activity in the Academy*. Mahwah, NJ: Lawrence Erlbaum.

Purdy, James P. 2014. "What Can Design Thinking Offer Writing Studies?" *College Composition and Communication* 65 (4): 612–41.

Roozen, Kevin. 2012. "Comedy Stages, Poets Projects, Sports Columns, and *Kinesiology 341*: Illuminating the Importance of Basic Writers' Self-Sponsored Literacies." *Journal of Basic Writing* 31 (1): 53–86.

Sandoval, William, and Philip Bell. 2004. "Design-Based Research Methods for Studying Learning in Context: Introduction." *Educational Psychologist* 39 (4): 199–201. http://dx.doi.org/10.1207/s15326985ep3904_1.

Schmuckler, Mark. 2001. "What Is Ecological Validity?: A Dimensional Analysis." *Infancy* 2 (4): 419–36. http://dx.doi.org/10.1207/S15327078IN0204_02.

Selzer, Jack. 1983. "The Composing Process of an Engineer." *College Composition and Communication* 34 (2): 178–87. http://dx.doi.org/10.2307/357405.

Sheridan, Mary, and Jennifer Rowsell. 2010. *Digital Literacies: Learning and Innovation in the Digital Age*. New York: Routledge.

Shipka, Jody. 2011. *Toward a Composition Made Whole*. Pittsburgh, PA: University of Pittsburgh Press.

Simon, Herbert. 1985. *The Sciences of the Artificial*. 2nd ed. Cambridge: MIT Press.

Sommers, Nancy. 1980. "Revision Strategies of Student Writers and Experienced Adult Writers." *College Composition and Communication* 31 (4): 378–88. http://dx.doi.org /10.2307/356588.

Strappers, Pieter Jan. 2007. "Doing Design as a Part of Doing Research." In *Design Research Now*, edited by Ralf Michel, 81–91. Basel, UK: Birkhäuser. http://dx.doi.org /10.1007/978-3-7643-8472-2_6.

Wysocki, Anne Frances. 2005. "awaywithwords: On the Possibilities in Unavailable Designs." *Computers and Composition* 22 (1): 55–62. http://dx.doi.org/10.1016/j.comp com.2004.12.011.

Chapter 3
THE THINGS THEY CARRY
Using Design-Based Research in Writing-Teacher Education

Tricia Serviss

ABSTRACT

While research about undergraduate source use proliferates, we know less about graduate-student source-use development. It is essential to understand how writing teachers themselves use and think about source use. This chapter describes a design-based pilot study of the citation knowledge and practices of ten graduate students through three methods: citation context coding, solicited reflective writing, and reiterative interviewing useful both for (1) data collection and analysis and (2) pedagogical interventions in graduate education. Chapter appendices include coding materials, interview questions, and analytic prompts.

INTRODUCTION

For writing studies scholars like me who focus on teacher preparation, terms like *teaching practicum* and *graduate-student orientation* stir up deep and pressing disciplinary tensions. We return to the same theoretical and practical questions as we do in the work of professionalizing ourselves as teachers: *How can we best prepare writing teachers, both novice and veteran? When and how should programming support their professionalization? How do we simultaneously prepare them both as emerging writers and writing teachers?* As we embrace digital writing, reading, and research tools even more fully, the cracks in our knowledge and strategies for preparing new writing teachers—writers and researchers themselves in formation—are not only exposed but beg repair. While our teacher-preparation programs historically focus upon pedagogical theory and practices in composition, pedagogical formation is typically packaged as separate and distinct from other kinds of graduate-student professionalization; we work with

DOI: 10.7330/9781607326250.c003

graduate students in great (local) need as they begin their teaching careers in one particular writing program with cultural and curricular expectations. Programmatic structures (decisions about graduate-program curriculum, faculty professionalization, etc.) with all their disciplinary negotiations have often encouraged the isolation of this "pedagogical" programming from the scholarly formation of graduate students as writers and researchers (pointed out by many scholars including Dobrin 2005; Miller 1991; Nystrand, Greene, and Wiemelt 1993).

After spending several years preparing new graduate students for their teaching careers at several different large research-intensive universities, this unnatural separation troubled me and called forth an intervention. I wanted to reform my approach to graduate education. I wanted to design a research project that would both inquire about how graduate students develop as writers/writing teachers and serve as a pedagogical intervention within graduate education. A design-based research methodological framework offered me a place to start. Prepared by the methodological work I've already done as one of the founding members of the Citation Project research team, I designed a pilot study driven by these questions: How do new writing teachers/graduate students conceptualize and develop citation practices? What strategies do they use when working with sources in their own academic writing? What beliefs influence that work? How do those beliefs and strategies play out in their pedagogical formation?

Earliest research in writing studies focuses on these kinds of challenges explicitly, studying how writers develop while also using our collective knowledge about writerly development to create pedagogically and curricularly sound writing-education programming (Alden 1913; Allen 1952; Bishop 1990; Braddock, Lloyd-Jones, and Schoer 1963; Corbett 1987; Denney 1918; Dobrin 2005; Faigley 1992; Gere 1985; Hesse 1993; Latterell 1996; Miller 1991; Pytlik and Liggett 2002). Questions about how to best professionalize writing teachers still abound as writing studies scholars conduct institutional research to learn different ways for writing programs to successfully prepare their newest writing teachers ("Doctoral Programs in Rhetoric and Composition: A Catalog of the Profession" 1994; Brown, Jackson, and Enos 2000; Chapman and Tate 1987; Dobrin 2005; Lauer 1980). Other scholars capture histories of teacher-preparation approaches, compiling foundational readings about the theories and pedagogical approaches that made up writing studies as the field developed (Miller 2009; Tate, Rupiper, and Schick 2000; Tate, Rupiper Taggart, Schick, and Hessler 2013; Villanueva 2003;). Yet there are fewer publications that offer research about *how* college writing teachers themselves develop. There are even fewer published studies about how graduate students develop as writers while preparing to teach writing. Invested in understanding how writers develop in all kind of contexts—classrooms, community spaces, and professional arenas—our disciplinary research about graduate students most often focuses on the best practices for their pedagogical formation (Beaufort 2007; Dobrin 2005) instead of and apart from their writerly development.

Graduate students, in this kind of scholarship, are presented as primarily the *audience* for research about how undergraduate students learn to write, how undergraduate students navigate digital resources and writing spaces, and other ongoing inquiries about undergraduates learning to write. I began this pilot project to inquire about writing teachers as both *subjects* and *agents* of developmental writing research. Scholarship supporting graduate-level composition practicums—compiled both for graduate students in the practicum (in readers such as *Cross-Talk*) and for the instructors of those practicums to consider (Dobrin 2005; etc.)—establish some of the "best practices" for these courses but leave room for more to be considered and proposed.

While I can turn to very useful research in English-education journals and general education research to learn about teacher development in a general sense, there is little research about the development of writer-teachers in the context of their parallel development as writers. Very useful studies of how undergraduate writers develop and transfer abound (Beaufort 2007; DePalma and Ringer 2011; Yancey, Blake, Robertson and Taczak 2014) and orient our gaze toward research that looks for the deployment and transformation of writing strategies and habits across contexts. I propose that we consider graduate students as one embodiment of such transcontextual research; graduate students move between their roles as emerging writer-researchers and professionalizing pedagogues most explicitly during their time in composition practicum courses and programming. Thus, this chapter describes how I established and enacted a pilot study of graduate-student citation practices, and I offer reflective suggestions about modification and expansion of this pilot focused on the formation of writing teachers across disciplines and institutions.

RESEARCH QUESTIONS AND DESIGN

Across two semesters, I taught a credit-bearing graduate seminar, Composition Pedagogy: Issues and Approaches, which was capped at fifteen students, at a large, public, research-intensive university. Inheriting the course from other writing program administrators (WPAs), I understood the course to have several goals including introducing the current issues, curricular objectives, and pedagogical practices important in writing studies; preparing new graduate-student teaching assistants to teach college-level writing throughout their careers and, particularly, in our first-year writing (FYW) program; and preparing them to enter the academic job market conversant in current composition pedagogy. Among the materials I shared with students in the course was Citation Project (a national collaborative research project studying how undergraduate students use sources in their academic writing across campuses) research (see Jamieson, this collection), including the article Rebecca Howard, Tanya Rodrigue, and I wrote about the initial pilot study (Howard, Serviss, and Rodrigue 2010).

As we discussed source-based writing, along with pedagogical strategies, several questions habitually emerged for me.

- How do graduate students write with sources in their own researched writing?
- What citation practices and epistemologies do entering graduate students use?
- How do they, as developing advanced writers, move between citation practices and epistemologies in different writing environments they encounter throughout their graduate education?
- Do their citation practices and epistemologies change as they move between their graduate education and their emerging teaching life?

I posed these questions to the graduate students in the class, and their interest in exploring them led me to develop a small study of graduate-student source use across two semesters designed to capture their developing skills, source use, metacognitive awareness, and what DePalma and Ringer (2011) call their "adaptive transfer" of various strategies across contexts. The study was guided by the features of design-based research, which brings together study of learning in naturalistic settings with the design and testing of pedagogical interventions (Brown 1992; Collins, Joseph, and Bielaczyc 2004; Design-Based Research Collective 2003). Perhaps the most important feature of design-based research methodology is simultaneity; the methodology required me to study student learning while also designing, deploying, and evaluating the utility of a particular pedagogical intervention. I wanted to meet graduate-student writers in authentic settings, studying how they develop and understand citation practices while working on actual tasks in their graduate education.

The last main feature of design-based research that guided the design of the pilot study is the notion that all research is reiterative, developed across several phases that ideally lead to the refinement of methods and tools. This methodology, along with the methods provided by grounded theory (Corbin and Strauss 1990; Glaser 1978; Glaser and Strauss 1967) and citation context analysis (Pecorari 2003; 2006; 2008; White 2004), framed my decisions about what graduate students would do, what data I would capture, and how I would process that data once in hand.

THE PILOT STUDY
Context and Purposes

The graduate students in the class volunteered to participate in the pilot study based on the criteria approved by my campus Institutional Research Board (IRB). I offered no compensation to students, and participation was not part of their grade for the course, either directly or indirectly. Initially, their participation in the project was to span both semesters of their first year in the graduate program, although I subsequently extended the study in a different form for their second year once all agreed to continue their participation.

Members of the pilot-study cohort first attended a series of workshops to learn about the Citation Project citation analysis coding methods; to practice coding student texts together; and to practice coding their own academic writing, sharing results with each other in the form of a debriefing discussion. The second phase involved participant reflection, via one-on-one interviews with me, in which participants explored a written reflection they wrote and brought to our interview for discussion. The third phase I developed required participants to code a second piece of their writing recently produced in a graduate course and discuss it in a reflective interview with me. I ambitiously planned to also visit participants in their own writing classrooms, observing them as they taught undergraduate students in their FYW classes about source use. Each phase of this study used a mixed-method approach, drawing on both qualitative and quantitative strategies to describe the data (surveys, coding results, reflections, and interviews) and discern useful patterns within that data. I had three main goals: (1) refining my research design and methods to allow for expansion of the study translocally, (2) developing better pedagogical strategies for teaching writing at the graduate level, and (3) preparing graduate students as researchers as they engaged in different methods and approaches embedded in the study (qualitative coding, use of surveys and interviews, coding interview transcripts, etc.).

My research design was premised upon transcontextual research goals, using the pilot to refine and plan expansion for the project.

Situating Participants Using Informal Surveys

Nine of the participants were enrolled in the masters of arts in English program, and one was studying for a masters of arts in education with an emphasis in secondary-language arts education; all ten of the graduate students were preservice teachers with various paraprofessional education experiences (tutoring, writing center work, summer-camp counseling, childcare, etc.). After volunteering for the study, these ten graduate students completed informal entrance surveys that asked them basic contextualizing questions (about educational background, familial background, career ambitions, etc.) as well as pointed questions about why they chose to participate in the study. The most typical explanation of interest in these surveys was pedagogical; participants primarily wanted to understand how undergraduates use sources and secondarily wanted to learn more about how to analyze their own citations as novice researchers.

DEVELOPING METHODS: MECHANISMS AND PROCEDURES
Learning to Code

Participants were asked to select and code a piece of their own recent academic writing for citation context analysis using Citation Project coding methods. After this practice workshop, participants gathered for our first individual coding workshop. They coded their own writing, conferring with each other and with me when they had difficulty using the coding methods. I did not help coders make interpretive decisions (about whether the citation moment was paraphrasing, summarizing, copying, or patchwriting); the workshops were instead a place to get guidance about how to use Citation Project coding methods themselves. The participants needed guidance from me in the most expected and common ways as they coded; they needed clarification about the definitions of the citation terms (*paraphrasing*, etc.) and help with application of those terms to actual writing. Participants frequently asked about what the CP definition of summary meant upon application, for example, which is a typical difficulty in conducting this kind of textual coding. Individual participants coded pages 4–10 of their own seminar papers, recording their results on a Citation Project coding sheet (See Appendix 3.C). At the end of the workshop, participants voluntarily reported their individual results to the larger community of participants; discussion naturally ensued as participants reflected on their own results and commented on the results of peers. Generally, this debriefing session was marked by a kind of emotional sharing as participants made realizations about their own writing, frequently through the filter of *morality* often associated with source use, authorship, and plagiarism conversations. After this community discussion, I offered participants writing prompts to provoke reflective writing (see Appendix 3.B) that they contributed to the data emerging from the study.

Analyzing Results Together

After this guided self-coding workshop, I generated categorical descriptions both qualitative (impressions of shared strategies such as challenging theoretical framework) and quantitative (tallying up the codes), looking for patterns across the cohort's coding results and reactions. I shared these results with the cohort, requesting that participants read through my descriptions before our individual interviews began. The interviews began with a set of questions I posed to every participant, some questions repeating from the intake survey they originally completed, some questions pursuing new ideas introduced in their reflections after the coding workshop, and some questions spontaneously posed during the interview to pursue an interesting idea participants shared (see Appendix 3.A for the questions I used at the start of the interview). Interviews were an opportunity to analyze initial descriptions and sort the data together, making the data collection and analysis process both a training tool for young researchers and a potential pedagogical intervention in their lives as writers. I repeated this same process with the same cohort a second time. Participants selected an additional recent academic research paper of their own, brought the paper and their sources to a guided self-coding workshop the entire cohort attended, and coded, debriefed, and wrote reflections at the end of the workshop. I collected these reflections, synthesized them into a master document, along with the cohort's collective coding results, and shared them with participants before meeting with them for a second round of individual interviews.

CREATING TRANSLOCAL CONTEXT FOR PARTICIPANTS
Including External Coders

External coders trained in CP citation context analysis double coded all twenty of the papers generated by the ten MA students across two semesters, discussed their codes, and then reconciled their results with one another to provide one reliable coding of each paper. The reconciled scores provided a second set of coded papers and data to be discussed. This double coding by a seemingly objective pair of coders as a design mimics the reconciliation practices developed by Citation Project researchers (see pages 50–52 in this collection). The comparison of the two coding sets (author codes and external codes) is where the coding methods diverge. In this pilot study, author codes proved to be unreliable; however, the differences between the data produced by the authors and external coders provided rich material for interviews and the impetus for further research. In fact, the lack of reliability in the author codes became one of the great affordances of the pedagogical intervention the study enacted. Awareness of different kinds of citation moves, as well as deeper metacognitive awareness of their own practices, became more important to the authors than attaining coding *reliability*.

Round One: Participants and External Coders Illuminate Ways Forward

At the end of the first semester, each of the ten participants in the pilot cohort coded six pages from their own essays, generating sixty pages of coded text that included eighty-six citations. The source material used in each of those citations was coded by the author and then double coded by two external coders (table 3.1 and table 3.2).

The main difference in the coding results in table 3.1 and table 3.2 appears in the categories of paraphrasing and patchwriting. The external coders found *patchwriting* where authors found *paraphrasing*. Although I had already introduced the ten participating authors to the term *patchwriting* as defined by the Citation Project glossary, they did not recognize patchwriting in their own writing, a typical struggle for developing academic writers. When I shared the comparative results in table 3.1 and table 3.2 with the authors, they were both surprised—and distressed—to learn the papers had moments of patchwriting. Typical reactions from authors included comments such as, "There must be a mistake. Let me code again with the [other] coders" (MA in English); "Someone isn't sure what patchwriting is and I'm freaking out when I think it might be me" (MA in education); "Oh my God. I turned this paper in for a grade in my [name withheld] seminar" (MA in English).

The external coders, doctoral students from the same campus serving as additional coders trained in Citation Project methods, were equally distressed by the differences they recognized between their codes and the participating authors' codes. These external coders, both veteran teachers (with four years of teaching experience each), explained

Table 3.1. Author codes (first term), n = 86

Predominant Use of Source Material within the Citation	Frequency	Percent	Cumulative Percent
Copying, cited but not marked as quotation	0	0.0	0.0
Copying, cited and marked as quotation	52	60.5	60.5
Patchwriting	**0**	**0.0**	**60.5**
Paraphrasing	**27**	**31.4**	**91.9**
Summarizing	7	8.1	100.0
Total	**86**	**100.0**	

Table 3.2. External codes (first term), n = 86

Predominant Use of Source Material within the Citation	Frequency	Percent	Cumulative Percent
Copying, cited but not marked as quotation	0	0.0	0.0
Copying, cited and marked as quotation	52	60.5	60.5
Patchwriting	**14**	**16.2**	**76.7**
Paraphrasing	**13**	**15.1**	**91.8**
Summarizing	7	8.2	100.0
Total	**86**	**100.0**	

feeling "nervous" and "anxious" in their own postcoding surveys. They reported being worried their findings might "sully the reputation of the participants and maybe [our institution]."

When I asked the external coders to comment on the coding results as scholar-teachers rather than concerned peers of the authors, their responses changed. External coder A respected the authors explicitly, commenting that the ten authors seemed to be "learning the discourse of their disciplines" and so "their source use relies heavily upon quotations." External coder A found this to be an "expected outcome for first-year graduate-student writers" and yet it was still "unsettling to see the results because we [external coders A and B] knew this would have various psychological consequences for the authors . . . as if they had failed as writers." External coder B offered a different perspective, writing, "I checked and double checked the patchwriting and paraphrasing codes to make sure I was being accurate" because these areas seem to "have the most at stake" for the graduate students as future educators and writers. The attention external coders A and B brought to the coding results was not entirely surprising to me given the arguments Howard (1993; 2001) has already made about patchwriting as perhaps a stage in writerly development and the revision process and given the initial results of the pilot study of the Citation Project (Howard, Serviss, and Rodrigue 2010) that recognized how students struggle with sources on the sentence level.

In fact, the presence of patchwriting in these papers was not a surprise at all given the findings of the Citation Project (Jamieson and Howard 2013) and the presence of patchwriting in professorial writing found by Miguel Roig (2001). Following Roig, this research suggests that phases of writerly development continue in cycles throughout the formation of academic writers. It is unlikely that academic writers ever move completely outside these recurring cycles of development that result from interactions with different kinds of unfamiliar sources and discourses. Therefore, awareness of these cycles—and useful tools for (self-)intervention—is key for all kinds of academic writers, not just first-year and sophomore undergraduate academic writers. By combining citation context analysis with interviews, two very different research methods, I was able to recognize useful relationships. Namely, I saw the potential value of peer coding as a professionalization tool for graduate-student teachers in particular. The additional layers of reflective writing and conversations I solicited from the external coders, initially data that seemed distinct from the author codes and reflections, helped me refine my methods, expand my research questions, and illuminate my path going forward.

Round Two: Pilot as Pedagogical Intervention

The pilot study, embracing design-based research methodology, functioned not only as a means to understand graduate-student writing better but also to pedagogically intervene and enhance the metacognition and development of those same writers. During the second term of the pilot study, both the authors and the external coders again coded sixty pages of student writing, this time with a total of 128 citation incidents. The comparative results of this second round of coding are described in tables 3.3 and 3.4.

During this second round, authors and the external coders again disagreed about the frequency of paraphrasing and patchwriting (nearly 10 percent difference in both categories). Theoretically, if the self-guided coding methods were functioning both to provide researchers with insights about how graduate-student writers use sources *and* to allow for pedagogically useful interventions into graduate-student writing development, I'd expect the coding results of this second round to reveal shifts in author awareness and source-use practices. First glance at tables

Table 3.3. Author codes, n = 128

Predominant Use of Source Material within the Citation	Frequency	Percent	Cumulative Percent
Copying, cited but not marked as quotation	0	0.0	0.0
Copying, cited and marked as quotation	52	40.6	40.6
Patchwriting	11	8.6	49.5
Paraphrasing	44	34.4	83.6
Summarizing	21	16.4	100.0
Total	128	100.0	

Table 3.4. External codes, n = 128

Predominant Use of Source Material within the Citation	Frequency	Percent	Cumulative Percent
Copying, cited but not marked as quotation	5	3.9	3.9
Copying, cited and marked as quotation	52	40.6	44.5
Patchwriting	22	17.2	61.7
Paraphrasing	34	26.6	88.3
Summarizing	15	11.7	100.0
Total	128	100.0	

3.3 and 3.4, working from this notion, were discouraging; I valued the data being collected but worried about the viability of self-guided coding as a pedagogical intervention.

Yet according to the external-coder results, the second set of papers included a 20 percent drop in direct quotation (from 61 percent to 41 percent), an increase in paraphrase (from 15 percent to 27 percent), and an increase in summary (from 8 percent to 12 percent). The move from excessive quotation to paraphrase is a key stage of development as writers learn to incorporate sources, suggesting a deeper engagement with sources and/or increased confidence in their ability to understand and reproduce the ideas themselves. The increased willingness to risk *not quoting* sources led to a slight (but not statistically significant) increase in patchwriting between the two semesters (from 16 percent to 17 percent, with an additional 5 percent coded as uncited copying). This data is also not surprising in light of Howard's claim that patchwriting is part of an attempt to paraphrase or summarize (Howard 1993).

What did surprise me, however, was my realization that self-guided coding was a productive pedagogical intervention. By guiding authors through coding of their own writing, I directed the authors' attention in very specific ways, providing them with definitions and therefore paradigms through which to analyze, develop, and (re)consider their own scholarly writing. Yet the pilot-study coding I describe here needed more context. For this study of graduate-student writing, the coding statistics became more valuable when synthesized with surveys, reflective writings, and interviews of not only the participants but of the external coders as well.

A (Surprise) Case Study

Pairing the qualitative data with the quantitative data collected about each author was crucial in making sense of the data generated by the two rounds of citation coding. Without this mixed-methods approach, this pilot study would be much less productive and much less promising for development into a larger study. It is precisely because of these different kinds of data that this project seems viable for expansion across different kinds of novice-writer contexts. I'll share a brief example of the value of this mixed-methods approach here via one case study that emerged from the study.

Author C, an English graduate student, reported that the study was deeply effective. She reported that the experiences she had as a participant manifested as an intervention into her development as a writer and researcher. During our second interview, she commented on her newfound awareness and "hesitation" to copy from (meaning *quote*) sources.

> I understand that close reading of text is foundational to doing the work of literary criticism I'm training for. But I think I got careful about using tons of block quotes in my seminar papers because my first paper was just a bunch of block quotes in the end . . . I think I was consciously trying not to do that much quoting with all my papers this semester . . . I was really embarrassed to see all my copying in blue last time. I would never reward that in my [general education literature course's] discussion section [where the student serves as a TA]. I'd give myself a low grade. . . . That is depressing but also maybe an important moment for me because it is a watershed or threshold moment now. You [Serviss] talk about threshold concepts in class, and I think this is a [long pause] threshold moment.

These interview comments reflect author C's individual coding results of her own writing (see table 3.5).

After coding this first paper (table 3.5), author C shared feeling "surprise" and "worry" about her own coding results, particularly the large amount of copying (all of which had quotation marks). Author C also

Table 3.5. Author C's coding of first term, n = 20

Predominant Use of Source Material within the Citation	Frequency	Percent	Cumulative Percent
Copying, cited but not marked as quotation	0	0.0	0.0
Copying, cited and marked as quotation	12	60.0	60.0
Patchwriting	0	0.0	60.0
Paraphrasing	4	20.0	80.0
Summarizing	4	20.0	**100.0**
Total	20	100.0	

Table 3.6. External coding of Author C's first term, n = 20

Predominant Use of Source Material within the Citation	Frequency	Percent	Cumulative Percent
Copying, cited but not marked as quotation	0	0.0	0.0
Copying, cited and marked as quotation	12	60.0	60.0
Patchwriting	3	15.0	75.0
Paraphrasing	1	5.0	80.0
Summarizing	4	20.0	**100.0**
Total	20	100.0	

celebrated the absence of patchwriting, a code the authors generally noted they feared in their reflective writing and interview. Author C's reactions to her own coding changed significantly once she learned what the external coders had decided about her writing (see table 3.6).

The results disturbed author C so much that we had an impromptu interview in my office soon after I shared the results. External coders agreed with author C's coding of copying and summarizing but found patchwriting where author C found paraphrasing, a common tension in the coding process. Author C described herself as "panicked" by the "presence of patchwriting . . . because it can be read as academically illegal, right?" At the end of the conversation, author C asked me to recommend more scholarship about patchwriting and plagiarism and declared the experience a "crisis intervention" into her own graduate education.

Author C's second-term paper codes, however, complicated things. The external coders reported that C's quotation dropped by a solid 50 percent (from 60 percent of all citations in term-one paper to just 30 percent in this second paper), while paraphrase increased from 5 percent to 20 percent and summary increased from 20 percent to 30

Table 3.7. Author C's coding of second term, n = 30

Predominant Use of Source Material within the Citation	Frequency	Percent	Cumulative Percent
Copying, cited but not marked as quotation	0	0.0	0.0
Copying, cited and marked as quotation	9	30.0	30.0
Patchwriting	0	0.0	30.0
Paraphrasing	12	40.0	70.0
Summarizing	9	30.0	**100.0**
Total	30	100.0	

Table 3.8. External coding of Author C's second term, n = 30

Predominant Use of Source Material within the Citation	Frequency	Percent	Cumulative Percent
Copying, cited but not marked as quotation	0	0.0	0.0
Copying, cited and marked as quotation	9	30.0	30.0
Patchwriting	6	20.0	50.0
Paraphrasing	6	20.0	70.0
Summarizing	9	30.0	**100.0**
Total	30	100.0	

percent. C's second paper also draws on significantly more sources (thirty in comparison to only twenty in the first term). Not surprisingly, patchwriting also increased from 15 percent to 20 percent, suggesting a slower learning curve than we (and especially author C) might expect.

Author C found these results encouraging: "The pilot is working the way you thought! We are learning to make better [rhetorical] moves by coding writing. I think I might even be becoming a better writer" but also "frustrating." Author C began the interview by saying, "I can't seem to see my own patchwriting! . . . Am I doomed?" I responded by returning to author C's survey responses from the first term. Author C commented then that a "threshold moment" was afoot. This allusion to our discussion of threshold concepts (something we talked about in the graduate course) prompted further conversation about author C's issue with self-identified overreliance upon quoting (copying) and difficulty in recognizing patchwriting. We discussed potential worry about an inability to investigate our own writing without the distractions of attachment and biases. Author C recalled the article "Personal Biases in Student Assessment" (Archer and McCarthy 1988) that we read together in our graduate seminar, particularly the idea of "empirical blindness" the authors call "bias" and equate to the "halo effect" (a term from social psychological educational research that suggests cognitive biases effect our judgment, even when we want to be impartial). Author C goes on to say,

> Do you think the halo effect might be working here? Like I didn't want to find patchwriting so I didn't? Or like I can't imagine research outside of my take as a lit student? . . . I only read as a literary critic? . . . [Pauses. Laughter.] That my efforts to become a literary critic . . . blinded [me] to my own writing strategies?

Author C further articulates this worry that a cognitive bias, perhaps based upon disciplinary values or writerly beliefs, is making it difficult for author C to understand the citation practices and epistemologies at play, let alone intervene in them.

Author C was not the only student to use reading material from the composition theory course, a very different learning context during the first term, to explain the coding results and subsequent changes in their writing and source use during the second term. Theory-based reflection was an unexpected move participating authors made. Transfer of these ideas suggested to me that research designed to intervene in educational development can make, perhaps, a more significant difference to participants than anticipated. The pilot study revealed that some application—some praxis—was occurring during the self-study and reflection processes, particularly in the interviews and reflective writing. The idea of teaching writing as a reflective activity is fundamental to writing studies, most notably described in George Hillocks's (1995) *Teaching Writing as Reflective Action*, a text often invoked because of his claims that writing is the best tool for learning. However, equally important is Hillocks's claim that writing is the best tool for learning when used to teach self-reflection on cognitive processes and learning practices (Hillocks 1995, 22). Following Hillocks, it seems that author C sees participation in the pilot study as exposing the value of reflective writing as potentially both a learning and teaching tool. Author C reached only one conclusion at the end of the second term: certainty that these research activities were "productive interventions" into both her writing life as a first-year graduate student struggling to write as a scholar and her pedagogical life as a beginning writing teacher who "now connects the struggles of writers [of various levels] together" across contexts.

DRAWING CONCLUSIONS: CONSEQUENTIAL TRANSITIONS

Refining a mixed-methods approach across two terms (using Citation Project coding, interviews, reflective writing, and comparative coding analysis) revealed things both about graduate-student writer/teaching development as well as possible methodological futures for the pilot study. Participating graduate students reported significant realizations about themselves as writers—and about writing itself—when prompted to analyze their own citation practices and epistemologies. Both rounds of the study required participants to analyze individual artifacts (their papers, their coding results), to engage in self-analysis (reflective writing), and respond to my inquiry questions in our interviews. I did not expect the study of the cohort's papers to affect the external peer coders *as well as* the participants themselves. This unexpected line of inquiry means I ought to develop ways to include peer coders more actively and intentionally in future iterations of this study. A kind of feedback loop between participating author coders and external peer coders emerged, challenging me to account—and allow—for that important avenue of interaction as I refine the study.

Nor did I expect the pilot study to offer opportunities to study discourse communities in formation. Yet the study did, in fact, create cohorts on multiple levels. These cohorts engaged in conversations and analyses that often moved beyond my simple questions because the participating authors and external coders are writers, researchers, and teachers in close contact themselves. In these conversations with one another, I heard them talk about happily veering from the research plans I designed, at times, in search of their own interests and in service of their own priorities. These conversations led me to consider issues of transition and transfer more closely and critically than before. I turned to King Beach's idea of consequential transitions (Beach 1999), which focuses not only on transfer, which he defines as "moving between" and "movement," but also on transition, which he defines as "how we experience continuity and transformation in becoming someone or something new—a student, a machinist, a bartender, a shopkeep, or a teacher—and how these consequential transitions may be a macrocosm of how we learn new tasks and problems" (Beach 1999, 102).

For Beach, transfer is movement and repositioning of things; transition is the transformation that results from such movement. His framework is key to appreciating the phenomenon the pilot study concretized. Participants became highly conscious of their citation practices and epistemologies across the different analytical activities of the study. Participants also—and this is very important—became consciously aware of the changes the interventions generated as a result. Beach illuminates this phenomenon, as he writes about what he calls "consequential transitions." These moments, Beach argues, happen "when transition is consciously reflected on, struggled with, and shifts the individual's sense of self or social position. Thus, consequential transitions link identity with knowledge propagation" (Beach 1999, 104). Beach's concept of consequential transition is helpful for me as I think about expanding this pilot further; the pilot study not only gathered descriptive data about how first-year graduate students use sources and think about that source use but also about how the vertical nature of the pilot study became a pedagogical intervention itself that prompted moments of consequential transition for participants. The pilot study's mixed-method design brought together different facets of participants' citation lives and asked them to engage in cross-talk with themselves and each other as writers/writing teachers.

The activities the pilot required of participants were designed to optimize the transformative moments consequential transitions, as Beach puts it, or threshold moments, as author C puts it, provoke. The mixed methods of the pilot study, as observation and intervention tools, offer a useful way to engage professionalizing writers/writing teachers in empirical study of their own writing. With that in mind, I would refine this pilot further in hopes of

1. using guided self-study methods to engage teachers in research *about* their own writing;

2. studying graduate students—particularly TAs across the curriculum—as writers as well as writing teachers;

3. triangulating data generated by graduate students about themselves alongside data generated by external analysis;

4. renewing attention to writing teachers as academic researchers and writers themselves;

5. reconceiving the methods of this pilot—particularly the interview questions and reflective-writing prompts (Appendix 3.A) to account for programmatic contexts, structures, and cultures.

APPENDIX 3.A
Basic Interview Questions (Pre- and Post-Coding)

These appendices may be downloaded from https://upcolorado.com/utah-state-university-press/item/3188-points-of-departure and used or modified for teaching or research purposes with attribution.

BACKGROUND INFORMATION (PRE-CODING)

1) What is a citation? What do we mean when we talk about "citations"? What about when we talk about "source use"? What about "research-based writing"?
2) What were you taught about these phenomena across your education?
3) How would you define plagiarism?
4) What citation style have you most frequently been asked to use? Do you know why you've been asked to use that style?
5) What are the features of MLA citation style? Values?
6) What is your greatest strength as a writer? As a researcher?

POST-CODING INFORMATION (POST-CODING)

1) Describe the coding process as you experienced it. Which moments were most significant for you? Why?
2) Describe your coding results. What did you find out about your writing? What do you think the results might mean?
3) What did you learn about the citation style you were using?
4) What did you learn about the different source use moves we've talked about (summarizing, paraphrasing, patchwriting, quoting)?
5) Did your coding experience reveal anything in particular to you about yourself as a writer? About how citations work?
6) What encouraged you, based upon the coding you did? What worried you?
7) What is a citation? What do we mean when we talk about "citations"? What about when we talk about "source use"? What about "research-based writing"?

APPENDIX 3.B
Coding Workshop Schedule and Prompts

INTRODUCTORY WORKSHOP SCHEDULE

1) Overview and discussion of the glossary, particularly definitions of summary, paraphrase, patchwriting, and copying. (20 min)
2) PowerPoint presentation of the coding steps with illustrative examples. (20 min)
3) Get acquainted with coding materials in pairs at their tables. (5 min)
4) Code one page sample paper (all have the same sample for this first coding exercise). (30 min)
5) BREAK
6) Rectify with your partner. (15 min)

7) Big group reporting and discussion. (30 min)
    a. Reflective prompt: What were the two most surprising moments of this first coding experience? Why?
8) Prepare your own writing sample for coding. (30 min)
9) Final prompt: What did you learn today about source-based writing? About coding as a research method? About yourself as an evaluative reader of undergraduate writing?

CODING WORKSHOP SCHEDULE AND PROMPTS
1) Overview of glossary and coding procedures.
2) Organizing and final preparations of your writing sample.
3) Code four pages of your own sample paper.
4) BREAK
5) Debrief with your partner.
    a. Reflective prompt: What surprised you as you coded your own writing? Did any noticeable patterns emerge in your writing?
6) Debrief with the large group.
    a. Collect data from all the coding sheets. Which citation moves happened the most across the cohort? Why those citations?

APPENDIX 3.C
Self-Guided Coding Sheets (Participant Version)

Guided Self-Study: CODING SHEET   Paper # (of 4):_____
Term_____ Year_____   Coder Name:_____
                                       Coding Date:_____

	Fill out these 3 columns			Mark if relevant	Mark an X in one, and only one, of these five columns					
Citation #	Page in the paper	Source used (source #)	Page in source	More than one type of source use in the citation	Copying *not* marked as quotation	Copying marked as quotation	Patchwriting	Paraphrasing	Summarizing	coder notes (optional)
1										
2										
3										
4										
5										
6										
7										
8										
9										
10										
11										
12										
13										
14										
15										
16										
17										
18										
19										
20										

References

Alden, Raymond MacDonald. 1913. "Preparation for College English Teaching." *English Journal* 2 (6): 344–56. http://dx.doi.org/10.2307/801562.

Allen, Harold B. 1952. "Preparing the Teacher of Composition and Communication—A Report." *College Composition and Communication* 3 (2): 3–13. http://dx.doi.org/10.2307/354272.

Archer, John, and Barry McCarthy. 1988. "Personal Biases in Student Assessment." *Educational Research* 30 (2): 142–45. http://dx.doi.org/10.1080/0013188880300208.

Beach, King. 1999. "Consequential Transitions: A Sociocultural Expedition Beyond Transfer in Education." *Review of Research in Education* 24 (1): 101–39.

Beaufort, Anne. 2007. *College Writing and Beyond: A New Framework for University Writing Instruction*. Logan: Utah State University Press.

Bishop, Wendy. 1990. *Something Old, Something New: College Writing Teachers and Classroom Change*. Carbondale: Southern Illinois University Press.

Braddock, Richard, Richard Lloyd-Jones, and Lowell Schoer. 1963. *Research in Written Composition*. Champaign, IL: NCTE.

Brown, Ann L. 1992. "Design Experiments: Theoretical and Methodological Challenges Creating Complex Intervention in Classroom Settings." *Journal of the Learning Sciences* 2 (2): 141–78. http://dx.doi.org/10.1207/s15327809jls0202_2.

Brown, Stuart, Rebecca Jackson, and Theresa Enos. 2000. "The Arrival of Rhetoric in the Twenty-First Century: The 1999 Survey of Doctoral Programs in Rhetoric." *Rhetoric Review* 18 (2): 233–242.

Chapman, David W., and Gary Tate. 1987. "A Survey of Doctoral Programs in Rhetoric and Composition." *Rhetoric Review* 5 (2): 124–86. http://dx.doi.org/10.1080/07350198709359143.

Collins, Allan, Diana Joseph, and Katerine Bielaczyc. 2004. "Design Research: Theoretical and Methodological Issues." *Journal of the Learning Sciences* 13 (1): 15–42. http://dx.doi.org/10.1207/s15327809jls1301_2.

Corbett, Edward. 1987. "Teaching Composition: Where We've Been and Where We're Going." *College Composition and Communication* 38 (4): 444–52. http://dx.doi.org/10.2307/357638.

Corbin, Juliet M., and Anselm Strauss. 1990. "Grounded Theory Research: Procedures, Canons, and Evaluative Criteria." *Qualitative Sociology* 13 (1): 3–21. http://dx.doi.org/10.1007/BF00988593.

Denney, J. V. 1918. "Preparation of College Teachers of English." *English Journal* 7 (5): 322–26. http://dx.doi.org/10.2307/800889.

DePalma, Michael-John, and Jeffrey Ringer. 2011. "Toward a Theory of Adaptive Transfer: Expanding Disciplinary Discussions of 'Transfer' in Second-Language Writing and Composition Studies." *Journal of Second Language Writing* 20 (2): 134–47. http://dx.doi.org/10.1016/j.jslw.2011.02.003.

Design-Based Research Collective. 2003. "Design-Based Research: An Emerging Paradigm for Educational Inquiry." *Educational Researcher* 32 (1): 5–8. http://dx.doi.org/10.3102/0013189X032001005.

Dobrin, Sidney. 2005. "Introduction: Finding a Place for the Composition Practicum." In *Don't Call It That: The Composition Practicum*, edited by Sidney Dobrin, 1–34. Urbana, IL: NCTE.

"Doctoral Programs in Rhetoric and Composition: A Catalog of the Profession." 1994. *Rhetoric Review* 12 (2): 240–389. http://dx.doi.org/10.1080/07350199409389043.

Faigley, Lester. 1992. *Fragments of Rationality: Postmodernity and the Subject of Composition*. Pittsburgh, PA: University of Pittsburgh Press.

Gere, Anne Ruggles. 1985. *Writing and Learning*. New York: Macmillan.

Glaser, Barney, and Anselm Strauss. 1967. *The Discovery of Grounded Theory*. London: Weidenfeld and Nicholson.

Glaser, Barney G. 1978. *Theoretical Sensitivity: Advances in the Methodology of Grounded Theory*. Mill Valley, CA: Sociology Press.

Hesse, Doug. 1993. "Teachers as Students, Reflecting Resistance." *College Composition and Communication* 44 (2): 224–31. http://dx.doi.org/10.2307/358840.

Hillocks, George. 1995. *Teaching Writing as Reflective Practice: Integrating Theories*. Language and Literacy Series. New York: Teachers College Press.

Howard, Rebecca Moore. 1993. "A Plagiarism Pentimento." *Journal of Teaching Writing* 11 (2): 233–46.

Howard, Rebecca Moore. 2001. "The Ethics of Plagiarism." In *The Ethics of Writing Instruction: Issues in Theory and Practice*, edited by Michael Pemberton, 79–90. New York: Ablex.

Howard, Rebecca Moore, Tricia C. Serviss, and Tanya Rodrigue. 2010. "Writing from Sources, Writing from Sentences." *Writing & Pedagogy* 2 (2): 177–92. http://dx.doi.org/10.1558/wap.v2i2.177.

Jamieson, Sandra, and Rebecca Moore Howard. 2013. "Sentence-Mining: Uncovering the Amount of Reading and Reading Comprehension in College Writers' Researched Writing." In *The New Digital Scholar: Exploring and Enriching the Research and Writing Practices of NextGen Students*, edited by Randall McClure and James P. Purdy, 111–33. Medford, NJ: Information Today.

Latterell, Catherine. 1996. "Training the Workforce: An Overview of GTA Education Curricula." *WPA: Writing Program Administrators* 19 (3): 7–23.

Lauer, Janet. 1980. "Doctoral Programs in Rhetoric." *Rhetoric Society Quarterly* 10 (4): 190–94. http://dx.doi.org/10.1080/02773948009390578.

Miller, Susan. 1991. *Textual Carnivals: The Politics of Composition*. Carbondale: Southern Illinois University Press.

Miller, Susan, ed. 2009. *The Norton Book of Composition Studies*. New York: Norton.

Nystrand, Martin, Stuart Greene, and Jeffrey Wiemelt. 1993. "Where Did Composition Come From?: An Intellectual History." *Written Communication* 10 (3): 267–333. http://dx.doi.org/10.1177/0741088393010003001.

Pecorari, Diane. 2003. "Good and Original: Plagiarism and Patchwriting in Academic Second Language Writing." *Journal of Second Language Writing* 12 (4): 317–45. http://dx.doi.org/10.1016/j.jslw.2003.08.004.

Pecorari, Diane. 2006. "Visible and Occluded Citation Features in Postgraduate Second Language Writing." *English for Specific Purposes* 25 (1): 4–29. http://dx.doi.org/10.1016/j.esp.2005.04.004.

Pecorari, Diane. 2008. *Academic Writing and Plagiarism: A Linguistic Analysis*. New York: Continuum.

Pytlik, Betty P., and Sarah Liggett. 2002. *Preparing College Teachers of Writing: Histories, Theories, Programs, Practices*. New York: Oxford University Press.

Roig, Miguel. 2001. "Plagiarism and Paraphrasing Criteria of College and University Professors." *Ethics & Behavior* 11 (3): 307–23. http://dx.doi.org/10.1207/S15327019EB1103_8.

Tate, Gary, Amy Rupiper, and Kurt Schick. 2000. *A Guide to Composition Pedagogies*. 1st ed. New York: Oxford University Press.

Tate, Gary, Amy Rupiper Taggart, Kurt Schick, and Brooke Hessler. 2013. *A Guide to Composition Pedagogies*. 2nd ed. New York: Oxford University Press.

Villanueva, Victor. 2003. *Cross-Talk in Comp Theory: A Reader*. 2nd ed. Urbana, IL: NCTE.

White, Howard D. 2004. "Citation Analysis and Discourse Analysis Revisited." *Applied Linguistics* 25 (1): 89–116. http://dx.doi.org/10.1093/applin/25.1.89.

Yancey, Kathleen Blake, Liane Robertson, and Kara Taczak. 2014. *Writing across Contexts: Transfer, Composition, and Sites of Writing*. Logan: Utah State University Press.

Chapter 4
STORIED RESEARCH
Using Focus Groups as a Responsive Method

Crystal Benedicks

ABSTRACT

This chapter describes a study of undergraduate source use at a small liberal arts college (SLAC) using mixed methods (coding survey and focus-group results). The study's findings promoted more intentional teaching and revision of academic-honesty policies. Data was taken from recursive student surveys (two years apart) and a series of first-year-student focus groups and fourth-year-student focus groups gauging their understanding and experiences with source-based writing. The methods used in this study will be of greatest interest to scholars designing data-driven studies using mixed methods, particularly those working at small liberal arts colleges where broad-based study of the entire student population is possible, there is a high degree of faculty independence, and administrative structures are relatively agile and flexible.

INTRODUCTION

The research project I describe in this chapter had two goals: capturing the ways students at a small liberal arts college (SLAC) think about source use and academic honesty, and prompting institutional change in response to these findings. My methodologies therefore had to be flexible enough to be responsive to things we heard from students along the way. Further, those methodologies also combined qualitative and quantitative data to provide a fuller understanding of student source use; I therefore used both qualitative and quantitative data-analysis strategies to prepare the results for faculty and administrators across the disciplines. This chapter is the story of the challenges and the promises of this kind of broad-based, dynamic inquiry.

Located in rural Indiana, Wabash College is a small liberal arts college for men. The student population numbers fewer than one thousand, all of them undergraduates. Like many small liberal arts colleges, Wabash's policies about any number of issues tend to be implicit rather than explicit, dependent on individual faculty choice and implementation rather than institutional policy. While this informality can foster great creativity and flexibility, it can also be disorienting, particularly for students navigating source use and academic honesty.

In my roles as Assistant English professor and Writing Across the Curriculum (WAC) Coordinator, I was and am often consulted about potential plagiarism cases. These rich and engaging conversations with colleagues revealed that, despite individual faculty members' genuine desire to help students become better writers and researchers, there were blind spots in our campus culture of responding to and talking about academic honesty. Although repeat plagiarists are punished with immediate expulsion, there has been little attempt to teach students why and how sources are used. Most classroom discussion of source use is either devoted to the mechanics of citation or to pedantic warnings about the moral failing that is plagiarism. I initiated this research project as a complement to the qualitative data we were garnering through our participation in the Citation Project as a way of deepening and texturizing those data with students' local experiences and knowledges. In other words, the goal was to find out what students (say they) know about source use and where and how they learned what they know. I hoped to use these surveys as a needs assessment for the community that would help me convince faculty, staff, and administration to address source use in the classroom in contexts other than the legalistic or the moral. I also hoped to revise and formalize the college's policy for responding to plagiarism issues. Before I could go about courting such changes, however, I had to know what it was exactly that needed change. My research essentially maps out the cartography of students' source-use attitudes, practices, and affects in one academic community.

FRAMEWORK

As an English professor whose doctoral work focuses on nineteenth-century poetry, I am prompted by my training to approach problems through narrative, conversation, close reading, and case studies. These "soft" methodologies are unlikely to persuade my colleagues in the sciences and social sciences, to say nothing of gaining traction in the increasingly data-driven world of writing studies or the assessment-driven world of higher education administration I navigate as a WAC coordinator. Thus, I attempted to get at my research questions by marrying quantitative research with narrative inquiry. The methodologies Wabash College developed for investigating its local culture of citation are a result of this disciplinary complementarity: I hope they can demystify such processes for other researchers whose inquiry questions span both humanities and social science ways of knowing. The work of Donald E. Polkinghorne (1998) in *Narrative Knowing and the Human Sciences* as well as Clandinin and Connelly (2000) in *Narrative Inquiry: Experience and Story in Qualitative Research* is relevant here, as these scholars point out that narrative offers a useful counterpoint to the accumulation of quantitative data. Recent scholarship in plagiarism studies—such as Susan Blum's (2009) study of college students' understandings of originality and success, *My Word! Plagiarism and College Culture*—seeks to understand student action and attitudes through qualitative methods such as interviews and classroom-observation sessions.

My small study contributes to these ongoing conversations. Ultimately I argue that understanding local student perspectives on source use is critical for campus communities because it allows colleges to adjust to meet the specific needs of their populations. Faculty, administrators, and staff who articulate the need for change based on demonstrated research about local student practices and attitudes stand a greater chance for community cooperation and success pursuing change this way than do those who advocate for change based on exterior research or decontextualized conviction.

METHOD

In 2008 the Citation Project collected student writing from multiple institutions in the United States, including Wabash College. As a result, Wabash College initiated the first stage of this research project by inviting Sandra Jamieson, a principal researcher for the Citation Project, to administer a survey about source-use habits and attitudes to the college's first-year students. We hoped the Citation Project would help us trace the roots of our "plagiarism problem" back to classroom practice and ingrained institutional traditions.

The survey was titled "What Is (and Isn't) Plagiarism?" (Appendix 4.A). It asked first-year students to consider twenty different actions and determine whether they constituted plagiarism. These ranged from fairly obvious acts of dishonesty (purchasing a paper online and submitting it as your own) to more nuanced situations (dual submission of a paper, or taking your main idea from *SparkNotes*, with or without citation). Finally, the survey asked students to look at excerpts of student writing in comparison to the sources referenced by the students and judge whether the student was representing the source fairly or not. The survey garnered 113 student responses. A fuller exploration of our findings is below; we learned quickly that student perceptions of academic honesty differed vastly from faculty perceptions.

To follow up on this survey, I partnered with the writing center, the Dean of Students' Office, and the college's Teaching and Learning Committee (the *we* of this chapter), a rotating faculty committee composed of representatives from each academic division whose charge is to lead pedagogical inquiry on campus. We facilitated a series of faculty conversations inspired by the results of the first survey. The main concern of the faculty in those meetings was how well students understand standard expectations for source use. The group confronted the realty that any consensus across disciplines about the nature of those expectations is impossible. This understanding both complicated and heightened our desire to learn more about how our students think about source use in general and academic honesty in particular. As a result of these faculty-driven conversations, we launched an internal survey of the student body (Appendix 4.B) in 2010. This digital survey had two purposes: gauging how well students understood Wabash's academic-honesty policy and determining where and how they were gaining this understanding. To do this, we asked questions similar to those posed in the original 2008 survey; however, we drew on the recent faculty discussions to identify and highlight potential gray areas and potential opportunities for instruction. For example, the newer survey asked probing questions about how students learned about academic honesty and gave students more options about whether certain uses of sources were appropriate. The 2010 survey asked students to rate the relative appropriateness of various source-use gray areas—so, for example, students could indicate not just whether or not it is ethical to ask a classmate to edit their paper but also whether such collaboration rises to the level of a "strike" (at Wabash, students get a strike for being found guilty of academic dishonesty and are expelled after two strikes). They were also asked to indicate the extent to which they perceived faculty to agree about what constitutes academic dishonesty. Of our roughly 850 students (at the time), 175, or just over 20 percent, answered the survey. Respondents were split among first-year students, sophomores, juniors, and seniors, with first-year students being the most strongly represented group (35 percent of respondents). Students from all three academic divisions (humanities, social sciences, and natural sciences and mathematics) responded.

In the second stage of our research, we initiated a series of five student focus groups to deepen our understanding of the resultant survey data (see Appendix 4.C for student-focus-group questions). Each focus group was composed of four to seven students, either all freshmen or all seniors, taken at random from the freshmen and senior student populations. Focus-group sessions each lasted an hour and were collaboratively led by two faculty members or administrators from the college's Teaching and Learning Committee, writing center, and dean of students' office. The purpose of the focus groups was to contextualize what we'd learned from the 2008 and 2010 surveys by inviting students to describe their experiences using sources at Wabash.

DISCUSSION OF METHOD

Coming to Methodology

In this collection (introduction, interchapters for parts 1 and 2), Tricia Serviss and Sandra Jamieson write about the anxiety of scholars who are interested in making their methods transparent yet are hindered by a fear of critique and the pressure to produce original work rather than reflecting on and refining methodological tools. In other words, writing studies is a field that preaches to students that the writing process is as important as or more important than the product, but tends to keep its own research methods under wraps and focus on the research products. As Serviss and Jamieson suggest in that discussion of transcontextual research, sharing what we actually do is something of an act of courage, just as asking a student to describe their writing process might reveal a lot of crumbled drafts in the wastebasket, a few late nights, a few false starts.

Much of my own reticence about my methodology is a holdover from my doctoral education in English, in which research means writing a book all by yourself. While this is a perfectly sound methodology, it is not always the one best suited to figuring out how students understand writing. Yet the single-author, theory-driven book has such a tight hold on the imagination of the humanities that it is often difficult to justify to self or tenure-and-promotion committees that more collaborative and open-ended methodologies "count." Many composition scholars are positioned as I am: at least partly trained in the humanities, comfortable with the methodologies of narrative and close reading. However, the field as a whole, as this book attests, is trending toward data-driven projects open for reproduction. Ideally, the field of composition needs and cultivates both data-driven and more humanist methodologies, although the fact that composition scholars are not regularly trained in both creates the conditions for mistrust or anxiety. In the research I describe here, I decided (or my experiences and training decided for me) to attempt a kind of mash-up, a blend of data-driven and qualitative research.

I entered this project relatively inexperienced in the art of data-driven research. I have a tattered copy of Mina Shaughnessy's (1977) *Errors and Expectations* and a subscription to *CCC*, but when we launched this study of student source-use practices, I was unprepared. In fact, almost everything I knew about this kind of research came from conversations and mentorships formed through the Citation Project as participants exchanged ideas at conferences, over e-mails, and even one late afternoon in the deserted food court of lower Manhattan's Fulton Street Transit Center, where Sandra Jamieson taught me to code student papers. Looking back, I wish I had learned more about other studies—and perhaps related research projects like the one I was about to attempt—before jumping in with both feet. Yet probably the most important insight I've personally/professionally taken from this research project is that anyone who is possessed of a question they feel passionately about, anyone willing to work hard at unfamiliar kinds of work, can do research—even replicable, data-driven research.

Flexibility, (In)coherence, and Lunch Money
In practice, my methodology was flexible, organic, and inclusive (sometimes to the point of disintegration, sometimes to the point of inspiration). When I invited Sandra Jamieson to campus, I did not realize I was beginning a conversation that would turn into a full-fledged, long-term study. We—a growing cohort of concerned faculty from across the disciplines, the dean of students' office, and the writing center—moved organically from surveys to focus groups to faculty development to policy change. The main questions and themes of each research stage suggested the questions and themes for the next—and the process as a whole allowed us to sustain large-scale change in teaching practice and institutional policy.

While a flexible, recursive methodology allows room for corrections midcourse, it also courts chaos. Perhaps the biggest challenge we faced was keeping a coherent vision of our research question(s) before us. When the major goal of a project is to prompt institutional change rather than or in addition to answering specific questions about students' practices and beliefs, it is crucial to balance flexibility of methodology with integrity of the overall vision. How can we be nimble and responsive to what we learn as we design methodologies but at the same time keep moving in a relatively consistent direction toward the goal of prompting change?

One result of this quandary is that I ended up trying to do too much with one research project. It would have helped if I'd developed two separate studies: one on students' knowledge about academic-honesty standards (which could be used to help revise institutional policy) and another to get at what students say about how and why they use sources (which could be used to drive faculty development). Because I did not do this, I ended up conflating source use with academic honesty in some of the survey questions when my goal was to expand the campus discussion of source use beyond academic honesty.

Another unexpected issue that came up for us had to do with marshaling resources for the project. Who would pay for the lunches and gift certificates we planned to use to incentivize students to participate? Who would help take notes in focus groups? One practical response to this issue was to form strategic partnerships. I worked most closely with the college's Teaching and Learning Committee, but that committee further partnered with the dean of students and his staff, who were motivated to participate because they most often felt the burden of responding to plagiarism cases. These partnerships allowed me access to material resources, and, perhaps most important, helped me broadcast this research project as a cross-disciplinary, whole-campus concern felt by us all—not just the pet project of the writing specialist. These issues, however, were unexpected and not initially considered as I designed the project and its pieces.

NOTES FOR REFINING AND EXPANDING THIS STUDY

The methodology I've described, a methodology based on strategic team building, recursive surveys, and open-ended focus-group-and-faculty conversation, was specifically designed to be effective in the residential SLAC atmosphere, where it is possible to garner rather intimate knowledge of the opinions and practices of the student body and where faculty and administrators and students live and work in close proximity. Moreover, institutional change at SLACs is most effective when it is perceived to come from the bottom up as a natural, organic reaction to what seems to be going on. In relying heavily on student voices and student perceptions, we hoped to persuade our colleagues to make changes in their teaching and administrating because they clearly saw the need for it. Our surveys led to invigorating data well illustrated by stories from the focus groups. We used these data to drive significant institutional change. In that sense, the methods of storytelling and hard listening worked. However, one challenge for anyone seeking to refine and expand such a study would be the difficulty of doing so on a bigger, more dispersed campus. In such a case, it may be most efficient to focus the study on one department/major/class/vector of student identity within the university rather than to attempt a holistic overview.

To those who might take up a study of student attitudes similar to this one, I'd recommend the following:

- Hone your research question in advance as much as possible, including operationalizing the terms central to that research question.
- Invite feedback from the faculty and administration as often as possible, and allow that feedback to shape your process even once underway.
- Form strategic partnerships with faculty and administrators who share your concerns, making your research project team based.
- Consider doing more focus groups and/or individual interviews with students. The stories we collected about student experiences learning to work with sources were remarkable and remarkably effective at helping faculty and administrators see the "human cost" of our under-teaching source use. This kind of information couldn't be collected through our survey mechanisms, and thus we needed more than one method to understand the phenomena.
- Don't fear unfamiliar data-driven research methods. RAD research methods can be acquired as you go; as in most things, you can learn by doing.

FINDINGS

The student surveys as a corpus revealed four main findings about our campus community.

- Students perceive collaboration among themselves as a gray area of academic honesty. They are unsure about the boundaries between productive mutual support and plagiarism.
- Students are overreliant on the mechanics of citation as a kind of "magic bullet" that can redeem them from any accusations of academic dishonesty. They demonstrate more concern for correct citation than for meaningful interaction with sources.
- Students learn about academic honesty in discipline/punish settings rather than in academic, scholarly settings (i.e., in the dean's office rather than in the classroom).

- Students perceive that their teachers are only "sometimes" clear about their expectations for academic honesty. Further, these teachers only "sometimes" appear to agree with one another about what constitutes academic dishonesty.

The focus groups further led to the following insights:

- These students associate their efforts to use sources with uncertainty, fear, and frustration: freshmen especially tend to believe they have not been educated about source use but are expected to be good at it.
- Many students are not aware of disciplinary differences in source-use standards.
- Some students are aware of developments and changes in the way they use sources over time, although they often cannot describe how these changes came about.

DISCUSSION OF FINDINGS

Our surveys and focus groups demonstrated a significant gap between faculty expectations and actual student practices and attitudes. Faculty were particularly struck by student attitudes about citation. In the 2008 survey, 84 percent of respondents believed that "submit[ing] a paper written in your own words but drawing heavily on the ideas in *SparkNotes* or some similar study guide (print or electronic) *with no citation*" counted as an act of plagiarism. However, the survey then asked students whether plagiarism had taken place if the writer had included a citation at the end of the paper in a bibliography or Works Cited page. In this case, only about 23–28 percent of students believed plagiarism had occurred, indicating instead that the hypothetical situation constituted an appropriate use of sources. Further, if the hypothetical student paper included in-text citations "throughout the paper wherever the source is used," only 10–16 percent of student believed plagiarism had occurred.

These findings were reinforced by the 2010 survey, in which 90 percent of respondents believed that "submitting a paper that relies heavily on an idea from *SparkNotes* or *Wikipedia*, but putting it in your own words—*with in-text citations throughout the paper whenever the source is used*" is "not academically dishonest." Students in this situation may understand the letter of the law (cite your sources, as often as possible), but they misunderstand the point of including other authors' voices and ideas in their paper. Few faculty members are as interested in a student's ability to paraphrase *Wikipedia* as they are in a student's ability to sustain a meaningful interaction with the work of other writers.

Focus-group interviews deepened our understanding of students' relationship to citation. One representative freshman noted his fear of being accused of plagiarizing because of a careless mistake or because he failed to cite something his professor thought should be cited. He worried that being accused of plagiarism would ruin his life: he'd be kicked out of college; he'd never get a job. It is important to note that this student and others like him considered themselves to be honest; their fear was that they would not be perceived this way. The danger in this kind of fraught self-consciousness is that fear of a misstep begins to undermine students' ability to develop as writers. As one freshman put it, "I find myself more worried about proper citation, rather than the content of my paper."

Moreover, focus-group interviews revealed that many students felt undereducated about source use, even though they understood the stakes to be high. One freshmen earned laughs and approval from the other members of his focus group by describing his Wabash source-use education this way: "It's like they hand you *Rules for Writers* [the required writing manual for all freshmen] and say, here you go, two strikes and you're out!" Similarly, one senior noted, to the approval of others in his focus group, that he often felt "by the time you hear about it [a rule you inadvertently broke], you're in the dean's office." One of his peers in the same focus group added that learning how to use sources properly at Wabash is "trial by fire, but it's a pretty big fire." One freshman explained that most of what he'd learned about source use in his one semester of college came from being reprimanded for doing it incorrectly. We came to a troubling conclusion based on the data at this particular institution: it appears that our community sometimes "teaches" by punishing.

None of these findings are particularly surprising: researchers across the nation are reaching similar conclusions. For example, Project Information Literacy researchers Head and Eisenberg (2010) have recently shown that research-assignment handouts given to students are heavy on mechanical instruction (how to find sources, how to cite correctly) but short on more substantive explanations about why research matters. Similarly, the results of the Citation Project suggest a failure to communicate to students why and how sources are used. Yet there is value and potential in learning how these macrofindings are reflected in our local cultures. Our research methods helped us make the case that this national problem affects our own college, which, like many SLACs, sometimes imagines it is unique and exempted from national trends. When we conduct studies designed to investigate the local culture and use methods that collect student voices and attitudes, we challenge some of the ingrained beliefs we may have about ourselves and therefore motivate global institutional change. Our research methods, and not just what they revealed, were important in prompting these changes. Because the leaders of the project worked collaboratively across disciplines and compiled qualitative as well as quantitative data, we were able to appeal not just to writing teachers, often the default audience for these issues, but to most faculty and administrators. Indeed, our ability to texturize data with student stories and student voices was compelling to most members of the institution.

However, our mixture of qualitative and quantitative methodologies was valuable not just because it was rhetorically effective. The data-driven and "soft" methodologies complemented and complicated each other. For example, when we discovered the surveyed students did not consider *Wikipedia*-inspired but correctly cited papers academically dishonest, some members of our research team wondered whether these students genuinely do not see the problem with unoriginal work, or whether the students were (correctly) claiming that these papers—quality aside—were not technically plagiarized. When we addressed the issue of source use in the focus groups, however, we learned that students do tend to be quite focused on and anxious about using "the correct" citations to avoid "punishment" rather than thinking about questions of originality. We further learned that this problem is not one of student immaturity, ignorance, or fecklessness but rather a situation faculty help create by failing to explain that the point of writing with sources has more to do with ideas than with getting your parenthetical citations in order. Here, the focus-group interviews clarified the results of the survey and helped us further identify the frameworks within which students seem to think about source use.

To correct our default pedagogy of mechanics and intimidation, Wabash College mobilized this local research project by ultimately revising its academic-honesty policy, including establishing a review board and required educational activities for students who misuse sources (activities individually designed on a case-by-case basis). We also launched a series of retreats and faculty discussions around better educating students on how and why scholars use sources. Finally, we created a booklet (print and online) to guide students through the intricacies of source-use standards, including gray areas, real-life case studies, and suggested assignments. These energies have filtered down to the students: as I write this, an article has just appeared in the student newspaper about the importance of understanding source use.

CONCLUSION

Throughout this chapter, I've highlighted the challenges we faced, particularly in maintaining methods that are recursive and responsive but also directed and goal oriented. I've discussed how we operated at the intersections of disciplinary ways of knowing. I've detailed the complications of conducting research specifically designed to provoke institutional change. I want to end, though, with two more personal conclusions about what I've learned as a researcher attempting RAD research and its methods for the first time. One of the biggest challenges for me as a writer, and one with which I continue to struggle, has been learning to write in the genres preferred for describing research—less like an English professor and more like a social scientist. This isn't just a matter of personal style; it gets at issues of audience and authority, tone and structure. Although learning to communicate in a different register is difficult, it is necessary for scholars who want to speak to the widest possible audiences in making claims for improving the way we teach and learn writing. Finally, engaging this process has tempered my academic's knee-jerk reaction against the culture of assessment, emphasizing the possibilities of writing assessment to both vary and allow for genuine inquiry. Rather than railing against it, we as composition scholars must find ways to work with it strategically, to design assessments, perhaps born from unfamiliar research methods, that make institutions genuinely better.

APPENDIX 4.A
Academic Honesty Survey Created by Sandra Jamieson, 2008

These appendices may be downloaded from https://upcolorado.com/utah-state-university-press/item/3188-points-of-departure and used or modified for teaching or research purposes with attribution.

FINAL data from Wabash first year students – based on 113 student responses.
Sandra Jamieson, Drew University, November 10, 2008

	Have you ever submitted something for a class that	Yes	No
1	you knew was in violation of the campus plagiarism rules?	13	110
2	you suspected might be in violation of the campus plagiarism rules?	24	89
	Do you think it is plagiarism if you	Yes	No
3	Copied <u>part, one, or more than one</u> answer from another person in an exam,	81	32
4	Got questions or answers from someone else before a quiz or exam or used unauthorized notes	51	62
5	Copied part of all of someone else's computer program, lab report, or math calculations	76	37
6	Fabricated or falsified lab data, research data, or any other "results" for a class	49	64
7	Copied or purchased a complete paper from someone else	100	13
8	Downloaded or purchased a complete paper from the internet	96	17
9	Worked closely with someone else on an assignment when told to work alone	42	71
10	Asked or paid someone to write, rewrite, or significantly revise part of a paper for you have written	76	37
11	Written a paper for someone else, or allowed someone to copy a paper or other work from you	92	21
12	Fabricated or falsified part of all of a bibliography or works cited list	70	43
13	Submitted a paper for one class that you have already submitted for a grade in another class	28	85
14	Submitted a paper written in your own words but drawing heavily on the ideas in *SparkNotes* or some similar study guide (print or electronic) (a) with no citation	95	18
	(b) with citation at the end of the paper in a works cited or bibliography	32	81
	(c) with in-text citation throughout the paper wherever the source is used	18	95
15	Submitted a paper written in your own words but drawing heavily on the ideas of someone else such as a classmate, friend, or writing tutor for the main argument and/or support (a) with no citation	77	36
	(b) with citation at the end of the paper in a works cited or bibliography	26	87
	(c) with in-text citation throughout the paper wherever the source is used	18	95

		Yes	No
16	Submitted a paper written in your own words but drawing heavily on the ideas of something you read for the main argument and/or support		
	(a) with no citation	78	35
	(b) with citation at the end of the paper	26	87
	c) with in-text citation throughout the paper wherever the source is used	11	102
	Do you think the student text to the left of each image is guilty of plagiarism	**Yes**	**No**
17	*Student text:* Studies show that children, as well as parents, in low-income families have very few assets, so eliminating asset tests for coverage could increase enrollment (Cox, Ray, and Lawler). / *Coded student text:* Studies show that children, as well as parents, in low-income families have very few assets, so eliminating asset tests for coverage could increase enrollment (Cox, Ray, and Lawler). / *Source: Cox, Ray, & Lawler* Studies have shown that most low-income families have few assets. Eliminating asset tests....	50	63
18	*Student text:* Also, to eliminate confusion and difficulty for a family, states with separate Medicaid and SCHIP programs should coincide their renewal times and conduct renewal by mail or telephone. / Sentence 9 / *Coded student text:* Also, to eliminate confusion and difficulty for a family, states with separate Medicaid and SCHIP programs should coincide their renewal times and conduct renewal by mail or telephone. / *Source: Cox, Ray, & Lawler* • Coincide Renewal Times for Medicaid and SCHIP. • In states with separate Medicaid and SCHIP programs, eliminate confusion for a single family by making the renewal times of family members who are Medicaid coincide with the renewal times for family members in SCHIP.... • Conduct renewal by telephone.... Mail-in renewal.	87	26
19	*Student text:* Also, to eliminate confusion and difficulty for a family, states with separate Medicaid and SCHIP programs should coincide their renewal times and conduct renewal by mail or telephone. (Cox, Ray, and Lawler). / Sentence 9 / *Coded student text:* Also, to eliminate confusion and difficulty for a family, states with separate Medicaid and SCHIP programs should coincide their renewal times and conduct renewal by mail or telephone. / *Source: Cox, Ray, & Lawler* • Coincide Renewal Times for Medicaid and SCHIP. • In states with separate Medicaid and SCHIP programs, eliminate confusion for a single family by making the renewal times of family members who are Medicaid coincide with the renewal times for family members in SCHIP.... • Conduct renewal by telephone.... Mail-in renewal.	42	71
20	*Coded Student text:* Gamblers also have the tendency to lie to trusted family members, counselors or others in order to cover up their gambling addiction. "This addiction is spreading. Teens are gambling away tuition. They're going to college, applying for education aid checks, and they're gambling away—and their parents don't know that they are not going to school (Deffner)." / *Source text (Deffner)* "This addiction is spreading," Phil says. "Teens are gambling away tuition. They're going to college, applying for educational aid checks, and they're gambling away—and their parents don't know that they are not going to school"	29	84

APPENDIX 4.B
Wabash College Academic Honesty Survey, 2010

1. Academic Honesty Survey   **Exit this survey**

The Teaching and Learning Committee is reviewing the College's academic honesty policy. Please help us by completing the following short survey. *Please note that we do not intend to review or alter the Gentleman's Rule.* We are specifically interested in reviewing the 'two strikes and you're out' policy. If you have any questions or concerns, please contact Dr. Crystal Benedicks at benedicks@wabash.edu or x6156.

This survey is completely anonymous, and honest perspectives on academic honesty will be the most helpful.

1. What level are you?
- Senior
- Junior
- Sophomore
- Freshman

2. What is your major?

3. Please explain Wabash's academic honesty policy to the best of your ability below. If you are not familiar with the policy, indicate that.

4. Where did you learn most of what you know about academic honesty standards at Wabash? Check all that apply.
- Student Orientation
- Freshman Tutorial
- ENG 101 (Composition)
- Other classes
- Living unit/friends
- Other:

138 CRYSTAL BENEDICKS

5. Do you consider the following hypothetical student actions to be academically dishonest? Do you think students should receive a "strike" for them?

	Academically dishonest and deserves a strike	Academically dishonest, but does not deserve a strike	Not academically dishonest
Purchasing a paper and submitting it as your own			
Working with a fellow student on a take-home exam			
Submitting the same paper for two different classes			
Failing to include a parenthetical citation or footnote, even if you put quotation marks around the quote and list the source in the Works Cited page			
Paraphrasing a source (that is, putting it in your own words) without including a footnote or parenthetical citation			
Copying another student's work on an exam			
Getting your paper "corrected" by a fraternity brother or parent			
Copying sentences or phrases from the textbook into your written work			
Submitting a paper that relies heavily on an idea from SparkNotes or Wikipedia, but putting it in your own words--*without citation*			
Submitting a paper that relies heavily on an idea from SparkNotes or Wikipedia, but putting it in your own words--*with a citation at the end of the paper in a Works Cited or bibliography page*			
Submitting a paper that relies heavily on an idea from SparkNotes or Wikipedia, but putting it in your own words--*with in-text citations throughout the paper whenever the source is used*			

Optional comment about any of the above:

[blank text box]

6. To what extent do you find that faculty agree with one another about what constitutes academic dishonesty?

                High Agreement   Some Agreement   No Agreement

Degree of Agreement:

Optional Comment:

[blank text box]

7. Do your professors clearly explain their standards for academic honesty in class?

                Always   Sometimes   Never

Clarity of Standards:

Optional Comment:

[blank text box]

8. Do you think the current "two strikes and you're out" system is fair?

    Yes

    No

What changes, if any, do you think should be made to the policy?

[blank text box]

9. Do you have any other comments about the policy?

[blank text box]

APPENDIX 4.C
Wabash College Focus Group Questions, 2011

1) How has your thinking about source use developed over your time at Wabash?

   (Follow-up: Where/how did you learn what you've learned?)

2) When it comes to proper source use and citation/documentation, what are the challenges you have faced? What about challenges with academic honesty in general?

   (Follow-ups: How did you deal with these challenges? What kind of useful help did you get/wish you'd gotten?)

3) How can the administration and staff at the college (including the Dean of Students, the Writing Center, and college publications like the website) clarify expectations of proper source use and academic honesty in general? How can individual faculty members do so?

   (Follow-up: Can you remember any particularly useful advice or guidelines given by a particular teacher or staff member?)

References

Blum, Susan D. 2009. *My Word: Plagiarism and College Culture.* Ithaca, NY: Cornell University Press.

Citation Project. n.d. Accessed January 19, 2012. http://site.citationproject.net/.

Clandinin, D. Jean, and F. Michael Connelly. 2000. *Narrative Inquiry: Experience and Story in Qualitative Research.* San Francisco, CA: Jossey-Bass.

Head, Alison J., and Michael B. Eisenberg. 2010. "Assigning Inquiry: How Handouts for Research Assignments Guide Today's College Students." Project Information Literacy Progress Report. http://projectinfolit.org. http://dx.doi.org/10.2139/ssrn.2281494.

Polkinghorne, Donald E. 1998. *Narrative Knowing and the Human Sciences.* Albany: SUNY Press.

Shaughnessy, Mina P. 1977. *Errors & Expectations: A Guide for the Teacher of Basic Writing.* New York: Oxford University Press.

Chapter 5

TERMS AND PERCEPTIONS
Using Surveys to Discover Student Beliefs about Research

Kristi Murray Costello

ABSTRACT

This chapter describes a study that explores and demystifies the perceptions, processes, and feelings of 330 first-year students about research-based writing (RW). Working within a writing program at a large public university in New York, the author describes the development of a student-survey mechanism across two fall terms as well as the relationships among those surveys, administrative duties, and resulting change in the institution.

INTRODUCTION

Numerous articles and studies about research papers in first-year writing (FYW) courses appeared in English journals beginning in the 1930s, many calling for abolition of the extended research paper in FYW (Larson 1982; Strickland 2004). These recurrent calls, combined with recent Citation Project findings (Howard, Serviss, and Rodrigue 2010; Jamieson and Howard 2011; The Citation Project 2012) and other works (Nelson 2011) have led some programs to eliminate the "research paper" from their curriculum altogether. Though discussions among FYW faculty at a public university in the State University of New York (SUNY) system echoed the same questions about the validity of the research paper, we remain unsure about students' research writing (RW) and need data to better understand our students. Given the university's admission standards, it initially seemed likely that students had been exposed to some of the steps and techniques of RW. Yet we wanted to open the "black box that largely conceal[s] the processes undertaken by the student" when writing with sources (Foster and Gibbons 2007).

Instructors and administrators of the FYW program wanted to find out more about our students, their prior experiences with research, and their RW processes, as well as their feelings about RW and then revise our RW curriculum accordingly. More specifically, we wanted to know the answers to several questions: Where, when, and from whom are students learning their RW strategies? What are their research strategies? Are those strategies effective? Thus, I piloted and refined two surveys of first-year writing students, one in fall 2010 and a follow-up survey in fall 2011, that sought answers to these questions.

FRAMEWORK

Like many of the participating Citation Project researchers who worked to code FYW student research papers, I coded undergraduate research papers and saw a real difference between what we ask students to do and what they actually produce in FYW (see Bodi 2002 for further description of such differences). As a result, I generated a series of questions relative to the work undertaken by reference librarians and information-literacy specialists like Bodi (2002), Leckie (1996), Valentine (1993), Head and Eisenberg (2010), and others. The good news is that studies like the Citation Project within writing studies are likewise shedding light on how and to what extent students engage with sources in their writing. The bad news is, as information-literacy specialists and resource librarians reiterate, we still have little data that explains why they engage in often ineffective practices.

The two surveys I administered at one SUNY campus are designed to collect and make meaning of such data. There are both similarities and differences between these surveys and those administered by Foster and Gibbons (2007), Head and Eisenberg (2010), and Valentine (1993). The major difference between my surveys and this trajectory of research within library science is that their studies are focused less on what can be done instructionally in students' writing courses and more on how institutional librarians can provide better resources for students or better encourage students to use such resources. Unlike the results of Alison Head and Michael Eisenberg's (2010) study, which showed "the reasons students procrastinate are no longer driven by . . . pre-internet fears of failure and a lack of confidence" (3), my 2011 survey suggests that students, at least on one campus, do procrastinate because of a lack of confidence. Barbara Valentine's (1993) study reported similar findings. My study contributes to this research tradition by exploring first-year students' perceptions and prior experiences with RW as they navigate FYW courses.

The 2010 and 2011 FYW research surveys are an extension of the 1982 composition study conducted by Robert Schwegler and Linda Shamoon. Schwegler and Shamoon (1982) interviewed instructors and students, "[becoming] acutely aware of differing views [held by students and instructors] of the research paper" (818), a sentiment also supported in Valentine's (1993) research. Unlike Valentine, however, who focused on library spaces, Schwegler and Shamoon (1982) focused their research on the writing. Schwegler and Shamoon asked students and instructors to address the "research process, the aims of research, the forms of research writing, and the appropriate evaluation standards for academic research papers" (818). They revealed a disconnect between instructor and student responses, concluding that "these contradictory perspectives . . . [explain] the dissatisfaction many instructors feel when they have finished grading a set of research papers and the irritation students feel when they receive a poor grade on a paper they were sure did all that a research paper is supposed to do" (818). I developed and deployed my surveys, therefore, to gauge the currency of such an interpretive stance in twenty-first-century FYW courses.

METHOD

Survey

The main mechanism of this study is a series of student surveys refined across two iterations one year apart. The first (2010) survey was taken by FYW students midway through the semester before formal research instruction began; the second (2011) survey was taken by students during the first week of similar FYW classes the next year.

The 2010 survey (see Appendix 5.A) included twenty questions about students' experience and confidence when engaging in college-level research and about their beliefs as to the purposes of research in FYW. The list included questions asking about

- previous experiences writing a research paper;
- amount of time spent writing research papers;
- amount of time and effort dedicated to understanding and finding sources;
- source incorporation into their own writing;
- kinds of sources sought and used;
- points of struggle with writing a research paper;
- perceptions of the aims of FYW research.

Some of these questions, particularly those pertaining to the kinds of sources used by students, align with survey questions posed by Foster and Gibbons (2007) and Head and Eisenberg (2010). Others, pertaining to students' information-seeking routines, are similar to Valentine's (1993) questions. However, unlike the surveys in these studies, the surveys I designed were mostly comprised of multiple-choice questions, a majority of which asked students to quantify their answers on a Likert scale as opposed to providing short-answer responses (see Appendix 5.A). Several of the questions' response options included the following range: not at all comfortable, somewhat comfortable, comfortable, and very comfortable. The survey design reflects the goal of shedding light on the extent to which students understand and depend upon such practices. After receiving IRB approval, the first survey was distributed to 138 FYW students in fall 2010. Then, a revised second survey was given to 192 additional students in fall 2011. The surveys were introduced to students by their writing instructors, who explained that survey responses would be both anonymous and inaccessible to instructors.

The 2010 survey was given to eight FYW classes (four Writing 110 courses and four Writing 111 courses) taught by four different full-time faculty; 136 FYW students participated. Just under half the students surveyed were enrolled in Writing 110: Seeing and Writing the World, a full-credit-bearing self-placement writing course created by the Writing Initiative in tandem with the Educational Opportunity Program, a program that provides academic, financial, and personal support to first-generation as well as low-income students. The course expands on the instruction students receive during the summer bridge program and serves as a precursor to the traditional FYW course, Writing 111: Coming to Voice. Seventy-two percent of Writing 110 students are Educational Opportunity Program students. Writing 110 is also open to Student Support Services students, another program that supports first-generation as well as low-income students. The remaining 16 percent of Writing 110 students have either requested entry into the course or are second-language learners served by the campus's English as a second language program. Ultimately this means that more than 83 percent of Writing 110 students are first-generation college students. The other sixty-four students surveyed in 2010 were enrolled in Writing 111, the FYW course more than 80 percent of first-year students opt to take.

The 2011 survey was administered similarly in twelve different FYW sections, yet this time during the first week of classes. Students surveyed were largely enrolled in FYW sections taught by full-time faculty with the exception of two sections of Writing 111 and two sections of Writing 110 taught by veteran teaching assistants with similar teaching experience.

Collection and Coding

Once all printed surveys had been collected from participating students, I manually recorded responses to multiple-choice questions into an Excel worksheet, gathering both discrete (distinguishing between Writing 110 and 111 survey results) and composite (combined) data. I relied upon open-coding methods described by proponents of grounded theory (Corbin and Strauss 1990) to recognize patterns in student perceptions as well as axial coding based on multiple contextual variables, including students' backgrounds (i.e., previous instruction), type of FYW course (Writing 110 or Writing 111), and reported practices. When open coding, I coded every response and every short-answer question, developing relevant themes as I went, such as lack of confidence. New categories were then added to the data sheets as the list of patterns expanded. While coding, I wrote informal theoretical memos to better understand and connect the data, memos I returned to once all the data had been tabulated. In these ways I used the practices proposed by grounded-theory researchers to systematize my data analysis.

Selective Coding

After this initial coding, I engaged in selective coding according to the following indicators:

- innovative practices (curriculum described as exceptional or innovative);
- problematic practices (curriculum described as subverting best practices);
- anxiety (student nervousness or discomfort); and/or
- misconception (the student's response perpetuated a myth about RW or higher education, from a faculty point of view).

My choice to determine these selective coding categories quickly was largely due to time constraints. As an administrator, I needed some results from this pilot study to share with the teaching community as a form of program assessment. The material realities of administrative life pushed me to limit the coding categories as early as possible to produce such time-sensitive results. Thus, my reiteration of distributing surveys in 2011 revised this process; I extended both the axial and open coding in attempts to generate more accurate and complete findings.

Both surveys were double coded at the selective coding stage. My coding partners and I coded each survey independently and then compared—and at times rectified—our findings, ensuring correctness of multiple-choice question tabulation and interrater reliability of short-answer question coding. To prepare for this double coding, my partners and I collaboratively coded and reconciled five to ten sample surveys to increase our interrater reliability. A more refined version of this pilot study will require the coding results be processed statistically to help uncover more nuance in terms of interrater reliability as well as to understand differently the confidence levels of students.

Discussion of Method

If I had been working with a quantitative research partner or a more experienced statistician throughout the pilot study, that partner likely would have pointed out that the initial 2010 survey was administered to more students enrolled in Writing 110 (55 percent) than Writing 111 (45 percent), a ratio that does not correlate with the institution's first-year writing course offerings. My sample represents the pre-general education credit-bearing course, Writing 110, more predominantly than it does our more populated general education course, Writing 111. This disproportionate ratio could skew the data and the meaning our FYW program assigned to the survey results. The annual Writing 111 enrollment is typically around one thousand eight hundred, nearly ten times the enrollment of Writing 110. However, I wanted to survey students from both courses to get a better idea of the perceptions and processes of all our first-year student writers, not just those who go directly into the more advanced course, Writing 111. In designing the pilot study, I decided not to differentiate between students in the two courses when compiling the data I wanted to ensure that the populations weren't compared in problematic ways. However, I quickly realized that without discrete data, in addition to composite data, I had limited what I could learn about how perceptions and processes vary based on linguistic, economic, and educational background. Likewise, creating only composite data also implicitly argued that our students, across courses and backgrounds, are similar enough to be defined by composite data to other instructors and administrators at my institution. These are all lessons learned through reiterative pilot-study processes that were invaluable to me as a researcher.

Learning from my previous mistake, I administered the 2011 survey to 192 first-year writing students—61 enrolled in Writing 110 and 131 enrolled in Writing 111, a balance that better represents the institution's actual FYW course enrollment. Further, data derived from Writing 110 and 111 students in the 2011 survey was analyzed both together and separately. The second survey, like the first, was distributed in the classrooms of experienced writing teachers. Similar to distribution of the 2010 survey, the 2011 distribution was premised on the idea that more experienced teachers could better adapt one class meeting to accommodate students completing the survey in class. The differences among the responses of Writing 110 and Writing 111 students are indeed illuminating and will be shared in a future work.

Additional questions evolved between the 2010 and 2011 surveys. Both the 2010 and the 2011 surveys were comprised of mainly multiple-choice questions, most of which asked students to plot their answers on varying Likert scales (Appendix 5.A and Appendix 5.B). However, based on some of the responses derived from the 2010 survey, the 2011 survey was expanded to include three additional short-answer follow-up questions. For example, students' responses to the question "When you are struggling with writing a research paper, which of the following do you typically do?" yielded what I found to be surprising results. I developed additional follow-up questions: "Revisit Question 16. Explain your response. For example, how often do you struggle with research papers and why? Why do you procrastinate, call your parents, or visit the Writing Center when you're struggling? If you rarely struggle with research papers, why do you think this is?" (see Appendix 5.B). In the 2011 survey, I also added a question asking students whether they had been instructed in how to use online databases to find scholarly articles (see Appendix 5.B). Next time I conduct this study, I will revise this question further, asking students in a multiple-choice question to differentiate among online search engines, such as Google, and online subscription databases, such as those accessed through universities and public libraries.

While I did not include my own students in the data, I did conduct the survey informally and orally with my FYW students in 2010 and thus was able to ask them follow-up questions not possible in a paper survey. This experiment inspired me to add questions to the 2011 survey. For example, when I asked students about their feelings regarding research and writing research papers, nearly half the students commented that at some point since entering college, they had felt angry or upset because high school had not prepared them for college-level RW. Many noted that their high-school teachers often said, "You'll learn that in college," yet what their high-school teachers neglected to mention is that, as opposed to teaching them this information, many of their college professors would expect them to know the information already. In fact, a student described how her high-school teachers and college professors often follow up mentions of such things as Google Scholar with an aside of "but you all already know about that." Nearly every student in the room identified with that student, nodding and raising their hands to contribute. Students shared that while they are known as a generation of technology experts, they actually have limited experience using technology for academic purposes. In fact, a show of hands revealed that out of my sixteen students, only three of them knew how to access Google Scholar. This conversation led me to ask, *if we're so often wrong about the extent of our students' familiarity with technology, might we also be wrong about their research experience?*, a question I hope to explore further in future research as a result of this pilot study.

FINDINGS

Both the 2010 and 2011 surveys revealed that very few students felt even "reasonably comfortable conducting college-level research and engaging in college-level research writing" (see Figure 5.1). In 2010, only a quarter of students surveyed felt reasonably comfortable conducting college-level research and engaging in college-level research writing, with only a couple of the 136 students referring to themselves as confident, even though the 2010 survey was completed eight weeks into the semester. In fact, not one student who took the 2010 survey considered themselves "very comfortable." In 2011, 8 percent of FYW students said they were "very comfortable conducting college-level research and engaging in college-level research writing." A quarter of the students surveyed considered themselves reasonably comfortable conducting college-level research; many of these same students referred to citation-style mechanics as the grounds of their confidence.

A lack of confidence was further supported by student responses about plagiarism and experience writing research papers (see Figure 5.2). In 2010, 84 percent of students surveyed tentatively answered the question asking them if they had ever engaged in intentional plagiarism (responding "I don't think so," "I hope not," or "possibly"). Only 16 percent of students answered resolutely, with 6 percent selecting "no" in answer to the question asking them if they had ever unintentionally plagiarized and 10 percent selecting "yes." Similarly, in 2011, 80 percent of students surveyed answered tentatively. Only 18 percent of students answered resolutely, with 7 percent saying "no" and 11 percent saying "yes" to engaging in unintentional plagiarism. In 2010, only 18 percent of students said they had never written a research paper before.

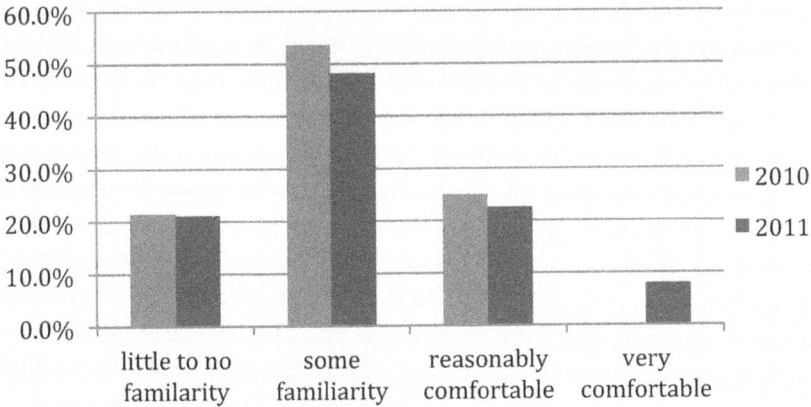

Figure 5.1. Familiarity with college-level research and writing. Students were asked to categorize their current familiarity conducting college-level research and engaging in college-level research writing.

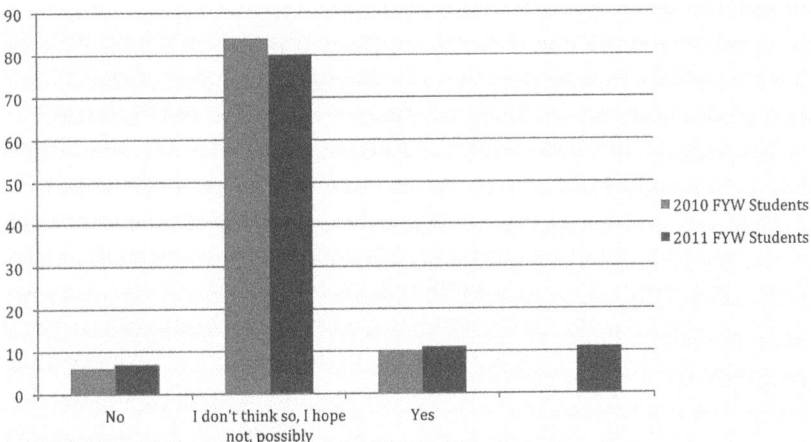

Figure 5.2. Unintentional plagiarism. Students were asked whether or not they had ever unintentionally plagiarized.

However, of the remaining 82 percent of students, nearly half chose option C, which was "Sort of. Explain."

Both the 2010 and 2011 surveys concluded by asking students what they hoped to gain from the upcoming research unit in their FYW course. Notable reoccurring responses included the hope for increased ease and avoidance of punishment with regards to plagiarism. More specifically, frequent responses revealed that students wanted to learn how to "make [their] paper[s] sound like . . . college paper[s]," "use sources properly so [they] won't be punished for plagiarism," "[create a] works cited perfectly to not get points off," "[learn] how to use information that is benefitting for [their] research," "write lengthy papers," and "correctly write a research paper and find the easiest way to do so."

DISCUSSION OF FINDINGS

In 2010, 82 percent of surveyed students noted that they definitively had or had "sort of" written a research paper before. Short-answer responses to the prompt "Explain" revealed that some students considered assignments such as reports on first ladies assigned in junior high to be "sort of" research. This led me to wonder whether some of the students who had chosen "yes" were also referring to similar assignments. To this end, I added a more detailed short-answer follow-up question to the 2011 survey: "Describe the kind of research papers you wrote and in what grade you wrote them. What kinds of topics did you explore? What kinds of sources were required?" (see Appendix 5.B). Analysis of 2011 data revealed that some students were indeed counting research projects from several years before, some even dating back to elementary school, as experience doing the kind of research expected at the university.

Similarly, in the 2010 survey, I asked students whether or not they had ever been instructed as to how to use online subscription databases. Though many students indicated yes, their responses to the later questions regarding how they seek sources seemed to suggest that their definition of online databases was different than I expected. This theory was further supported in the aforementioned roundtable discussion I had with my students in fall 2010 regarding their experiences with research. Thus, the 2011 survey asked students to be more specific, revealing that many students did consider being taught how to use Google and/or *Wikipedia* in fourth or fifth grade as previous research experience. Thus, my perception of research *was* very different than my students' beliefs about research.

While the study revealed numerous other findings, the key findings at the end of this pilot phase are perhaps ones we already suspected— that students largely lack confidence when it comes to research and RW; simultaneously, they do not see the value of research and research-based writing. What this study added to the conversation, however, is not only evidence that many of our students see research and RW more as an opportunity to shore up proof for their ideas than an opportunity for learning but also that many students who participated in the study, particularly those who were confident about their research and RW skills, were actually confused as to what faculty recognize as university-level research and RW.

CONCLUSION

I began this study in an attempt to answer what seemed like simple questions: Where, when, and from whom are students learning their RW strategies? What are their research strategies? Are those strategies effective? However, before I could effectively find answers to these questions, I had to know what and how to ask—two things I could not have done without the information and clarity provided by the 2010 survey—and the additional 2011 iteration of that survey. Thus, this study taught me as much about developing credible research mechanisms as it did about the subject of my inquiry—research practices and beliefs of first-year undergraduates.

At the end of the pilot study, these surveys illustrated students' lack of confidence and experience with research and RW, implicitly reiterating what many of us already know; FYW programs are enriched by frequent data-driven needs assessments of their students. The 2010 and 2011 surveys enabled this one program to learn about our students' research and writing processes and perceptions in nonevaluative, comfortable environments. The surveys led to renewed focus on research in FYW courses. The lessons of the pilot study, however, extend beyond this one institution's classroom. Drafting, implementing, and analyzing the 2010 and 2011 surveys have inspired and informed me not only as a teacher and administrator but also as a researcher. To refine the design of this study I would

- ensure the student sample size is reflective of the institution's course offerings;
- obtain student surveys from the classrooms of faculty members with varying backgrounds and experience;
- conduct and collect surveys digitally;
- refine my survey questions, relying less on short-answer questions, which necessitate qualitative coding, and more on detailed multiple-choice questions.
- recruit research partners invested in creating more illustrative coding schemes and conducting double-blind coding on all materials.

In sum, while I learned a lot about students' writing and research processes and perceptions at one institution, in many ways, the most valuable aspect of the 2010 study was that it helped me better craft and conduct the 2011 study as a research mechanism with potentially trans-contextual research affordances.

APPENDIX 5.A
2010 First-Year Writing Research Study

These appendices may be downloaded from https://upcolorado.com/utah-state-university-press/item/3188-points-of-departure and used or modified for teaching or research purposes with attribution.

DIRECTIONS

Please clearly circle the letter that correlates to the response that best coincides with your perspective. Do note that in responding to this survey, you acknowledge that your comments may be used in institutional and/or personal research. You are in no way obligated to participate in this survey, but please know that if you do, your responses are absolutely anonymous and neither your participation in this survey nor your responses will be linked to you personally or affect your grade in this course. Thank you for your participation and your willingness to assist us as we work to improve the quality of first-year writing Research Instruction. If you have any questions or concerns about this research, please direct them to Dr.X at x@x.edu.

1. How would you categorize your familiarity with conducting college-level research and engaging in college-level research writing before entering the university?
    A. I had little to no familiarity with conducting college-level research and engaging in college-level research writing
    B. I had some familiarity with conducting college-level research and engaging in college-level research writing
    C. I was reasonably comfortable conducting college-level research and engaging in college-level research writing
    D. I was very comfortable conducting college-level research and engaging in college-level research writing

2. Prior to enrolling in your first-year writing course, had you ever written a Research Paper?
    A. Yes
    B. No
    C. Sort of. Explain. _____

3. What was the longest paper you had ever written before beginning college?
    A. 1–4 pages
    B. 5–8 pages
    C. 8–10 pages
    D. 10–15 pages
    E. 15+ pages

4. Had you ever been instructed as to how to use online databases to find scholarly articles?
    A. Yes
    B. No
    C. Sort of. Explain. _____

5. How do you choose a topic for a research paper?
    A. I try to choose a topic which has already been discussed in class and thus, one I know the teacher will approve
    B. I choose a topic in which I already have a background and sufficient knowledge
    C. I choose a topic in which I already have a background and interest, but about which I have not formulated specific opinions
    D. I try to choose topics which have not previously been discussed in class, but which pertain to the content of the course
    E. I try to choose topics about which I have already previously written papers or read articles
    F. Often my instructor either chooses or strongly encourages me to do a specific topic because I struggle with topic selection

6. Which one of the following descriptions best characterizes how you typically begin when writing a research paper?
    A. I sit down at the computer and type, engaging in online research as needed
    B. I sit down at the computer with my research and type
    C. I compile and read my research, and then I begin writing the paper
    D. I compile and read my research, formulate detailed notes and/or outlines, and then, with a clear idea and focus in mind, begin writing my paper

7. Where do you find sources? (circle all letters that apply)
    A. Online search engines such as Google or Yahoo
    B. Local Newspapers and magazines
    C. National newspapers and magazines
    D. Textbooks
    E. Library databases
    F. General and Informational webpages such as *Wikipedia*
    G. Print journals accessed from the library
    H. Library book stacks
    I. Friends and/or family
    J. Online web pages and resources such as government sites and organization sites

K. Professors and/or TAs
L. Other, specify:_____

8. After being assigned a research paper, when do you typically develop your thesis?
   A. After I have decided on a topic, but before compiling any sources
   B. After I have decided on a topic and compiled my sources, but before I have finished reading my sources
   C. After I have decided on a topic, compiled, and read my sources
   D. After I have begun writing my paper

9. When given a writing assignment that requires 3 or more sources, when do you typically begin doing your work?
   A. Three or more weeks before the due date
   B. Two weeks before the due date
   C. One week before the due date
   D. Three days before the due date
   E. Two days or less than before the due date

10. When using sources for a research paper, how much time do you spend reading and understanding each source?
    A. Two hours or more
    B. One hour
    C. 30 minutes
    D. Less than 30 minutes apiece

11. While reading each source, do you: (mark all that apply)
    A. Take notes as you go
    B. Summarize the entire source when you are done
    C. Underline important ideas or points in the source
    D. Make comments in the margins of the text
    E. Write down quotes that support your thesis/argument
    F. Do nothing until you are actually writing the paper
    G. None of the above

12. How comfortable do you feel quoting from sources in your writing?
    A. Very comfortable
    B. Comfortable
    C. Uncomfortable
    D. Very uncomfortable

13. How comfortable do you feel paraphrasing text from sources in your writing?
    A. Very comfortable
    B. Comfortable

C. Uncomfortable
D. Very uncomfortable
E. The only time I use sources in my writing is when I quote directly from the text.
F. I never use sources in my writing.

14. How comfortable do you feel summarizing sources in your writing?
    A. Very comfortable
    B. Comfortable
    C. Uncomfortable
    D. Very uncomfortable
    E. The only time I use sources in my writing is when I quote directly from the text.
    F. I never use sources in my writing.

15. When you are struggling with writing a research paper, which of the following do you typically do? (Circle all that apply)
    A. Procrastinate
    B. Speak to classmates and/or parents
    C. Speak to my instructor
    D. Despite struggles, overcome them by submerging myself in my work
    E. Visit the campus Writing Center or utilize other campus resources
    F. I have never struggled when writing a research paper

16. When do you create your Works Cited list and/or incorporate in-text citations into your paper?
    A. As I compile sources, I add them to the Works Cited
    B. As I use sources in my paper, I add them to the Works Cited and create in-text citations
    C. After I have completed my paper, I formulate a Works Cited page and insert in-text citations
    D. I often do not create a formal Works Cited page or use in-text citations due to lack of guidance, time constraints, paper requirements, or other situational issues

17. How comfortable do you feel formatting an MLA Works Cited page and in-text citations?
    A. Not at all comfortable
    B. Somewhat comfortable
    C. Comfortable
    D. Very Comfortable

18. Do you think that you have ever unintentionally plagiarized?
    A. Never
    B. I don't think so
    C. I hope not, but I'm not confident in my understanding of the definition of plagiarism
    D. Possibly
    E. Yes

19. Have you ever intentionally plagiarized?
    A. Never
    B. Once or twice
    C. Occasionally, but only when I was desperate
    D. I hope not, but I'm not confident in my understanding of the definition of plagiarism
    E. On more than two occasions, I have plagiarized
    F. I plagiarize frequently

20. What do you most hope to learn about research or research writing in your first-year writing course?

APPENDIX 5.B
2011 First-Year Writing Research Study

DIRECTIONS

Please clearly circle the letter that correlates to the response that best coincides with your perspective. Please only circle one letter even if your first impulse is that your opinion lies in between two answers. Do note that in responding to this survey, you acknowledge that your comments may be used in institutional and/or personal research. You are in no way obligated to participate in this survey, but please know that if you do, your responses are absolutely anonymous and neither your participation in this survey nor your responses will be linked to you personally or affect your grade in this course. Thank you for your participation and your willingness to assist us as we work to improve the quality of first-year writing Research Instruction. If you have any questions about this research, please direct them to Dr. X at xxx.edu.

1. How would you categorize your familiarity with conducting college-level research and engaging in college-level research writing before entering the university?
    A. I had little to no familiarity with conducting college-level research and engaging in college-level research writing

B. I had some familiarity with conducting college-level research and engaging in college-level research writing
C. I was reasonably comfortable conducting college-level research and engaging in college-level research writing
D. I was very comfortable conducting college-level research and engaging in college-level research writing

2. Prior to enrolling in your first-year writing course, had you ever written a Research Paper?
    A. Yes
    B. No
    C. Sort of. Explain. _____

3. Describe the kind of research papers you wrote and in what grade you wrote them. What kinds of topics did you explore? What kinds of sources were required?

4. What was the longest paper you had ever written before beginning college?
    A. 1–4 pages
    B. 5–8 pages
    C. 8–10 pages
    D. 10–15 pages
    E. 15+ pages

5. Had you ever been instructed as to how to use online databases to find scholarly articles?
    A. Yes
    B. No
    C. Sort of. Explain. _____

6. How do you choose a topic for a research paper?
    A. I try to choose a topic which has already been discussed in class and thus, one I know the teacher will approve
    B. I choose a topic in which I already have a background and sufficient knowledge
    C. I choose a topic in which I already have a background and interest, but about which I have not formulated specific opinions
    D. I try to choose topics which have not previously been discussed in class, but which pertain to the content of the course
    E. I try to choose topics about which I have already previously written papers or read articles
    F. Often my instructor either chooses or strongly encourages me to do a specific topic because I struggle with topic selection

7. Which one of the following descriptions best characterizes how you typically begin when writing a research paper?
   A. I sit down at the computer and type, engaging in online research as needed
   B. I sit down at the computer with my research and type
   C. I compile and read my research, and then I begin writing the paper
   D. I compile and read my research, formulate detailed notes and/or outlines, and then, with a clear idea and focus in mind, begin writing my paper

8. Where do you find sources? (circle all letters that apply). Then, write a number "1" next to the type of source you use first, a 2 next to the source you use second, and then write a check next to the source you feel you use most. Please make sure these marks and their correspondences are clear.
   A. Online search engines such as Google or Yahoo
   B. Local Newspapers and magazines
   C. National newspapers and magazines
   D. Textbooks
   E. Library databases
   F. General and Informational webpages such as *Wikipedia*
   G. Print journals accessed from the library
   H. Library book stacks
   I. Friends and/or family
   J. Online web pages and resources such as government sites and organization sites
   K. Professors and/or TAs
   L. Other, specify:_____

9. After being assigned a research paper, when do you typically develop your thesis?
   A. After I have decided on a topic, but before compiling any sources
   B. After I have decided on a topic and compiled my sources, but before I have finished reading my sources
   C. After I have decided on a topic, compiled, and read my sources
   D. After I have begun writing my paper

10. When given a writing assignment that requires 3 or more sources, when do you typically begin doing your work?
    A. Three or more weeks before the due date
    B. Two weeks before the due date
    C. One week before the due date
    D. Three days before the due date
    E. Two days or less than before the due date

11. When using sources for a research paper, how much time do you spend reading and understanding each source?
    A. Two hours or more
    B. One hour
    C. 30 minutes
    D. Less than 30 minutes apiece

12. While reading each source, do you: (mark all that apply)
    A. Take notes as you go
    B. Summarize the entire source when you are done
    C. Underline important ideas or points in the source
    D. Make comments in the margins of the text
    E. Write down quotes that support your thesis/argument
    F. Do nothing until you are actually writing the paper
    G. None of the above

13. How comfortable do you feel quoting from sources in your writing?
    A. Very comfortable
    B. Comfortable
    C. Uncomfortable
    D. Very uncomfortable

14. How comfortable do you feel paraphrasing text from sources in your writing?
    A. Very comfortable
    B. Comfortable
    C. Uncomfortable
    D. Very uncomfortable
    E. The only time I use sources in my writing is when I quote directly from the text.
    F. I never use sources in my writing.

15. How comfortable do you feel summarizing sources in your writing?
    A. Very comfortable
    B. Comfortable
    C. Uncomfortable
    D. Very uncomfortable
    E. The only time I use sources in my writing is when I quote directly from the text.
    F. I never use sources in my writing.

16. When you are struggling with writing a research paper, which of the following do you typically do? (Circle all that apply) Next, place a "1" next to the one you do first.

A. Procrastinate
B. Speak to classmates and/or parents
C. Speak to my instructor
D. Despite struggles, overcome them by submerging myself in my work
E. Visit the campus Writing Center or utilize other campus resources
F. I have never struggled when writing a research paper

17. Revisit Question 16. Explain your response. For example, how often do you struggle with research papers and why? Why do you procrastinate, call your parents, or visit the Writing Center when you're struggling? If you rarely struggle with research papers, why do you think this is?

18. When do you create your Works Cited list and/or incorporate in-text citations into your paper?
    A. As I compile sources, I add them to the Works Cited
    B. As I use sources in my paper, I add them to the Works Cited and create in-text citations
    C. After I have completed my paper, I formulate a Works Cited page and insert in-text citations
    D. I often do not create a formal Works Cited page or use in-text citations due to lack of guidance, time constraints, paper requirements, or other situational issues

19. How comfortable do you feel formatting an MLA Works Cited page and in-text citations?
    A. Not at all comfortable
    B. Somewhat comfortable
    C. Comfortable
    D. Very Comfortable

20. Do you think that you have ever unintentionally plagiarized?
    A. Never
    B. I don't think so
    C. I hope not, but I'm not confident in my understanding of the definition of plagiarism
    D. Possibly
    E. Yes

21. Have you ever intentionally plagiarized?
    A. Never
    B. Once or twice
    C. Occasionally, but only when I was desperate
    D. I hope not, but I'm not confident in my understanding of the definition of plagiarism

E. On more than two occasions, I have plagiarized
F. I plagiarize frequently

22. What do you most hope to learn about research or research writing in your first-year writing course? Are there any lessons of research that you feel instructors assume you know when you don't?

References

Bodi, Sonia. 2002. "How Do We Bridge the Gap between What We Teach and What They Do: Some Thoughts on the Place of Questions in the Process of Research." *Journal of Academic Librarianship* 28 (3): 109–14. http://dx.doi.org/10.1016/S0099-1333(01)00302-0.

Corbin, Juliet, and Anselm Strauss. 1990. "Grounded Theory Research: Procedures, Canons, and Evaluative Criteria." *Qualitative Sociology* 13 (1): 3–21. http://dx.doi.org/10.1007/BF00988593.

Foster, Nancy, and Susan Gibbons, eds. 2007. *Studying Students: The Undergraduate Research Project at the University of Rochester.* Rochester, NY: Association of College and Research Libraries.

Head, Alison, and Michael Eisenberg. 2010. "Lessons Learned: How College Students Seek Information in the Digital Age." *Project Information Literacy,* 1–42. http://projectinfolit.org/pdfs/PIL_Handout_Study_finalvJuly_2010.pdf.

Howard, Rebecca Moore, Tricia Serviss, and Tanya Rodrigue. 2010. "Writing from Sources, Writing from Sentences." *Writing & Pedagogy* 2 (1): 177–92.

Jamieson, Sandra, and Rebecca Moore Howard. 2011. "Report of Citation Project Findings: Binghamton University in a National Context." Report.

The Citation Project. 2012. http://site.citationproject.net/.

Larson, Richard L. 1982. "The 'Research Paper' in the Writing Course: A Non-Form of Writing." *College English* 44 (8): 811–16. http://dx.doi.org/10.2307/377337.

Leckie, Gloria J. 1996. "Desperately Seeking Citations: Uncovering Faculty Assumptions about the Undergraduate Research Process." *Journal of Academic Librarianship* 22 (3): 201–8. http://dx.doi.org/10.1016/S0099-1333(96)90059-2.

Nelson, Jennie. 2011. "The Scandalous Research Paper and Exorcising Ghosts." In *The Subject Is Research: Processes and Practices,* edited by Wendy Bishop and Pavel Zemliansky, 3–11. Portsmouth, NH: Boynton/Cook.

Schwegler, Robert A., and Linda K. Shamoon. 1982. "The Aims and Process of the Research Paper." *College English* 44 (8): 817–24. http://dx.doi.org/10.2307/377338.

Strickland, James. 2004. "Just the FAQs: An Alternative to Teaching the Research Paper." *English Journal* 94 (1): 23–28. http://dx.doi.org/10.2307/4128843.

Valentine, Barbara. 1993. "Undergraduate Research Behavior: Using Focus Groups to Generate Theory." *Journal of Academic Librarianship* 19 (5): 300–4. http://dx.doi.org/10.1016/0099-1333(93)90026-2.

Points of Departure 2
DEVELOPING DESIGN-BASED LOCAL AND TRANSLOCAL STUDIES

One of the main assertions embodied in this collection is that we can make real progress toward establishing ethical, productive RAD writing studies research by orienting ourselves in two explicit directions: (1) making renewed commitments to the idea that research projects are *processes* as well as *products* that convey findings and theories and (2) pursuing the idea that research ought to be designed and presented in anticipation of eventual transcontextual—as well as local—utility. Such possibilities for departure are illuminated by Tricia Serviss, Kristi Murry Costello, and Crystal Benedicks in chapters 3, 4, and 5 in part 2. These chapters reveal some of the possibilities of design-based research methods in their design and deployment of pilot studies, focusing on the reiterative and collaborative nature of research processes within a community of stakeholders. All three researchers collaborated with others—with administrators and instructors in writing programs, with students in first-year writing (FYW) courses, with other researchers and coders along the way—to generate varied kinds of texts and tools (using surveys, conversation, focus groups, written reflections, and student citation context analysis coding) to understand source use dynamically in a local context. All three of these researchers incorporated students into the research processes, establishing their research as not only investigations of student learning but also as *interventions* into the learning of students, faculty, and campus writing cultures as well. What does such an approach expose or advance? Where might we go from here?

One useful direction seems to be the use of action research; chapters 3, 4, and 5 use action-research approaches to inquire about how

DOI: 10.7330/9781607326250.c005a

communities understand and engage with sources in academic-writing contexts. This action-research orientation involves members of communities of practice to better understand and resolve problems of practice they struggle to overcome, like source misuse in academic writing, and allows the part 2 contributors to also begin to articulate meaningful pedagogical interventions. Although the Citation Project citation context coding described in chapter 1 propelled the studies Serviss, Costello, and Benedicks undertook, the research is very different. The action-research orientation that shapes their method focuses primarily on participants and actors (students, faculty, administrators) rather than on learning artifacts (such as student texts) at the heart of the Citation Project. The different iterations of action research presented in part 2 diverge in the particular inquiry questions posed and methods used to investigate them but converge in their identification of fruitful pedagogical interventions we might design—and study—as we continue the study of source use in writing studies.

DBR RESEARCH AS INTERVENTION

Low-Stakes Inquiry into Student Source Use:
Research as Pedagogical Intervention

Each contributor was able to access student understandings and experiences of source use because they created low-stakes learning experiences that positioned faculty as researchers working in direct collaboration with students. The research projects were inquiries about how learning was happening—or failing to happen—in communities of practice in ways contributors found to be low stakes and naturalistic. Such was also the case with the LILAC Project described in chapter 2; however, that study, like the Citation Project, was motivated by a desire to understand what writers *do*, not to imagining different outcomes based upon pedagogical interventions. These three chapters all in some way embed pedagogy within the research process, focusing on the research as engagement with students as well as inquiry about their processes.

Serviss asked participating graduate students to use Citation Project citation context analysis coding to describe their own academic writing. Participants used coding methods to determine how they were using sources rather than to evaluate how successfully they use sources. In orienting participants toward *description* rather than assessment of source use, the research prompted participants to generate their own questions about how and why they used sources across different contexts. Participant coding of their own writing while in conversation with

Serviss transformed coding from description of source use to proactive engagement with participants. The purpose of the interviews that followed the coding sessions was not for elaboration on or clarification of practices that had been observed but to provide interaction with the participants and function as an intervention. Dialog with participants evolved from verifying participant coding decisions to drawing out participant beliefs and prompting self-reflection. The interviews put critical reflection practices into play as Serviss and the participants collaboratively used specific questions to tease out the most useful questions emerging from author coding. This kind of elicitation of input from participants in collaboration with Serviss as the researcher suggests additional inquiries to consider: How might *collaborative critical reflection* help a community of practice—like graduate-student writers—to identify the most pressing problems of practice they must confront? How might FYW curricula incorporate *collaborative critical reflection* into those communities of practice? How might faculty development initiatives incorporate such *collaborative critical reflection* practices and strategies into WAC and WID programming?

In chapter 5, Costello describes a study that has important overlaps and similarities with that conducted by Serviss. Costello generated student surveys that weren't tied directly to the assessment of student learning but instead were a kind of additional curriculum, making the endeavor low stakes for participating students, participating faculty of those students, and the writing program housing them all. This design of the survey tool evolved while in use. Costello eventually used the survey as a kind of interview opportunity with her own FYW students, providing a low-risk opportunity for that learning community to talk about perceptions and practices related to source use together *separately* from assessment. In this way, students and faculty collaborated to determine *the needs* of the learning community, allowing students to participate quite actively in any intervention Costello—and the wider writing program—might create in response. The explicitly inquiry-driven nature of the research initiated by these local pilot studies emphasized *discovery* over *evaluation*, turning what we might typically understand as merely data collection into strategic pedagogical interventions. Her chapter presents us with some potentially valuable ways forward as we ask, how else might we revise our summative assessment methods into more formative learning tools within writing programs?

In a similar low-stakes fashion, Benedicks used the affordances of focus groups to not only capture student understandings (and misunderstandings) of one campus's expectations and policies about source use but also to create opportunities for different constituencies of the community to inquire together across their usual contexts. Faculty found themselves inquiring with students rather than *instructing* them. Students found themselves influencing policies at their own institution rather than *following* them. The research method of the focus group allowed for interventions in the learning and understanding of all the constituencies involved. In this way, Benedicks's main research method was an intervention into learning by design. By participating in the focus groups, the participants and their understandings were altered. This pilot study prompts us to ask even more questions about this kind of learning intervention on multiple levels simultaneously: How is participants' learning about source use transformed when they become investigators of the phenomenon themselves? How might participants understand research differently as a result of their participation in focus groups—or other learning interventions—that require them to engage in research in ways that challenge what research actually *is*?

Metacognitive Interventions

Serviss, Costello, and Benedicks generated data and initial findings that imply that metacognitive awareness is crucially important for writers who want to use sources in increasingly sophisticated and productive ways in their academic writing. For Serviss, the metacognitive self-awareness and self-regulation of graduate students as teachers and scholars in training emerged as a key tool for graduate-student education. For Benedicks, metacognitive self-awareness of faculty and students as related, interdependent groups emerged as a key outcome from her use of surveys and focus groups. For Costello, the use of surveys across several terms—and in dialog with students who provided immediate feedback about the survey design—illuminated the potential for widespread metacognitive self-regulation within first-year-student communities via survey and FYW community dialog.

The contributors to part 2 converge in their calls for developing pedagogical interventions into the metacognitive lives of students and teachers alike, asking us to continue considering

1. how different research methods can help us access the metacognitive life of student writers as they interact with sources;
2. how collaborative inquiry with entire communities of practice can help us identify ways to model metacognitive self-awareness and self-regulation about source use;

3. how different conceptual frameworks—distributed cognition and embodied cognition, for example—can help us present metacognition about source use to writers more dynamically.

DEPARTURE POINTS: SOME PARTICULAR WAYS FORWARD

These chapters raise additional questions others are invited to explore, not by replicating the research as we traditionally think of that term (and as RAD researchers sometimes employ it) but by developing research projects that reproduce the central goals of design-based research and work toward involving and changing participants rather than just collecting information from them. Such projects might explore such questions as:

1. How can we best teach metacognitive awareness in writing classrooms surrounding source use and integration? Design-based research developed to address this question might not only present models and heuristics for pedagogical use in teaching metacognition but also involve action research that investigates the affordances and limitations of such models. Researchers might draw on the methods described by Serviss while also being conscious of the local context of their research.

2. How can we design research projects so they also help faculty become more metacognitively aware of disciplinary and individual source-use beliefs and practices and utilize professional-development programming as possible pedagogical interventions into faculty learning about source use? Costello's method might inform a project like this, and the materials she provides in her appendix could be adapted for local use.

3. How might we design writing program administration research, particularly research geared toward assessing programmatic outcomes and student learning, to both gather information and become a strategic intervention into source-use epistemologies and practices of students and faculty alike. For this kind of research, the multiphased process described by Benedicks could be adapted or adopted, or only part of that process might be employed. As with the other possibilities identified here, it is essential for local context to shape the design of the research and for the needs of local participants to help it evolve. Such research will generate data that can be compared transcontextually, but in most cases that data will take second place to the interventions involved in gathering it.

These three chapters help us imagine the many avenues of research—and interventions—still to be pursued. Yet the opportunity for replication and data generation should not be forgotten, as these three chapters highlight; these contributors all expanded ongoing research in new localities, working to replicate some methods (Serviss) while also looking to expand our understanding of existing research data (Costello and Benedicks). They reimagined what it means to conduct RAD research most notably by working in collaboration with stakeholders in particular communities. As research continues to be designed in collaboration with writing teachers in different contexts—teachers in secondary education, in FYW education, in graduate education—more data will be produced that helps us better understand how academic writers develop across time and contexts, allowing our research to both investigate and intervene sooner and more effectively in both student and faculty learning about source use.

PART 3

Exploring Information Contexts

Interchapter 3
WHAT DOES THRESHOLD-CONCEPT RESEARCH OFFER WRITING STUDIES RAD RESEARCH?

> *A threshold concept can be considered as akin to a portal, opening up a new and previously inaccessible way of thinking about something. It represents a transformed way of understanding, or interpreting, or viewing something without which the learner cannot progress. As a consequence of comprehending a threshold concept, there may thus be a transformed internal view of subject matter, subject landscape, or even worldview.*
>
> (Meyer and Land 2003, 412)

Seeking to understand why some students succeed in specific disciplines while others do not, Erik Meyer and Ray Land posited that there are key—or threshold—concepts in every field that must be understood and incorporated into one's thinking before one can move forward in that field (Meyer and Land 2003). Once these conceptual "thresholds" have been crossed, learners can build on the knowledge made accessible by them and progress to the next threshold, gaining ever-deeper understanding and mastery as they go. Every teacher has experienced the frustration of explaining information or instructions to students who seem to understand in the moment but are unable to internalize the lesson, repeat the action a second time, or apply information in a different context. Teachers and researchers have also experienced for ourselves and in our pedagogy that moment when suddenly a concept not only makes sense but also helps explain a host of other concepts. That moment is what Meyer and Land (2003) describe in terms of threshold-concept theory. When a learner struggles, it may be because a threshold concept remains unrealized or external to the learner, yet in many cases, the theory suggests, these threshold concepts are so obvious to those of us who passed through them long ago that we don't think of them as things we need to teach explicitly (Atherton 2013). When we do focus on key concepts, they often become a form of "troublesome knowledge" for students (Perkins 1999), requiring rethinking and sometimes challenging their entire worldview. For this reason, some students (and faculty) do not actually embrace these new ideas but rather mimic the behavior and discourse attached to those concepts without being transformed by them.

The challenge presented by threshold-concept theory, Land, Meyer, and Smith (2008) suggest, is to identify the threshold concepts in any field, identify the areas of resistance, and design a curriculum that helps students both to gain the necessary new knowledge and to allow themselves to be changed by it (x). Much writing studies research does exactly this, but as recent scholars have noted (Adler-Kassner and Wardle 2015; Yancey 2015), the field has not *named* this knowledge or practice or theorized it in the systematic way threshold-concept theorists propose. Seeing our research as frequently focused on identifying writing thresholds allows us to connect studies and develop larger theories about student writing. It also allows us to think of pedagogical interventions in a more focused way and explore the concepts necessary for learning. Land, Meyer, and Smith (2008) note the value of developing a transactional curriculum based on "co-inquiry . . . between subject experts, students, and educational researchers" (xx) to help us understand the ways threshold concepts work in each discipline and genre. Such co-inquiry will develop research strategies to help us uncover the threshold concepts we take for granted, identifying challenging areas for student writers and for faculty across genres and disciplines.

As suggested above, threshold-concept theory also itself functions as a conceptual threshold through which we can rethink existing writing studies research. While researchers did not set out to apply threshold-concept theory or to explore threshold concepts per se, a great deal of the research in our field actually uncovers them and helps us realize what students need to understand before they can do anything else. David Bartholomae's (1985) articulation of the ways students need to "invent the university" before they can write for it is an example of a threshold concept in writing studies, expanding our understanding of audience and purpose and helping us realize the complexity of seemingly simple assignments. Mina Shaughnessy's (1977) understanding of error worked the same way, moving us away from superficial correction and transforming the teaching of writing and basic writing theory, as did Mike Rose's (1985) work on writer's block. Such studies impact the field because of what they reveal about student learning, their self-reported resistance to new ways of thinking, the strategies they employ as they confront and navigate new ideas, and the ways researchers themselves can reconceive these things. By looking through and beyond local context, research that uncovers threshold concepts important to student learning provides deeper understanding of the learning process, better preparing faculty for troublesome and challenging moments at its core.

When articulated this starkly, the idea sounds commonplace to most of us in the fields of writing studies and information literacy, but that is because, as Noel Enthwistle (2008) observes, this belief in the importance of understanding how students approach learning has "become a threshold concept for university teachers in opening up their thinking about how their own teaching can best support students' understanding" (21). At some point, we did not believe it. Then we did. Now we can't really remember what it was like not to believe it. However, while few would argue against the idea, not all teachers adapt their pedagogy based on what they know—and believe—about learning. Like students in a similar situation, these resistant faculty occupy what threshold-concept theorists call a *liminal space* between knowing and acting: the space just before they step across the threshold into a new concept. Glynis Cousin (2006) describes this space as a moment of oscillation between old understandings and new ones, which often begins with mimicry—"ritualized performance" (Meyer and Land, 2005)—of what will eventually become ways of being and knowing, a holding back from the transformative moment for as long as possible in what we might describe as a last effort to remain in a familiar comfort zone.

Useful research in writing studies invites those on the threshold to join researchers who already occupy that new conceptual space from which such research can occur. Once we teachers and researchers cross that threshold, we step into a space from which we can transform our own pedagogy and research questions, along with the institutional policies, practices, and contexts in which we coexist. But that act of *stepping over* is part of an individual transformation; it cannot be imposed from above or demanded as an employment condition. In such cases, faculty may appear to have made the necessary transformation—teaching writing as a process for example, or not circling every error—but researchers such as David Perkins (1999) show these faculty are really just poised at the threshold in that liminal space, likely to step back into old ways once the attention shifts away from them. To help prevent this stepping back, we need more research that moves from questions about discourses that impede movement across specific thresholds to information about those impediments, providing us with the information we need to understand and change our own practices and develop policies and pedagogies to help our students and colleagues.

For academics, such transformation is frequently powered by data and research that compel us to make that step, but at first the theories and concepts it reveals often appear "*troublesome*" (Perkins 1999) "'alien' or [even] counter-intuitive" (Land, Meyer, and Smith 2008, x), exposing connections between things we previously thought of as separate (reading and writing, researching and reasoning). Land, Meyer, and Smith (2008) explain that because threshold concepts are generally in this way "*integrative* (exposing . . . previously hidden interrelatedness)" (x), once we allow ourselves to be transformed by them, that change is "*irreversible*"—we cannot unknow what we have learned. For this reason, they remind us, this stepping over a threshold and allowing new knowledge to be internalized is an act of courage. Such a process is experienced similarly by students, teachers, and researchers, and it is only once this transformation has occurred within parts of an institution that real and lasting institutional change can occur.

The six features of threshold concepts identified by Land, Meyer, and Smith (2008) and used to explain threshold-concept theory here and by most people who talk about them are listed below. If teachers understand these six features, they will be better able to work with those students suspended in the liminal space (Land, Meyer, and Smith 2008, x), who experience new knowledge about writing and research as "troublesome" (Perkins 1999) and who understand but have not yet internalized the concepts at the heart of college-level writing and information literacy. They—we—are also more likely to understand the importance of discovering and articulating necessary thresholds and guiding students across them. Threshold concepts are, they tell us:

- transformative—changing our perception of things
- integrative—revealing connections and shedding light on existing knowledge
- irreversible—remaining with us and unlikely to be forgotten or unlearned
- troublesome—challenging accepted ideas and seeming counterintuitive
- bounded—serving as "boundary-markers for the conceptual spaces" (x)

- discursive—causing a shift in the language we use to articulate the new knowledge and our relation to it

APPLICATIONS OF THRESHOLD CONCEPTS

The first large-scale application of threshold-concept theory in a writing studies-related context was by the Association of College and Research Libraries (ACRL) in its "Framework for Information Literacy for Higher Education," filed by the ACRL Board in February 2015 "as one of the constellation of information-literacy documents from the association" (ACRL 2015). The document lists six threshold concepts necessary for successful information literacy, along with discussion and guidelines for implementing the framework in higher education. Some have begun to map the old information-literacy standards onto the new framework (see for example Jamieson 2016; Maid and D'Angelo 2016), but much research is needed both applying the new framework to existing research findings and conducting new research in relation to it. The frameworks identified by the ACRL are:

- Authority is constructed and contextual
- Information creation as a process
- Information has value
- Research as inquiry
- Scholarship as conversation
- Searching as strategic exploration

While these are listed separately and can be addressed in any order, the document stresses that they are "a cluster of interconnected core concepts . . . conceptual understandings that organize many other concepts and ideas about information, research, and scholarship into a coherent whole" (Association of College and Research Libraries 2016, 2). They are, in the words of Land, Meyer, and Smith (2008) "*integrative* (exposing . . . previously hidden interrelatedness)" (x). The document presents them as concepts for those teaching information-literacy skills to recognize and teach and as explicit ways of thinking for students to learn. Researchers can also use them to test attitudes and practices and to structure and organize or reorganize research findings.

This multiple use of threshold-concept theory provides rich opportunities for research and possibilities for strengthening pedagogy and practice. Research on the ways threshold concepts motivate and limit teacher behavior is essential as we move forward in this field. But the findings of existing studies like those by Shaughnessy, Bartholomae, and Rose can be understood as moments when threshold concepts were identified and presented as a way to challenge teachers to think differently and move beyond liminal spaces or comfort zones in our teaching so we could help students move forward. As with the ACRL, the first step is to identify threshold concepts for a field. Linda Adler-Kassner and Elizabeth Wardle have begun that process for writing studies, using a "refined crowd-sourcing" method (Adler-Kassner and Wardle 2015, xiv), listing multiple threshold concepts and including chapters that discuss how each concept can facilitate or impede progress. For example, Doug Downs and Liane Robertson argue that writing courses should be explicitly designed to teach threshold concepts as a way of teaching for transfer by helping students "reconsider prior knowledge about writing in light of new experiences and knowledge" (Downs and Robertson 2015, 105). Rebecca Nowacek and Bradley Hughes argue the same for courses designed to train writing tutors (Nowacek and Hughes 2015). Such essays do double duty, helping faculty recognize the role of threshold concepts in learning so they can cross a threshold themselves and then prompting them to revise standard pedagogy to accommodate the new awareness. Adler-Kassner and Wardle's collection, as its title indicates, is focused on "naming what we [already] know." There is still much need for consciously designed and replicable data-driven research about the threshold concepts that facilitate and block the development of writers, researchers, and teachers.

PLANNING RESEARCH FROM THRESHOLD CONCEPTS

Research planned to not just understand what students do but also get at the threshold concepts that may be preventing them from succeeding has been a hallmark of our field since long before we had a name for that block, as previously noted. Consciously focused research into threshold concepts must similarly begin with where students are rather than where we think they are or should be. The research can then focus on why some students appear unable to move beyond forms of writing, researching, or integrating sources that depend on methods they learned in high school in spite of additional instruction in college. It can also focus on what facilitates movement beyond these various liminal spaces. Other research can study faculty concepts of writing and research and the ways they talk about these processes and guide students across the relevant thresholds.

One might argue that all the chapters in this collection seek in some way to uncover threshold concepts. Indeed, the Citation Project research that inspired much of the other research here is centered on an understanding of what happens when students have not yet internalized the concept of scholarship as a conversation between sources—a concept now included on the ACRL list as well. Citation Project research also uncovers the impact of faculty and librarians *not* explicitly teaching the concepts of scholarship as conversation and research as inquiry as a way to help students reconsider and move beyond prior knowledge of what a research paper should be. Glynis Cousin (2008) describes threshold-concept theory as focused on "the kind of complicated learner transitions learners undergo" (264), and the chapters in this collection in some way all focus on what is necessary for those transitions to occur.

The three chapters in this section invite readers to think more explicitly about threshold concepts in action and to identify and name research findings as such. The section begins with a study of what students do (Breuch and Larson), followed by a study of what students say about what they do (Olsen and Diekema), and then a study of what faculty tell students about what they want them to do (Kleinfeld). While none of these chapters names the object of study as threshold concepts or arranges findings according to them, the findings map easily onto threshold-concept theory. They provide examples of the ways new knowledge can be *troublesome*, leaving students stuck in liminal spaces unable to make conceptual moves or perceive key information-literacy concepts as *integrative*. The research in these chapters also reveals the need for faculty to more explicitly identify concepts students must internalize before they can succeed and to introduce students to the discourse that frames those concepts. By highlighting the impact of students' inability to recognize concepts so essential to writing and to information literacy—let alone transform their practices accordingly—this research helps us understand threshold theory itself and invites researchers to explore other concepts necessary for success. Each chapter also demonstrates the ways new research can build on previous studies by replicating key aspects of them and modifying others—the model of replicable research presented in this collection and described as "approximate replication" by researchers interviewed by Congjun Mu and Paul Kei Matsuda (Mu and Matsuda 2016).

In "Research and Rhetorical Purpose: Using Genre Analysis to Understand Source Use in Technical and Professional Writing," Lee-Ann Kastman Breuch and Brian N. Larson explore the rhetorical purposes for which sources are used in research reports within a specific genre and in so doing build on research by the Citation Project described in Chapter 1 of this volume that explored the manner in which students incorporate source material. They base their research on John Swales's IMRAD superstructure (introduction, method, results, and discussion), which they point out has a long history in the textbooks and curricula of technical communications (183), focusing on source use in the results and discussion sections of the papers studied. Each of the eight "moves" identified by Swales (see their Appendix C) functions as a threshold concept students must understand in order to write successful research reports, and their findings indicate a need for more attention to these concepts in professional and technical communications courses. Their finding, that students may have had difficulty comparing sources and using them to position their research, suggests a need to focus more attention on the ACRL information-literacy frameworks and on *why* writers use sources, not just *how* they use them.

Breuch and Larson discuss their method and (in their appendices) provide the writing prompt and guidelines for coding the resulting reports, along with definitions and examples to guide coders. As we more fully discuss in "Points of departure: Using Existing Research to Think Beyond the Local," follow-up research might apply a version of this method to other contexts, expand the sample size, focus on other moves, or adapt the method to other aspects of research reports or other genres.

Like Breuch and Larson, M. Whitney Olsen and Anne Diekema also developed their research in response to previous research, in this case research into the sources students select as they develop researched papers. In "Asking the Right Questions: Using Interviews to Explore Information-Seeking Behavior," they observe that there is more research into the use of traditional sources than into the use of electronic sources, prompting their research into the latter. They focus on understanding why students make the information-seeking choices they do, and their findings map clearly onto the ACRL "Framework for Information Literacy for Higher Education" (Association of College and Research Libraries 2015). The research reveals that the students in these two institutions have not *integrated* any of the IL concepts into their way of thinking and talking about research. It thereby demonstrates the need for instruction in all six frameworks in order to *transform* the students' understanding of information-seeking beyond the high-school strategies they describe, which leave them unable to conduct or write about research as expected at the college level.

As they note in their conclusion, Olsen and Diekema present their research and findings as a prompt for further research. They place their findings in the context of previous studies (such as those by Head

2013), noting where they reproduce results and where further research is needed. To facilitate that further research, they provide a thorough discussion of their method and their interview questions (Appendix 3.A) to help other researchers broaden and expand their work to other contexts and students—as we discuss more fully in "Points of departure: Using Existing Research to Think Beyond the Local."

The same strategy of building on previous research and also calling for additional research frames the final chapter in this section, Elizabeth Kleinfeld's "Just Read the Assignment: Using Course Documents to Analyze Research Pedagogy." Kleinfeld began with the findings of the Citation Project and asked why students did not appear to understand the basic concepts necessary for successful research. While Breuch and Larson explored student writing to trace what students do with sources, and Olsen and Diekema interviewed students to understand how they talk about their research methods, Kleinfeld explores what faculty tell students about research. She notes that using various research methods, other researchers (Leckie 1996; Schwegler and Shamoon 1982; Valentine 2001) have found a disconnect between the ways faculty and students think and talk about researched writing, and sets out to explore whether such disconnect can still be observed in more recent course documents. In other words, she traces the missing threshold concepts back to the course artifacts we might expect to introduce students to concepts that are to be enacted in their papers.

Building on studies of syllabi by Dan Melzer (2003) and research assignments by Head and Eisenberg (2010), Kleinfeld collected and analyzed a range of course documents from twenty-four institutions, looking for intersections and omissions in the way the research process was framed and described. Her findings suggest faculty may not understand the importance of introducing concepts they expect to drive student writing, indicating a need for threshold-concept theory to shape faculty development and curricular design. The coding sheet and definitions she provides (Appendix 3.A and Appendix 3.B) could be used in such faculty development to invite instructors to explore their own course documents, or as Kleinfeld suggests, they could be applied or expanded as part of a larger study of how and where threshold concepts central to information literacy and student researched writing are discussed and encouraged.

Threshold-concept theory provides both an explanation of the struggles student writers experience as they engage with sources and a broader understanding of the pedagogies that must be developed to help them cross the knowledge thresholds necessary for their success. While writing studies and library faculty may be able to "name what we know," as Adler-Kassner and Wardle (2015) put it, we also need to name what students do not know and what we need to help them know. Like our students, though, many teachers *know* and can name the concepts at the heart of information-literacy and writing studies pedagogy but may still be stuck in that liminal space before the threshold; until they have crossed that threshold and internalized the concept, they will not enact it in their teaching practices. For this reason, it is not enough to simply study what students do. We must also study the ways faculty and pedagogy shape what students do—and what they are not yet able to do. And this also requires more of the kind of research discussed in this collection. Section 3 ends with "Points of Departure: Using Existing Research to Think Beyond the Local," which discusses ways the research methods employed in these chapters may be applied to other research questions and contexts and suggests ways to use them to replicate or generate additional research.

References

Adler-Kassner, Linda, and Elizabeth Wardle, eds. 2015. *Naming What We Know: Threshold Concepts of Writing Studies.* Logan: Utah State University Press.

Association of College and Research Libraries. 2015. "Framework for Information Literacy for Higher Education." http://www.ala.org/acrl/standards/ilframework.

Association of College and Research Libraries. 2016. "Framework for Information Literacy for Higher Education." http://www.ala.org/acrl/sites/ala.org.acrl/files/content/issues/infolit/Framework_ILHE.pdf.

Atherton, James, S. 2013. How Do People Get It? Doceo. http://www.doceo.co.uk/tools/threshold_3.htm.

Bartholomae, David. 1985. "Inventing the University." In *When a Writer Can't Write: Studies in Writer's Block and Other Composing-Process Problems,* edited by Mike Rose, 134–65. New York: Guilford.

Cousin, Glynis. 2006. "An Introduction to Threshold Concepts." *Planet* 17 (December): 4–5. http://dx.doi.org/10.11120/plan.2006.00170004.

Cousin, Glynis. 2008. "Threshold Concepts: Old Wine in New Bottles or a New Form of Transactional Curriculum Inquiry?" In *Threshold Concepts Within the Disciplines,* edited by Ray Land, Jan Meyer and Jan Smith, 264. Educational Futures: Rethinking Theory and Practice Series 16. Rotterdam: Sense.

Downs, Doug, and Liane Robertson. 2015. "Threshold Concepts in First-Year Composition." In *Naming What We Know: Threshold Concepts of Writing Studies,* edited by Linda Adler-Kassner and Elizabeth Wardle, 105–21. Logan: Utah State University Press.

Enthwistle, Noel. 2008. "Threshold Concepts and Transformative Ways of Thinking within Research into Higher Education." In *Threshold Concepts within the Disciplines,* edited by Ray Land, Jan Meyer, and Jan Smith, 21–36. Rotterdam: Sense.

Head, Alison, J. 2013. "Learning the Ropes: How Freshmen Conduct Course Research Once They Enter College." Project Information Literacy Research Report. http://dx.doi.org/10.2139/ssrn.2364080.

Head, Alison J., and Michael B. Eisenberg. 2010. "Assigning Inquiry: How Handouts for Research Assignments Guide Today's College Students." Project Information Literacy

Report. http://www.projectinfolit.org/uploads/2/7/5/4/27541717/pil_handout_study_finaljuly_2010.pdf.

Jamieson, Sandra. 2016. "What the Citation Project Tells Us about Information Literacy in College Composition." In *Information Literacy: Research and Collaboration across Disciplines*, edited by Barbara D'Angelo, Sandra Jamieson, Barry Maid, and Janice R. Walker, 117–41. Perspectives in Writing Series. Fort Collins, CO: WAC Clearing House and University Press of Colorado.

Land, Ray, Jan H. F. Meyer, and Jan Smith. 2008. Editor's Preface in *Threshold Concepts Within the Disciplines*, edited by Ray Land, Jan Meyer and Jan Smith, ix–xxi. Educational Futures: Rethinking Theory and Practice Series 16. Rotterdam: Sense.

Leckie, Gloria J. 1996. "Desperately Seeking Citations: Uncovering Faculty Assumptions about the Undergraduate Research Process." *Journal of Academic Librarianship* 22 (3): 201–8. http://dx.doi.org/10.1016/S0099-1333(96)90059-2.

Maid, Barry, and Barbara D'Angelo. 2016. "Threshold Concepts: Integrating and Applying Information Literacy and Writing Instruction." In *Information literacy: Research and Collaboration Across Disciplines*, edited by Barbara J. D'Angelo, Sandra Jamieson, Barry Maid, and Janice R. Walker, 39–52. Perspectives on Writing. Fort Collins, CO: WAC Clearing House and University Press of Colorado.

Melzer, Dan. 2003. "Assignments Across the Curriculum: A Survey of College Writing." *Language and Learning Across the Disciplines* 6 (1): 86–110.

Meyer, Jan H. F., and Ray Land. 2003. "Threshold Concepts and Troublesome Knowledge: Linkages to Ways of Thinking and Practising within the Disciplines." In *Improving Student Learning—Ten Years On*, edited by Chris Rust, 412–24. Oxford: Oxford Centre for Staff and Learning Development (OCSLD).

Meyer, Jan H. F., and Ray Land. 2005. "Threshold Concepts and Troublesome Knowledge (2): Epistemological Considerations and a Conceptual Framework for Teaching and Learning." *Higher Education* 49 (3): 373–88. http://dx.doi.org/10.1007/s10734-004-6779-5.

Mu, Congjun, and Paul Kei Matsuda. 2016. "Replication in L2 Writing Research: *Journal of Second Language Writing* Authors' Perceptions." *TESOL Quarterly* 50 (1): 201–19. http://dx.doi.org/10.1002/tesq.284.

Nowacek, Rebecca, and Bradley Hughes. 2015. "Threshold Concepts in the Writing Center: Scaffolding the Development of Tutor Expertise." In *Naming What We Know: Threshold Concepts of Writing Studies*, edited by Linda Adler-Kassner and Elizabeth Wardle, 171–85. Logan: Utah State University Press. http://dx.doi.org/10.7330/9780874219906.c011.

Perkins, David. 1999. "The Many Faces of Constructivism." *Educational Leadership* 57 (3): 6–11.

Rose, Mike. 1985. *When a Writer Can't Write: Studies in Writer's Block and Other Composing-Process Problems*. New York: Guilford.

Schwegler, Robert A., and Linda K. Shamoon. 1982. "The Aims and Process of the Research Paper." *College English* 44 (8): 817–24. http://dx.doi.org/10.2307/377338.

Shaughnessy, Mina. 1977. *Errors and Expectations: A Guide for the Teacher of Basic Writing*. New York: Oxford University Press.

Valentine, Barbara. 2001. "The Legitimate Effort in Research Papers: Student Commitment versus Faculty Expectations." *Journal of Academic Librarianship* 27 (2): 107–15. http://dx.doi.org/10.1016/S0099-1333(00)00182-8.

Yancey, Kathleen Blake. 2015. "Introduction: Coming to Terms Composition/Rhetoric, Threshold Concepts, and a Disciplinary Core." In *Naming What We Know: Threshold Concepts of Writing Studies*, edited by Linda Adler-Kassner and Elizabeth Wardle, xvii–xxxi. Logan: Utah State University Press. http://dx.doi.org/10.7330/9780874219906.c000a.

Chapter 6
RESEARCH AND RHETORICAL PURPOSE
Using Genre Analysis to Understand Source Use in Technical and Professional Writing

Lee-Ann Kastman Breuch and Brian N. Larson

ABSTRACT

This chapter describes a pilot study of student research-based writing in a technical and professional writing course designed for college-level juniors and seniors across the curriculum; fifteen analytical research papers are coded based on the rhetorical move John Swales (1990) calls "reference to previous research" to increase our understanding of how students use sources to introduce, support, or compare/contrast ideas and previous research. Student papers in this study overwhelmingly used sources to support main ideas, occasionally used sources to introduce ideas, often in the form of topic sentences, but rarely used sources to compare/contrast ideas. The frequency of support instances and the infrequency of compare/contrast instances may suggest students had difficulty using sources to position their research, whereas they had no trouble using source excerpts to support main ideas in their writing. Local impacts of this study included several discussions among instructors about the purpose of the analytical-report assignment in our technical and professional writing course as well as suggestions for pedagogical intervention and ongoing programmatic assessment as a result of the pilot study.

INTRODUCTION AND FRAMEWORK

In this chapter, we address student research writing in the context of a technical and professional writing course at a large public university.

DOI: 10.7330/9781607326250.c006

Specifically, we examine how students situate references to previous research in analytical reports. Our study addresses the question, *for what rhetorical purposes do students integrate sources into research reports?* This inquiry was inspired in part by recent work in the Citation Project regarding the ways students integrate sources into research writing. When Howard, Serviss, and Rodrigue (2010) examined eighteen student texts for instances of paraphrases, patchwriting, summary, and direct quotes, their analysis supported the hypothesis that students frequently "patchwrite" and that student papers often fail to summarize research (182). They propose a further research agenda, one to explore use of research by students in advanced writing courses, writing within their majors, and writing in specific genres (189). Our study responds to this call by examining writing in an advanced technical and professional writing course that reaches students in several disciplines across our university.

Our inquiry also responds to a call for research in technical-communication pedagogy from some scholars who have criticized technical-communication textbooks and curricula for failing to adequately address research methods and writing. For example, Joanna Wolfe (2009) argues that instructional textbooks in technical communication include ample material on formats or genres but rarely address techniques and strategies to communicate research results. She suggests that instructors must do a better job preparing students to use the IMRAD (introduction, method, results, and discussion) superstructure, illustrate data more clearly, discuss surprising results, and acknowledge errors and limitations of their studies (368–69). In a similar vein, Rachel Spilka (2009) points out the lack of research activities in technical-communication curricula. In a nation-wide survey of 114 technical-communication programs, Spilka found that only 35 percent of the programs surveyed included courses or activities involving research (527). While the assertions made by Spilka and Wolfe about technical-communication textbooks and curricula are on point, we note that neither Wolfe nor Spilka examined student research writing. Our research, then, is designed to extend theirs and focus on the writing produced by students in technical and professional writing courses rather than the pedagogy that led to that writing.

While some scholars have questioned generic application of the IMRAD superstructure to decision-making reports (see Rude 1995), IMRAD has a long history in technical communication and is commonly advocated in textbooks and curricula. It is associated with science writing and the scientific research article (see Bazerman 1988; Berkenkotter and Huckin 1995; Swales 1990), and as John Swales (1990) argues, the IMRAD superstructure, or what he refers to as the "Research Article" (RA), reaches across disciplines and therefore plays a powerful role in published research writing. Swales devotes attention to how disciplinary differences emerge in published research and the *rhetorical moves* common in RAs. Such opportunity for genre analysis also inspired our study.

We were specifically interested in Swales's description of rhetorical moves in the results-and-discussion sections of research articles. Swales (1990, 172–73) identifies eight rhetorical moves within results sections: background information, statement of results, (un)expected outcome, reference to previous research, explanation, exemplification, deduction and hypothesis, and recommendation. Many scholars have used this framework to analyze rhetorical moves in the results sections of published articles or professional-writing samples (see Dudley-Evans 1993; Hafner 2010; Holmes 1997; Rude 1995; Swales 2004); however, few studies have analyzed student research writing for these moves. Vijay Bhatia (1993, 93) includes a helpful comparison of professionals' and students' writing of research articles (RA) and discusses the extent to which student writing (such as a lab report assignment) might represent a "sub-genre" of the professional RA. However, he focuses on the introduction sections and not results and discussion, where students often synthesize their findings.

While Swales examines rhetorical moves in results sections of published research, we wanted to apply the model to student research writing. By using genre analysis, we extend the findings of Howard, Serviss, and Rodrigue (2010) in several ways. First, where that study and the expanded study by Jamieson and Howard (2013) describe the *manner* in which students integrate research sources into their writing (through direct quotes, paraphrases, patchwriting, or summary), our project examines the *purpose* of source integration. Second, our study looks at an upper-level professional and technical writing course rather than first-year writing. This leads to a third extension: the connection with professional and technical communication pedagogy and student research writing.

In the balance of this chapter, we describe the technical-communication class where we collected our data and the methods of data collection and analysis we applied. We then review how students positioned the rhetorical move Swales calls "reference to previous research," which in this case involved three purposes: introducing new ideas or topics, supporting ideas or claims, and comparing/contrasting references. We review the results of our coding in these three subcategories, discuss our findings with reference to examples of student writing, and conclude with recommendations for further study.

METHODS

To investigate the use of reference-to-previous-research moves in student research papers, we collected a sample of student writing from the University of Minnesota's WRIT 3562W Technical and Professional Writing course in spring semester 2011. This course enrolls junior and senior undergraduate students and is required by several academic majors across the university. We typically offer between fifteen and twenty sections of the course each semester, each enrolling twenty-four students.

The analytical report generally accounts for 20 percent or more of the semester's grade. It can best be described as a problem-solving report in which students articulate a research question, gather primary (interview or survey) research and secondary (popular or scholarly) research, and articulate findings and recommendations using a variation of the standard IMRAD superstructure of a scientific report (introduction, methods, results, and discussion). The assignment is the culmination of several smaller assignments, including a formal progress report, and in preparation, students also read a chapter about analytical reports from the required textbook, *Technical Communication Today* by Richard Johnson-Sheehan (2010), in which Johnson-Sheehan notes that "the [IMRAD superstructure] is a common one, but the sections of analytical reports can be arranged and combined in a variety of ways" (271). (A typical version of the assignment description appears as Appendix 6.A.)

In the spring 2011 semester, we arranged with instructors of the course to obtain eighty randomly selected papers from sixteen sections, each of which had between twenty and twenty-four students, giving us five papers randomly selected from each section. We also collected from each instructor the assignment description for the analytical report or proposal assignment. The University of Minnesota IRB Human Subjects Committee determined that this study was exempt from review under federal guidelines (IRB Study 1009E90112).

In a larger analysis of these samples, we analyzed the results, discussion, and conclusion sections of thirty student papers for evidence of eight rhetorical moves based on Swales (1990) and Bhatia (1993). Of these thirty student papers, only fifteen papers employed the IMRAD superstructure. Thus, while this chapter describes the method used for the complete study (all thirty papers), we report only on one part of that analysis: the single rhetorical move reference to previous research as it occurred in the fifteen papers that employed the IMRAD superstructure. Coders analyzed the thirty student papers at three levels: (1) IMRAD superstructure, (2) rhetorical moves in results section, and (3) reference-to-previous-research moves. First, four coders holistically assessed each student paper's conformity to the IMRAD superstructure (*Y* for yes and *N* for no). Observed agreement was 0.83; coders initially disagreed on five of the thirty papers. Disagreements were resolved during conferences among the coders to establish consensus codes on all the papers. (The coding guide for this phase appears as Appendix 6.B.)

Second, the same four coders performed an atomistic assessment of 2,943 units/sentences in thirty student papers for membership in categories based on the rhetorical moves we adapted from Swales (1990) and Holmes (1997). Table 6.1 illustrates the final rhetorical-moves coding scheme. Coders had two training sessions to prepare for coding; however, agreement among coders was difficult to establish. The coding scheme was adjusted after training sessions and the resulting observed agreement was 0.57. Coders met to resolve any remaining disagreements and established consensus for all codes.

The third analysis involved a close examination of the reference-to-previous-research rhetorical move in the papers coders had identified as conforming to the IMRAD structural convention—fifteen papers total. We did this coding without the assistance of our graduate-student coders. See table 6.5 for an overview of these papers. Given these fifteen papers, we began an examination of the units previously coded as Move 4: reference to previous research. We first coded the placement of each Move 4 within its respective paragraph, noting whether it occurred in the beginning, middle, or end of the paragraph. Then we coded each Move 4 for purpose. Swales's description of the reference-to-previous-research move involves the subcategories comparison, or comparing previous research with the focus of the student's research project, and support, or using references to support the student's research project (Swales 1990, 173). To these, we added a third subcategory of introduce, or using a reference to previous research to introduce a new idea or topic. Through these subcategories we wanted to learn more about how students were positioning references to previous research. Table 6.2 shows the coding scheme for reference to previous research.

We made no effort to judge interrater reliability at this stage, partly because we allowed for multiple subcategory codes per unit and partly because we found during our discussions that we were regularly agreeing on the subcategories.

Table 6.1. Rhetorical move coding scheme

Move 1: Background Information

Information that strengthens the main discussion by articulating the purpose of the study, reiterating information from previous sections, highlighting theoretical information, asserting importance of the subject matter at hand, or reminding the reader of technical information.

Move 2: Statement of Results

A statement about the subject matter of the student's study that articulates the main idea(s) and contribution(s) of the student's analytical report, that presents a claim of the student, or that represents an interpretation by the student of such a claim or of a Move 3 or Move 4 unit. A statement in this category is not reporting findings of primary or secondary research completed by the student but rather is an assertion about the subject matter of the study.

Move 3: Statement of Findings from Primary Research

A statement that articulates a discovery or finding based on primary research completed by the student, such as surveys, polls, or interviews.

Move 4: Reference to Previous Research

A statement that refers to any secondary source, such as journal articles, books, or Internet sources. (See discussion of subcategories below.)

Move 5: Explanation and Examples

A statement that offers any reasons for results, including any surprising or unexpected results. Explanatory statements may also demonstrate analysis or argument that connects findings from primary or secondary research to statements of results. Examples reflect instances (rather than summaries) that support explanations, including anecdotal information, stories, or other illustrations that support explanations.

Move 6: Generalization and Limitation

A statement that addresses generalizability of results of the study the student is conducting or addresses limits on its validity or generalizability. Statements in this category can include references to limitations in the present study the author is conducting, or it can include references to limitations in a secondary study the author reviews.

Move 7: Recommendation

A statement that addresses the need and directions for future research, specifically future research studies on the same or similar topic. Statements in this category may also address future actions that can be taken as a result of findings, or calls to action.

Move 0: None of the Above

Statements that do not reflect any of the previous categories. This includes rhetorical signposts or metatext, transition sentences between paragraphs or sections, rhetorical questions, and headers (unless headers exhibit characteristics of a particular move). This category includes sentences that have characteristics of more than one Move.

DISCUSSION OF METHODS

Adaptations to the Coding Scheme

Close textual analysis yielded many insights about student writing; the process was tedious, however, and we experienced several challenges.

Table 6.2. Coding scheme for subcategories of Move 4, reference to previous research

Code	Description
Compare or Contrast	Comment on how source information is similar or different from other information
Support	Comment on how source strengthens, explains, develops, or illustrates idea at hand.
Introduce	Use of source to introduce a new topic or idea in the paper
Other	Anything other than the three previous categories

First, the rhetorical moves we adapted from Swales (1990) are closely associated with the IMRAD superstructure in ways that did not always map easily onto student writing. For example, half our initial thirty-paper sample did not use the IMRAD superstructure, presenting a conflict between the collective rhetorical moves Swales found in published research and what we found in student writing and necessitating adaptations of the coding scheme to better suit the purposes of student writing.

UNITS OF ANALYSIS

A second challenge of our textual analysis involved determining the unit of analysis for coding. Swales (1990) identifies a series of eight rhetorical moves in the results sections of research articles, but these moves could be multisentence spans of text (see for example, the "sample move-step analysis" from Swales 1990, 139). If a coder had to select a span of text as a rhetorical move and then code the span for the move, interrater reliability would require an assessment of whether two coders selected the same spans and then an assessment of whether the span was coded as the same move. There are techniques for assessing the former, and they can address questions about what to do with partial matches or overlapping selections. For example, the span selections could be compared using pairwise F-scores with either a strict or lenient assessment of partial overlaps (see Cunningham, Maynard, and Bontcheva 2011; Larson 2015, 248). We chose to avoid those difficulties by using the approach of Richard Holmes (1997), who used sentences as coding units and applied a modified version of Swales's list of moves.

Coder Training and Interrater Reliability

A third challenge was coder training and interrater reliability. After Lee-Ann collected a random sample of eighty final projects from the course in question in spring 2011, the second author joined the project as a research assistant. Thanks to grant funding, two other graduate students were available to assist with the coding, resulting in four coders. We assessed interrater (or intercoder) reliability with regard to the coding, as we considered that effort important in establishing transparency (Breuch, Olson, and Frantz 2002). We based the coding for the atomistic sentence/unit analysis closely on the moves described by Swales for results sections: background information, statement of results, (un)expected outcomes, reference to previous research, explanation, exemplification, deduction and hypothesis, recommendations. This list is complex, and we directed coders to assign one, and only one, code for a move to each sentence/unit. To prepare for the training, all four coders read excerpts of chapter 7 of Swales (1990), all of Holmes (1997) and Wolfe (2009), and the then-current version of the coding guide (Appendix 6.C). All four coders then completed a training session on ten sample papers using the draft coding guide.

The observed agreement between our two graduate-student coders on the training papers was 0.53. (Because we had already examined the training papers, agreement during training was calculated only for the two additional coders.) Because we were dissatisfied with that level of agreement, we wanted to examine where problems appeared, and an excellent tool for that is a "confusion matrix" or "contingency table" (Jurafsky and Martin 2009). Table 6.3 presents the confusion matrix displaying the graduate students' codes. A confusion matrix can be created automatically from data records using the pivot-table function of popular spreadsheet software. To interpret it, recognize that the first row represents those units coder 1 identified as Move 0, and each column represents the move categories to which coder 2 assigned the same units. The shaded cell represents those units on which the coders agreed, sixty-one times in the case of Move 0. The second cell indicates the number of cases in which coder 1 assigned the unit to Move 0 but coder 2 assigned it to Move 1, four times in this instance. Using the ratios of category agreement described in the confusion matrix, we calculated the Kappa statistic for our graduate-student training at 0.42, which means they obtained only 42 percent of the possible nonchance agreement (Carletta 1996).

The confusion matrix in table 6.3 provided insights into those categories that were proving most difficult for our coders. For example, of the 208 units coder 1 identified as Move 4, coder 3 put 33 in Move 2, suggesting that the coding guide was unclear on some point(s) that would aid in choosing between these two categories.

Table 6.3. Confusion matrix from coding training

	Coder 2 Codes										
Coder 1 Codes	0	1	2	3	4	5	6	7	8	9	Totals
0	61	4	43		5		15	3	1	13	145
1	12	12	5				6				35
2	12	8	103		8		39	5		9	184
3				12	1					1	14
4	6	8	33	1	147	2	8			3	208
5	6	1	11	2	7			1			28
6	1	1					1				3
7	4	1	31		13			4		6	59
8									10	1	11
9	1		8		1			1		37	48
Totals	103	35	234	15	182	2	69	14	11	70	735

Regarding Move 4: reference to previous research (the subject of this chapter's analysis), we found that there was sometimes disagreement between Move 4: reference to previous research and Move 2: statement of results. While these were the most frequently coded moves, we noticed that student writers used them in different ways, thus making the coding difficult. One of the complexities arose from what we meant by Move 2: statement of results. Was it about stating a claim or assertion or simply stating a finding from primary or secondary research? For example, when students summarized sources, were those summaries considered a result of their research or simply a citation? Our final interpretation of this category was to agree with Swales's description of statement of results as a claim or assertion of findings, and with Swales's description of references to previous research as ways to compare, contrast, or support a study (Move 4). However, students used sources in many cases as part of their findings—"so and so found this" and "this author suggested this." Students rarely used language to position the work of previous authors against or for their current study. They simply reported it, often summarizing the work. In addition to this complexity, we noticed the inadequacy of the student summaries of previous work. Sometimes students failed to include citations, leading us to suspect plagiarism. In some cases, students included long paraphrases of several sentences with a parenthetical citation only at the end of the paragraph, making our sentence-level coding difficult. In short, students demonstrated varying levels of sophistication regarding the ways they summarized or shared previous research in their reports. Each of these factors complicated our coding.

We revised the coding guide again, based on the discussions and complexities we experienced in coder training. The final coding guide reflects the categories as stated in table 6.1. We were dissatisfied with the level of agreement in our second round of coding; agreement had slightly but not significantly improved. We recognized several causes for the problem: first, we had a large number of categories, which makes agreement less probable as a statistical matter. Second, rhetorical function is a complex thing, and different readers see a given sentence as serving different functions. Third, we required that units be assigned to single categories, and it seems quite likely that units can serve more than one function on our list.

To overcome these difficulties, we held coder conferences. We scheduled meetings of each pair of coders and required them to reach consensus on a single move code for each unit. Each coder spent four to six hours in such meetings, but the result was the assignment of a single move for each unit in our data set. Despite the relatively low interrater reliability on the original coding, the coders reached consensus codes. Once we had established agreement on codes, we focused attention on Move 4: reference to previous research and created subcategories that related to Swales's (1990) original descriptions of compare, contrast, or support. As mentioned earlier, we added introduce as a subcategory, as we often found citations used to begin a paragraph or new idea. Assigning these Move 4 subcategories was relatively straightforward and yielded consistent intercoder agreement.

Advice for Those Who Might Build on our Research

We learned much from our textual analysis and offer several suggestions for anyone conducting similar research, including the following:

- Create a coding guide and revise it to reflect any changes.
- Select individual rhetorical moves rather than the collective set to allow for more flexibility.
- Ask students about rhetorical purpose regarding how they referenced previous research.

First, we learned that the coding guide is an essential tool and that it is most effective when it clearly reflects relevant and concrete examples.

We revised our coding guide multiple times: our first version reflected Swales's rhetorical moves in brief form; our second version included adaptations to the categories that better fit the student papers (see table 6.1); our third version expanded the second version to include clear category descriptions and four to five concrete examples per category. (This final coding guide appears as Appendix 6.D.)

Second, we would not recommend applying Swales's (1990) collective rhetorical moves to student papers, as the set was intended for published research and not student writing. Applying all moves also introduced the potential for greater coder disagreement. Yet, specific rhetorical moves such as Move 4: reference to previous research were highly relevant to student writing, and close examination of that move allowed us to learn about the ways students were citing research. Thus, we recommend selecting specific moves rather than replicating Swales's collective set of rhetorical moves. To provide more context for using rhetorical moves in academic texts, we recommend reading Swales (1990), Holmes (1997), and Howard, Serviss, and Rodrigue (2010) as essential starting points.

Finally, we learned that our textual analysis could have been enhanced by asking students about their intentions as writers. In hindsight, student reflection about their own writing would have provided valuable information about the ways students were citing research, and it would have provided an important perspective. For example, using discourse-based interviews modeled on Odell, Goswami, and Herrington's (1983) work, we could have asked students to explain the choices we found so predominant. Doing so before our coding might have provided different categories for coding the references to research. Doing so after our coding might have provided insights into students' choices and purposes when referencing research.

FINDINGS

The results and discussion sections of the papers were segmented into units generally consisting of one sentence per unit, though a unit could consist of an image or an item in a numbered or unnumbered list instead. There were 1,405 units in the fifteen IMRAD papers. As table 6.4 shows, Move 4: reference to previous research was the second most common category, at 20.3 percent. This percentage reflects the overall frequency of this move across all samples—each sample varied significantly in the frequency and use of references to previous research.

A closer look at the subcategories of Move 4: reference to previous research shows that references were used most often to *support* a topic

Table 6.4. Frequency of coding categories in IMRAD papers

Category Number and Name	Raw Frequency	Relative Frequency (%)
Move 1: background information	40	2.8
Move 2: statement of results	218	15.5
Move 3: statement of findings from primary research	284	20.2
Move 4: reference to previous research	286	20.3
Move 5: explanation and examples	144	10.2
Move 6: generalization and limitation	17	1.2
Move 7: recommendation	97	6.9
Move 0: none of the above	319	22.7
Total	1,405	99.9

or idea expressed in the paper (n = 252) as opposed to using the reference to *compare/contrast* (n = 21) or to *introduce* an idea (n = 54). See table 6.5 for an overview of the fifteen IMRAD papers and the distribution of these Move 4 subcategories in them. These frequencies speak in part to rhetorical purpose, or how students were using references in their papers.

An analysis of how Move 4 was placed in paragraphs provides further insight. Units found in the middle and end of paragraphs (middle sentence and last sentence) were more likely to be instances of support or comparison. Units found in the first sentence were more likely to be instances of introduction to a topic or idea. Figure 6.1 shows the distribution of Move 4 sentences within paragraphs for each paper. (Note the absence of papers 013, 074, and 079, which had no Move 4 units.) While placement was not identical across authors, there was a pattern of more frequent uses of Move 4 in the middle sentences of paragraphs, which matched the frequency data of instances of support' for Move 4. Below we discuss some patterns of individual writers, such as using references to previous research to introduce, support, or compare/contrast ideas.

In the papers in which students used a significant number of Move 4 units to begin paragraphs, they usually did so to introduce a topic and sometimes also to provide some support for the claim in the paragraph. Here is an example of a paragraph in which the student used this approach:

> In November 2010, the *Marshall Independent*, as well as Minnesota Public Radio, reported on a new study being done by MNSCU to gauge the alignment of courses between Minnesota West Community and Technical

Table 6.5. Overview of IMRAD papers and presence of Move 4 and its subcategories

Paper # and topic	Units Coded	Move 4 (#/% total)	Subcategories of Move 4 (#/% of total)			
			Support	Compare	Intro	Other
5. Marketing university campus as transfer destination	59	7 (12%)	4 (57%)	2 (29%)	3 (43%)	0 (0%)
6. Fluctuating milk prices	103	49 (47%)	43 (88%)	1 (2%)	10 (20%)	2 (4%)
11. Title IX	65	25 (38%)	21 (84%)	1 (4%)	4 (16%)	0 (0%)
13. Management style and employee satisfaction	71	0 (0%)				
16. Effect of thin models on teen eating disorders	54	14 (26%)	13 (93%)	3 (21%)	3 (21%)	2 (14%)
27. Effect of music listening on exercise	93	28 (30%)	23 (82%)	0 (0%)	9 (32%)	0 (0%)
31. Choice of dogs as pets	82	42 (51%)	36 (86%)	4 (10%)	9 (21%)	5 (12%)
35. Effect of listening to music on student grades	59	6 (10%)	5 (83%)	1 (17%)	0 (0%)	0 (0%)
38. Website usability	192	16 (8%)	13 (81%)	0 (0%)	3 (19%)	2 (13%)
52. Dangers of tanning	166	57 (34%)	57 (100%)	9 (16%)	5 (9%)	0 (0%)
55. Raw-milk-related illness	103	33 (32%)	29 (88%)	0 (0%)	7 (21%)	0 (0%)
73. Evaluation of non-profit event	109	4 (4%)	3 (75%)	0 (0%)	1 (25%)	0 (0%)
74. Curriculum changes in computer science	163	0 (0%)				
78. Alcohol sales at university stadium	57	5 (9%)	5 (100%)	0 (0%)	0 (0%)	0 (0%)
79. Effect of stress and procrastination on student performance	29	0 (0%)				
Totals	1,405	286	252	25	54	11

College and SMSU [Move 4/introduce]. This was consistent with Dr. Onyeaghala's statements as well as what I was beginning to believe about the appeal of SMSU to community college students [Move 5].

Paper 05/units 0084–0085

As this example demonstrates, Move 4/introduce units could occur at the beginning of a paragraph as a kind of topic sentence. And more often than not, these moves consisted of a source paraphrase. We noted

Using Genre Analysis to Understand Source Use

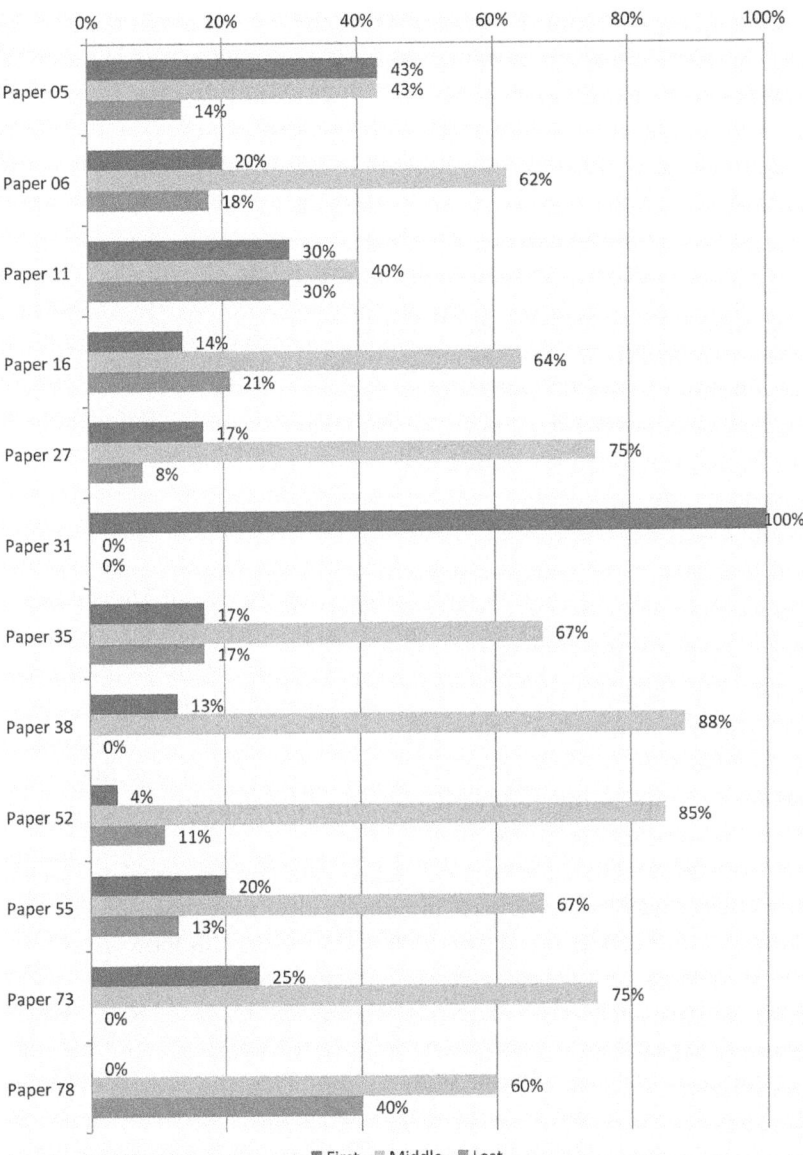

Figure 6.1 Distribution of Move 4 units

that in these instances, the paraphrase substituted for the student's voice in introducing a new topic through a topic sentence.

As we noted above, Move 4 was most frequently made to support ideas or topics in a paper. We began to notice common patterns among frequent "support" users. The simplest of these consisted of paragraphs entirely made up of references to secondary sources and paragraphs in which all the units were secondary sources except that the first or last sentence was in the student's voice. This excerpt comes from paper 06, whose author frequently had complete paragraphs made up of nothing but Move 4 units:

> The Federal Milk Marketing Orders were established in 1937 to help market milk from the producer to the processor [Move 4/introduce/support]. FMMOs are used to set a minimum price in which processors pay producers for raw fluid (Grade A) milk [Move 4/support]. The price that is established is a uniform "blend" price that is a weighted average of the class prices [Move 4/support]. The price also varies by a schedule based on the traditional supply and demand of dairy products. The Federal Milk Marketing Orders help to regulate about 75% of the milk produced in the United States (Dairy Fluid, 26) [Move 4/support].
>
> Paper 06/units 0174–0178

This is the most common pattern of all for the use of Move 4 units, and the authors of papers 27, 31, and 55 all practiced it regularly. A second pattern similar to the first consisted of a topic sentence in the student's voice (usually Move 0 or Move 2) followed by the balance of the paragraph consisting entirely of Move 4 units. The authors of papers 06 and 16 used this practice frequently. It was less common to find Move 4/support units at the ends of paragraphs, although papers 11 and 78 frequently used them in this way.

The least common use of Move 4 was compare/contrast, or placing references to previous research in conversation with other research or observations made by the author. The author using this move steps back and comments critically on research as it compares to previous studies or other evidence. This move was rarely practiced in our samples; however, a few students used one or two more sophisticated approaches for integrating the voices of others with the students' own. First, the authors of papers 05, 35, and 52 interspersed references to secondary sources with interpretive comments and claims of their own. This excerpt is from paper 35:

> Comparing the results of the background research and the empirical survey, there are many similarities and potential for new research projects to develop beyond this research report [Move 0]. First, every single participant regardless of student status, gender, and GPA listened to music during designated homework times (though the amount of time varied) [Move 1 (repeating previously presented results)]. This is comparable to what society is reflecting through the creation of headphones and portable music devices in addition to designing stores that music can overtake the

entire space (Lincoln, 2005) [Move 4/compare]. Second, it was found in the empirical survey that while there was a most preferred and least preferred music genre, there was not a significant difference between response numbers of the music genres [Move 2]. This is another reflection of societal changes of preferred music genres due to rises of technology [Move 0]. Technology makes music accessible, so humans are able to explore and develop personal musical tastes [Move 0]. Lastly, it is not surprising that college students are listening to music during designated homework times because music has been proven to influence behavior in previous studies and has current research interest for the Department of Homeland Security (Department of Homeland Security, 2009) [Move 4/support]. While it is speculative to conclude that listening to music may increase concentration levels during designated homework times, it would not be entirely surprising if a reputable study concluded it as fact [Move 0].

Paper 35/units 956–963

The Move 4/compare statement above demonstrates how this student author placed sources in conversation with one another. In this case, the author compared her primary survey research on the topic of music listening to a secondary source (Lincoln) on the prevalence of music devices. This kind of connection reflected an analysis useful to the remainder of her argument. Again, this move was rarely visible among our samples.

DISCUSSION OF FINDINGS

As we digest these findings, we return to our research question, *for what rhetorical purposes do students integrate sources in research reports?* Using genre analysis as described by Swales (1990), we structured our study around his rhetorical moves for results sections, focusing on Move 4: reference to previous research. We divided this move into three subcategories: introduce, support, and compare/contrast. Our findings suggest that of these subcategories, references were most frequently used to support a main idea or topic in student writing (252 instances), whereas references used to introduce an idea (54 instances) or compare/contrast (21 instances) were far less frequent. These findings, and our textual-analysis method, have generated several observations and questions about student use of citations among our samples.

First, we observe that the frequent use of citations to support main ideas (Move 4/support) corresponds well to Swales's finding that using sources for support is a standard and expected rhetorical move in academic writing. In fact, of the eight moves Swales outlines, Move 4 was the second most frequent rhetorical move we coded in our student samples. In addition, among the subcategories of introduce, support, and compare/contrast, support was by far the most frequent. The samples we reviewed for this study consistently demonstrated an awareness of and effort from students to incorporate secondary sources in support of a main idea or argument. We consider the frequency of Move 4/support statements encouraging, for it demonstrates student awareness of integrating sources to build written arguments. But this frequency does not necessarily reflect sophistication. For example, we did not examine the Move 4/support statements for correctness of citation format or accuracy of content; our results suggest only that students frequently made efforts to integrate sources for support.

However, the same observation cannot be made about instances of Move 4/compare statements and Move 4/introduce statements. The infrequency of the former suggests that students rarely place sources in conversation with one another, possibly because they do not know how to integrate sources in this way, or perhaps because they do not consider it important to their analytical research paper. Students did not often mingle their own interpretations with source findings and rarely articulated themes or trends among their sources. Students also rarely used sources to present alternative or opposing viewpoints; they used them to support main points rather than rebut them. Students' use of Move 4/introduce statements to introduce main points further illustrated the use of sources to develop a main point; however, they also illustrated how students constructed topic sentences using source references rather than articulating their own topic statements. We hypothesize that using sources to introduce topics in this way may dilute the student's authorial voice in research papers.

To better understand these findings, we reviewed the directions students in the Technical and Professional Writing course were given in the assignment description and grading criteria for the analytical report. (A commonly used assignment description appears as Appendix 6.A.) What we found was disappointing: the common assignment description notes students will analyze their data and sources, but it says nothing about what that effort entails. One implication is that instructors should provide further detail and explanation about this work in the assignment sheet (see also Head and Eisenberg 2010; Kleinfeld, this volume).

IMPLICATIONS AND FUTURE RESEARCH

We set out to discover what rhetorical purpose references to sources served in our students' analytical reports. We found that Move 4: reference to previous research was the second most common rhetorical move in our students' papers and that the great majority of those references to previous research served the purpose of supporting the claims or arguments the student was making. In fact, our finding that compare/contrast moves were rarely seen among student papers suggests that, in terms of rhetorical purpose, these undergraduate writers think of citations primarily in terms of supporting a position they have stated in their writing. Student writers in our sample rarely discussed themes or patterns evident in previous research. This almost unvarying purpose for references to previous research suggests students in this study may have had difficulty positioning their work in the context of previous scholarship. Or, as we learned from reflecting on our own assignment, students may have simply done exactly as we asked and found sources that aligned directly with their arguments.

These findings, we believe, suggest a greater need to help students develop a stronger authorial voice based on an overall perspective of the research they are citing. We are reminded of Wolfe's (2009) critique of technical-communication textbooks and her suggestions that students need more help discussing and integrating data in research papers. The same argument could be made regarding research papers that rely heavily on secondary sources—students need more help discussing and integrating sources in a way that demonstrates critical thinking.

On this point, we shared our data analysis with our local instructor community, which resulted in several discussions about how to better help students critically analyze sources in the contexts of their arguments. Many instructors noted the importance of students having stronger familiarity with their sources. One change we discussed was to strengthen an existing proposal assignment (meant to precede the analytical report) to include an annotated bibliography of sources that would be used for the analytical report. Another suggestion was to incorporate a stronger literature review section in the analytical report assignment. We reasoned that these additions might give students the opportunity to engage more deeply with sources and to observe patterns, themes, and disagreements among sources. We felt it was important that students engage with their sources early and often so they could more completely enter the conversation of scholarship. In addition to a more robust proposal assignment, instructors also articulated ideas for smaller, low-stakes assignments that would ask students to reflect on sources or share their findings with other students. If such changes are introduced, a follow-up study could analyze their impact in comparison with this data.

Our conversations with instructors yielded other helpful insights. For example, we discussed strategies to help students talk about their sources beyond a single paraphrase or quote to support a main point. Could students question the sources? Could they compare and/or contrast opposing views from sources? Could they explain the cited reference more deeply? Such strategies could potentially help students "unpack" their sources by encouraging them not only to *articulate* main points but also to *illustrate* and *explain* how those sources contribute to the overall argument at hand. One instructor noted that he'd like to share Swales's rhetorical moves along with examples so students could see what rhetorical moves might accomplish. We considered sharing our coding guide for this purpose because it includes explanations and examples of the rhetorical moves. Another idea was to have students analyze their own writing using Move 4: reference to previous research to further understand the ways they are using references in their writing. Each of these ideas offered great direction for strengthening attention on how students use research references.

In addition to local impacts of this research, our pilot study opened directions for future research. The pilot study involved tedious steps regarding coding, but we believe any second attempt could run more smoothly, especially if coding for specific rhetorical moves rather than trying to apply them all. We imagine future studies revisiting Move 4: reference to previous research using a new data set, perhaps as part of an ongoing assessment of student writing in this advanced writing course. We imagine inviting students to participate in an analysis of their own writing, perhaps by sharing with them the rhetorical moves and asking them to comment on their own purposes and choices for using references. Finally, we imagine how this research might be more fully integrated into our technical-communication programs, in terms of both undergraduate writing and graduate-student research. In sum, we found our study an important first step for building a more robust assessment program of student writing in our undergraduate program, and we look forward to exploring these new avenues.

APPENDIX 6.A
Assignment Description

These appendices may be downloaded from https://upcolorado.com/utah-state-university-press/item/3188-points-of-departure and used or modified for teaching or research purposes with attribution.

You have chosen a topic and have reported on the progress of your project in a progress report/activity report. In this assignment you will demonstrate your ability to follow the necessary steps for research: define a research question, develop a research methodology, gather information using that methodology, and analyze the information (see Figure 23.3 and Chapter 7). You will then demonstrate your ability to write an analytical report based on that research. Your report will follow the general analytical report structure—Introduction, Methodology, Results, Discussion, Conclusions and/or recommendations—the IMRAD structure. (Chapter and figure references are to Johnson-Sheehan 2010)

APPENDIX 6.B
Final Coding Guide for Holistic Assessment of Student Papers' Conformity with IMRAD Structure

Examine each of your student texts for the existence of IMRAD structure. An Excel spreadsheet will be provided for you to record your results. Please provide a "yes" or "no" indicating whether the IMRAD structure is present. The IMRAD structure resembles Introduction, Method, Results and Discussion. The Results and Discussion section may be labeled different things such as "Findings," "Results," "Results and Discussion," "Conclusion." More important than the headings used in the paper, the "Results" and "Discussion" must do two things: (1) make a statement of results, which may be interpreted as a claim or finding (or multiple claims or findings) and (2) provide an explanation of the statement of results, no matter how short or long that explanation is.

- For a "yes" code, the document must have evidence of all IMRAD sections. For example, there must be an introduction with background information, an explanation of methods, sharing of results and some kind of discussion of those results. The prose is more important than the headings/titles. For example, if sections of text indicate introduction, methods, results, and discussion, but are not labeled as such in headings or are labeled differently, the paper would still receive a "yes" code.
- For a "no" code, the document will have left out one or more of the IMRAD sections. For example, if an introduction is provided as well as results and discussion, but the methods section is absent, the document gets a coding of "no." If results are shared, but discussion of those results is absent, the document would receive a "no" code.

APPENDIX 6.C
First Draft Coding Guide for Atomistic Assessment of Sentences/Units

(Note that references are incomplete, as that is how they appeared in the draft.)

- **Move 1. Background information.** Information that strengthens the main discussion by restating main points, highlighting theoretical information, or reminding reader of technical information. Reference: See Swales, p. 172.
- **Move 2. Statement of results.** Statement of claim and findings. This statement may occur more than once. Reference: Swales p. 172, and Wolfe p. 368 "Interpret data and draw conclusions" p. 368.
- **Move 3. (Un)expected outcome.** Address any surprising results. Reference: Swales, p. 173, and Wolfe, p. 369, "Acknowledge errors, flaws, and unexpected or unfortunate results."
- **Move 4. Reference to previous research.** Swales describes this as the most common move after Move 2. Sub-types include comparison with present research or support for present research. Reference: Swales p. 173.
- **Move 5. Explanation.** Offer reasons for results, including any surprising or unexpected results that may differ from literature; acknowledge error something different from literature. Wolfe suggests that the writer should "present data in a way that leads reader to conclusion" (368). Swales suggests that this category overlaps somewhat with Move 3. Reference: Swales p. 173, and Wolfe p. 368.
- **Move 6. Exemplification.** Swales suggests that "Examples are most often used to support an explanation" (173).
- **Move 7. Deduction and hypothesis.** Claim about generalizability of results. Reference: Swales, p. 173.
- **Move 8. Recommendation.** Statements about need and directions for future research. Swales' comment that this section is often missing because US scientists don't want to tip their hat about their future directions. Reference: Swales, p. 173.

APPENDIX 6.D
Final Coding Guide for Atomistic Assessment of Sentences/Units

References to three-digit numbers are to the unique identifiers of the papers we used for developing the coding guide training coders; page numbers refer to pages in those documents.

MOVE 1. BACKGROUND INFORMATION.

Information that strengthens the main discussion by articulating the purpose of the study, reiterating information from previous sections, highlighting theoretical information, asserting importance of the subject matter at hand, or reminding reader of technical information.

EXAMPLES:

- "The purpose of this study was to find if caffeine had any effect. . . ." 002 p. 11

- "The effects of caffeine on academic performance are an important concept." 002 p. 11

MOVE 2. STATEMENT OF RESULTS.

A statement about the subject matter of the student's study that articulates the main idea(s) and contribution(s) of the student's analytical report, that presents a claim of the student, or that represents an interpretation by the student of a such a claim, or of a Move 3 or Move 4 unit. A statement in this category is not reporting findings of primary or secondary research completed by the student, but rather is an assertion about the subject matter of the study.

EXAMPLES:

- "However the limited evidence shows that caffeine has a negative impact on academic performance." 002
- "Relating to my question of what the effects are in pregnant women if they consume artificial sugars, we can conclude that it there will most likely not be any effects by consuming the sugar. Although it is suggested to not consume the artificial sugars during pregnancy to be sure that there will not be any bad effects." 018 (both coded as Move 2)

MOVE 3. STATEMENT OF FINDINGS FROM PRIMARY RESEARCH.

A statement that articulates a discovery or finding based on primary research completed by the student such as surveys, polls, or interviews.

EXAMPLES:

- "Sense of privacy in a workplace . . . is important to every generation that was interviewed." (Referring to interviews the student conducted.) 017 p. 8
- "[1] <LBimage imagetype="chart" > figure 1: Cumulative GPA of all Participants < /LBimage > [2] As you can see from the pie chart the majority of the participants have a 3.0 to 3.4 GPA. [3] A 3.0 grade point average is equivalent to a B average. [4] Participants with a 3.5 to 4.0 GPA make up 30% of the date." 002 ([2] and [4] report the results of the student's survey; those results are presented in a pie chart in [1]; all three are thus coded Move 3. [3] is coded Move 0, because it's unclear where the student came by this information.
- "In my interview with <redact></redact>, she explained to me that there are not any recommendations to not use artificial sugars during pregnancy." 018 (the student reports the comments of an informant the student interviewed; the information gleaned from this interview is thus coded Move 3)

MOVE 4. REFERENCE TO PREVIOUS RESEARCH.

This category includes statements that refer to any secondary source, such as journal articles, books, or internet sources. Statements in this category can manifest in a variety of ways:

- Reference that summarizes, paraphrases, or quotes previous research from a secondary source.
- Reference that compares and/or contrasts previous research with the study presently conducted by the student.
- Reference that articulates the way in which a previous article supports the study presently conducted by the student.

EXAMPLES:

- "The article *Encouraging Healthy diet is elementary in Lansdownw*, by Brain Conlin, looks at how foods are laid out in the lunchroom." 020 p. 7 (source attributed sentence)
- "Many studies have investigated the research of caffeine intake on academics and the results show that caffeine as negative impacts . . ." 002 p. 11
- "Also, brain science studies have shown that social interaction accelerates learning, decision making and long term memory (Williams 2009)." 003 p. 6 (cited source)
- "'There is no universal experience of childhood, experiences are rather social constructs which are the result of a complex interplay of historical, social and cultural factors' (Jha, 207)." 023 p. 7 (quoted source)

"Unfortunately. . . . the results [from secondary research] were extremely minimal regarding apparel design job listings." 009 p. 10–11 (though this sentence does not report specific secondary source results, it reflects the student's review of such sources)

MOVE 5. EXPLANATION AND EXAMPLES.

Statements in this category offer any reasons for results, including any surprising or unexpected results. Explanatory statements may also demonstrate analysis or argument that connects findings from primary or secondary research to statements of results. Examples reflect instances (rather than summaries) that support explanations, including anecdotal information, stories, or other illustrations that support explanations.

EXAMPLES:

- "[1]According to my survey, one of the most popular perceptions of child labor was the lack of implementation of current laws already in place . . . . [2] As discussed in the introduction, India has a long history of passing laws and taking a proactive stance on this issue. [3]

However, the government is not able to fully implement these laws as the issue is not getting any better. [4] This could be a results of lack of national funds to punish employers or rather the large amount of bribery and corrupt throughout the government."(Sentence [1] is Move 3, Sentence [2] is move 1, but sentences [3]-[4] are Move 5.) 023 p. 7

- "To me this seemed strange." (Referring to a result of the student's primary research.) 020 p. 7
- "Surprisingly, of everyone I surveyed, no one believes financial support was a contributor to the child issue problem." 023 p. 8
- "As I was reading this article I remember a conversation with an elementary teacher that I had." 020 p. 7
- "Because they cause snow to melt quicker, it reduces the amount of chloride dispersed in the environment." 041 p. 11

MOVE 6. GENERALIZATION AND LIMITATION.

Statements in this category address generalizability of results of the study the student is conducting or address limits on its validity or generalizability. Statements in this category can include references to limitations in the present study the author is conducting, or it can include references to limitations in a secondary study the author reviews. A statement explaining why some state of affairs is a limitation should be coded as Move 6 (rather than Move 5).

EXAMPLES:

- "This problem also affects external validity because since the scores did not measure what they were supposed to it cannot be applied to the population." 002 p. 11
- "Because I focused most of my research in Minnesota, I was not able to compare/contrast as I would if I looked fully at the whole US." 020 p. 6
- "A major problem of the study was that the experimenter used a questionnaire in order to collect data." 002, p.11 (referring to the student's primary research)
- "Effects from a rat could end up being slightly different in a human being." 018 p. 7 (referring to secondary research)
- "[1] A major problem of the study was that the experimenter used a questionnaire in order to collect data. [2] There was minimal demographic data collected on the subjects. [3] Detailed information was not obtained." 002 (though [2] and [3] don't overtly criticize the study, they *explain* the criticism in [1])

NOTE: "These are clear examples of the benefits social networking can have on specifically workers but could definitely be applied to the productivity of students." 003 p. 6 (this is the student's claim and thus

Move 2; here she generalizes from workers to students, but does not comment on generalizability)

MOVE 7. RECOMMENDATION.

Statements in this category address need and directions for future research, specifically future research studies on the same or similar topic. Statements in this category may also address future actions that can be taken as a result of findings, or "calls to action."

EXAMPLES:

- "In the future, the experimenter should use a more detailed questionnaire in order to properly assess the relationship between caffeine consumption and academic performance." 002 p. 11
- "Further research needs to begin at the core of this issue and alleviating the burden children have at supporting their families as such a young age." 023 p. 8
- "The Career Center should become more active in social media and include GoldPass in this process as a way of increasing advertisement to employers and businesses." 009 p. 13
- "My recommendations to other businesses and CEOs, keep the energy of your company, keep creating and if there is some difficulties looks like unsolved." 012 p. 11

MOVE 0. NONE OF THE ABOVE.

Statements that do not reflect any of the previous categories. This includes rhetorical signposts or 'metatext,' transition sentences between paragraphs or sections, rhetorical questions, and headers (unless headers exhibit characteristics of a particular move). Statements in this category will vary, and often may have some similarity to a particular category, but not enough to code it cleanly as that category. For example, statements of personal reflections or beliefs about the study might fall into this category, rather than Move 2 "statement of results." This category includes sentences that have characteristics of more than one Move. If a sentence firmly reflects one move, but has hints of a second, please code the first move and describe the second move in the "notes" space.

EXAMPLES:

- "Thank you for your interest on this issue and if you have any further questions or comments regarding this report please do not hesitate to call me . . . ." 023 p. 8
- Photograph in 012 p. 7.

- "I edit it into Excel form for clearly view." 012
- "What are the reasons for child labor: The poor economic status of India? The lack of implementation of current laws? Western greed for lower prices? Or just the simple difference in childhood definition between cultures." 023 p. 6

References

Bazerman, Charles. 1988. *Shaping Written Knowledge: The Genre and Activity of the Experimental Article in Science.* Madison: University of Wisconsin Press.

Berkenkotter, Carol, and Thomas Huckin. 1995. *Genre Knowledge in Disciplinary Communication: Cognition/Culture/Power.* Hillsdale, NJ: Lawrence Erlbaum.

Bhatia, Vijay K. 1993. *Analysing Genre: Language Use in Professional Settings.* London: Longman.

Breuch, Lee-Ann Kastman, Andrea M. Olson, and Andrea Frantz. 2002. "Considering Ethical Issues in Technical Communication Research." In *Research in Technical Communication,* edited by Laura J. Gurak and Mary M. Lay, 1–22. Westport, CT: Praeger.

Carletta, Jean. 1996. "Assessing Agreement on Classification Tasks: The Kappa Statistic." *Computational Linguistics* 22 (2): 249–54.

Cunningham, Hamish, Diana Maynard, and Kalina Bontcheva. 2011. *Text Processing with GATE.* Sheffield: University of Sheffield Department of Computer Science.

Dudley-Evans, Tony. 1993. "Variations in Communication Patterns between Discourse Communities: The Case of Highway Engineering and Plant Biology." In *Language, Learning, and Success: Studying through English,* edited by G. M. Blue, 140–47. London: MacMillan.

Hafner, Christoph A. 2010. "A Multi-Perspective Genre Analysis of the Barrister's Opinion: Writing Context, Generic Structure, and Textualization." *Written Communication* 27 (4): 410–41. http://dx.doi.org/10.1177/0741088310377272.

Head, Allison J., and Michael B. Eisenberg. 2010. "Assigning Inquiry: How Handouts for Research Assignments Guide Today's College Students." Project Information Literacy Progress Report. . http://projectinfolit.org/pdfs/PIL_Handout_Study_finalvJuly_2010.pdf. http://dx.doi.org/10.2139/ssrn.2281494.

Holmes, Richard. 1997. "Genre Analysis, and the Social Sciences: An Investigation of the Structure of Research Article Discussion Sections in Three Disciplines." *English for Specific Purposes* 16 (4): 321–37. http://dx.doi.org/10.1016/S0889-4906(96)00038-5.

Howard, Rebecca Moore, Tricia Serviss, and Tanya K. Rodrigue. 2010. "Writing from Sources, Writing from Sentences." *Writing & Pedagogy* 2 (2): 177–92. http://dx.doi.org/10.1558/wap.v2i2.177.

Jamieson, Sandra, and Rebecca Moore Howard. 2013. "Sentence-Mining: Uncovering the Amount of Reading and Reading Comprehension in College Writers' Researched Writing." In *The New Digital Scholar: Exploring and Enriching the Research and Writing Practices of NextGen Students,* edited by Randall McClure and James Purdy, 109–32. Medford, NJ: Information Today.

Johnson-Sheehan, Richard. 2010. *Technical Communication Today.* 3rd ed. New York: Pearson.

Jurafsky, Daniel, and James H. Martin. 2009. *Speech and Language Processing: An Introduction to Natural Language Processing, Computational Linguistics, and Speech Recognition.* 2nd ed. Prentice Hall Series in Artificial Intelligence. Upper Saddle River, NJ: Pearson Education.

Larson, Brian. 2015. "Gender/Genre: Gender Difference in Disciplinary Communication." PhD diss., University of Minnesota, Minneapolis, MN.

Odell, Lee, Dixie Goswami, and Anne Herrington. 1983. "The Discourse-Based Interview: A Procedure for Exploring the Tacit Knowledge of Writers in Nonacademic Settings." In *Research on Writing: Principles and Methods*, edited by Peter Mosenthal, Lynne Tamor, and Sean A. Walmsley, 221–36. New York: Longman.

Rude, Carolyn D. 1995. "The Report for Decision Making: Genre and Inquiry." *Journal of Business and Technical Communication* 9 (2): 170–205. http://dx.doi.org/10.1177/1050651995009002002.

Spilka, Rachel. 2009. "Practitioner Research Instruction: A Neglected Curricular Area in Technical Communication Undergraduate Programs." *Journal of Business and Technical Communication* 23 (2): 216–37. http://dx.doi.org/10.1177/1050651908328882.

Swales, John M. 1990. *Genre Analysis: English in Academic and Research Settings*. Cambridge: Cambridge University Press.

Swales, John M. 2004. *Research Genres: Exploration and Applications*. Cambridge: Cambridge University Press. http://dx.doi.org/10.1017/CBO9781139524827.

Wolfe, Joanna. 2009. "How Technical Communication Textbooks Fail Engineering Students." *Technical Communication Quarterly* 18 (4): 351–75. http://dx.doi.org/10.1080/10572250903149662.

Chapter 7

ASKING THE RIGHT QUESTIONS
Using Interviews to Explore Information-Seeking Behavior

M. Whitney Olsen and Anne R. Diekema

ABSTRACT

This chapter reports on an interview-driven qualitative research study of first-year writers' information-seeking behaviors. Informed by a synthesis of literature from the humanities and information science, we arrived at key exploratory findings by recruiting eleven first-year writing students from two universities (five at one and six at the other); interviewing them using a semistructured methodological approach; and processing the transcribed interviews using thematic analysis (Boyatzis 1998). The study indicates that students continue to be Google dependent and to prefer secondary sources. They demonstrate a behavior we call *funneling* as they conduct their information searches (beginning with expansive search terms and moving toward more specific terms and expectations at the end of their research) as well as reliance upon people as information sources, favoring friends and family members over faculty and information professionals.

INTRODUCTION

In 1993, Charles Schroeder wrote, "I am suggesting that an overall understanding of how students learn and where they are in the process can help us meet the needs of the new students who sit in our classrooms" (Schroeder 1993, 26). His suggestion is as true now as it was more than twenty years ago: as teachers, we must understand our ever-changing groups of students in order to help them. Today's writing students are mired in a conflicting world of computers and pens, smart phones and paper, and digital and physical information. Before writing instructors can ask students to research, it is imperative to understand their information behavior. In their article "Information Behavior," Karen Fisher and Heidi Julien write that human information behavior involves many complex factors: people's information needs, the context of the information needs, how people seek information, their formal and informal information collection, and what they do with the information (Fisher and Julien 2009). That description provides a basis for the research described in this chapter.

Information behavior is fluid and context dependent (Attfield, Blandford, and Dowell 2003, 435; Boyd 2004, 82); different user groups exhibit different information-seeking behaviors (Boyd 2004, 82). First-year writing students comprise a large and diverse information-user group dispersed across the United States. These facts make this group particularly compelling to study in terms of information behavior since their writing classes, in many ways, are representative of their campuses and the undergraduate information user group as a whole. In spite of previous research (e.g., Downs and Wardle 2007; Li and Casanave 2012), we still have much to learn about first-year writing students' information behavior and undergraduate students' information use in general. Yet instructors are repeatedly challenged to teach students information skills without an empirical understanding of their students' contexts or practices. This chapter introduces a small pilot study designed to revisit questions from earlier research about the information-seeking behavior of first-year writing students. It is our hope that explicit discussion of our research methods will provide a foundation for future researchers to replicate or expand the study and that the findings themselves—especially where they correlate with findings from other studies—will provide writing instructors with a better understanding of the information-seeking strategies of their students and the pedagogical strategies they might adopt in response.

FRAMEWORK

Jamieson and Howard (2011) note that how students research and cite is underresearched, especially as such practices relate to the rapidly expanding role of digital information. While it is generally assumed that all the information readily available on the Internet has increased, a parallel increase in plagiarism has been proven difficult to measure (Walker 2010). What is clear, however, is that undergraduate students still cite books and journals from local library collections (Hendley 2012; Jamieson 2016). Thus, we present a framework for understanding the information-seeking behavior of undergraduates based on literature from information science and the humanities. For the purposes of this chapter, we define university writing courses as required, general education, lower-division writing classes aimed at teaching incoming college and university students to write in formal and/or academic modes (e.g., first-year composition, freshman writing, and so on). This study focused on students enrolled in classes that required them to conduct research for their writing assignments. With online information resources such as digital libraries, websites, and blogs playing a more prominent role among all information user groups, it is important that researchers and practitioners understand the new role of digital information seeking among undergraduate writing students in addition to the contemporary face of their nondigital information-seeking behaviors. This study investigated the following questions:

1. Where do undergraduate writing students go for information?
2. How do undergraduate writing students arrive at information sources?
3. How and why do first-year composition students use their favored sources of information and choose not to use other sources of information?

METHODS

Basic Description

This study draws on qualitative methods of data collection and analysis. We selected naturalistic methods, interviews in particular, because we felt they were the best way to gather exploratory data that would reveal both students' search and use processes, as well as the context for that process on a granular level. We gathered data through eleven-question semistructured interviews (see Appendix 7.A) at two large public universities in the United States in the spring of 2012. We chose semistructured interviews because this approach allows more flexibility than fully structured interviews while still providing uniformity of the data we collected. The data for this research study were collected in the context of a class, which resulted in rich data because the students were in the process of searching for information to write their papers. The drawback to holding in-person interviews was a smaller sample size, which didn't necessarily allow us to generalize these findings to the entire population of first-year writing students.

Eleven students volunteered to participate, five at institution 1, and six at institution 2. All interviewees were white; seven were male, and four were female. To preserve as much of the instructional and task-orientation context as possible, all interviews were conducted on students' respective campuses. The interviews were conducted with individual participants in a private room; one researcher interviewed the student and the other observed the interview via Skype (videoconferencing software), asking relevant follow-up questions at the end of the interview. Students were aware of the second researcher's presence. Interviews were audio recorded to document interviews in their entirety and to facilitate future transcription. Each interview lasted approximately thirty minutes. We employed thematic analysis and an inductive approach to analyze students' responses to the interview questions (Boyatzis 1998). This process involved transcribing the audio recordings of student interviews, during which process we took note of interesting phenomena and trends, which informed our initial coding scheme. After the transcription process, we used the initial coding scheme to code the transcribed interviews. The coding scheme was extended with additional codes as needed, and the researchers clarified the different codes to achieve consistency. As such, this study used inductive codes, derived directly from the interview data, developed from the bottom up (Boyatzis 1998).

Expanded Discussion of Methods

To arrive at these methods, we first developed our interview guide (see Appendix 7.A) based on the research questions that shaped the study. Next, both researchers identified a suitable quiet, private location to interview participants. At institution 1, the researcher used her office. At institution 2, where the researcher shared an office, the researcher requested a room from her department and was granted one in the conference room of the department's main office.

Students who were enrolled in a single class at each institution self-selected for participation in this study. At institution 1, the researcher solicited student participants by contacting an instructor in the English department by e-mail, who then advertised verbally in one section of first-year writing and collected sign-ups by e-mail. Students at institution 2 were solicited via e-mail by their instructor, one of this study's researchers, and invited to use a website to choose an interview date and time. At both institutions, students were offered a nominal amount of extra credit, with additional opportunities for extra credit existing in both classes.

Next, the researchers followed a standard procedure to prepare for the interviews. For each interview, the researcher printed a clean copy of the interview guide, leaving space on the page for notes, which we handwrote on the page as needed. Each researcher turned on her computer, then opened and tested the audio-recording software. We used Audacity, a free audio-recording and editing package available at sourceforge.net. Then, the researcher logged into Skype for the other researcher to attend the interview in both audio and visual formats.

When the student arrived, the researcher welcomed the student, explained the purpose of the research, provided and explained the informed-consent form and asked the student to sign it, then started the audio recording. The interview followed a semistructured format, with the interviewer asking a question from the guide, allowing the student to respond, then asking follow-up questions or probing certain points further as needed. When the interview was completed, the researcher turned to the second researcher attending via Skype and asked if there were any questions they would like to pose. Once the interview was over, the interviewing researcher ended the audio recording, thanked the student, offered a candy bar as thanks for their help, and accompanied them to the door.

Once all participants had been interviewed, the researchers listened to the recordings using headphones and typed up the interviews verbatim in word-processing software. Doing our own transcriptions had the benefit of getting us much closer to the data than we could have if we had paid others to transcribe for us. When transcriptions were complete, we met to discuss emergent themes, inspired by the methods outlined by Richard Boyatzis (1998) and the detailed knowledge of the interviews that developed from the intensive transcription process. Arriving at a consensus for a theme allowed us to define it as a code, which was added to a digital coding sheet in a word-processing program. We used the first coding sheet to locate examples of the codes in the interviews, and as additional codes emerged, we met, arrived at a consensus, and added the code to the coding sheet. We also did additional coding passes of the transcriptions already analyzed. When all transcriptions and codes were exhausted, we concluded our analysis.

Limitations of This Method and Recommendations for Follow-Up Studies

Data were collected on students' campuses, in academic buildings and rooms, and in the case of institution 2's students, by their instructor. It is possible this approach would cause students to give answers colored by their positioning in the academic setting. Future research might investigate this influence by conducting similar interviews in more informal settings and/or having the interviews conducted by the students' peers or researchers from other institutions.

A larger sample size from more sites would help balance any skew caused by location, institutional practices, or policies or pedagogical interventions by individual faculty or librarians. This study was small and basically exploratory; future studies might replicate it in different populations, with larger sample sizes and/or using other questions or methods.

We interviewed eleven first-year writing students from two large, public universities in the United States regarding their information behavior. The small sample size and qualitative methodology were intended to capture as much of writing students' information-seeking context as possible, but what we gained in nuance we lost in scale. While it is not possible to generalize these findings to larger populations of first-year writing students and undergraduate students, this approach provides an important exploratory snapshot into the world of undergraduate researchers in the second decade of the twenty-first century, building on and updating earlier studies and suggesting areas for further research.

The qualitative nature of our research does not lend itself to meaningful numerical data but is best understood within the larger categories that identify trends and areas for further research. Future researchers might add a larger-scale survey to interviews, as does Project Information Literacy (see Head and Eisenberg 2009), or expand the model of focus groups and individual follow-up interviews (Valentine 1993) to multiple sites.

SUMMARY OF FINDINGS

Although we asked eleven interview questions (see Appendix 7.A), and follow-up questions where relevant, our goal was to answer the three broad questions discussed above. Approaching our findings in this way offers an opportunity to imagine local studies on one aspect of information literacy, a concept that might block or facilitate research behavior (see Serviss and Jamieson, interchapter 3 in this volume, 171–181), or relevant pedagogies. The findings replicate and update prior research, as shown in the detailed discussion of findings later in this chapter.

1. Where Do Undergraduate Writing Students Go for Information?

Our thematic analysis turned up interesting phenomena and trends. These emerged from the data and led to sometimes surprising findings, such as a heavy reliance on friends and family members in the information-seeking process. When looking for sources, students in this sample largely went to the following information resources[1] in their information-seeking processes: Google, *Wikipedia*, news websites, friends and family members, class notes, and select subscription databases. Only a few students reported using physical libraries, librarians and information professionals, content experts, books, or magazines, a significant update from research conducted at the beginning of this century, such as that by Fescemyer (2000) and Rowland and Rubbert (2001), which found that students are strongly attached to print materials, especially books. This progression is reflected in the literature, with studies published in 2005 finding students split between searching for information digitally and physically (Callinan 2005; Twait 2005) and more recent research correlating with our findings (Head 2013).

2. How Do Undergraduate Writing Students Arrive at Information Sources?

For the most part, undergraduate writers arrived at information sources for their papers by using resources they had "always" known about or been taught about in their high-school or college classes. Based on their descriptions, students tended to define specific information seeking as simply having a topic in mind and going generally in search of related information; very few students described actually seeking a particular source type or even having particular expectations for what they would find. First-year writers largely began their search processes by casting a wide net, typing in their topic in its broadest form, such as *childhood obesity*, or *war in Iraq*. Their search terms sometimes became more specific as they uncovered more information in the course of their search or if something in particular piqued their interest.

3. How and Why Do First-Year Composition Students Use Their Favored Sources of Information and Neglect or Choose Not to Use Other Sources of Information?

Students appear to use the sources they do because they are familiar and accessible. Once students feel comfortable using an information resource, they use it regularly and search it until they perceive they have exhausted all it has to offer (whether or not that is actually true). Students also tend to use sources they feel they clearly understand, and these are typically secondary sources. One way to understand this trend is to imagine students' neglect of sources as a combination of ignorance and unwillingness to venture outside the information resources with which they are comfortable or to adopt new information-seeking behaviors.

In general, weaknesses in first-year writing students' information behavior appear to be their heavy reliance on a limited number of information resources and their tendency to engage with only part of these resources; constraints on their time and their reluctance to invest too much time in their writing assignments; inability to generate productive searches; dependence on family and friends as information sources while ignoring librarians and faculty; and employment of easier-to-use (secondary) source types. Such limits suggest first-year students have yet to grasp the concept of research as inquiry or indeed any key aspects of information-literacy instruction. Dedicated lesson plans and course activities in composition courses could form a significant part of the solution to these weaknesses (see for example the recommendations in Head [2013] based on Project Information Literacy research). More research is needed to develop adequately complex and practical plans to assist first-year writers as the large and omnipresent group they are.

DETAILED DISCUSSION OF FINDINGS IN THE CONTEXT OF PRIOR RESEARCH

Our findings for this population of FYW students are in line with findings in other studies of undergraduate students more generally, and while we did not replicate the research questions in other studies, we did design them to be in dialogue with and, where relevant, update other research along the lines of the representation of RAD research as a process articulated in this collection (see Serviss, introduction to this volume, 3–23). Students in our study grounded their information-seeking behaviors in the Google search, appearing to operate in distinct comfort zones developed from the instruction they'd received in various classes. They preferred secondary sources, which they often did not read fully. They reported being nervous about their use of *Wikipedia*, yet they used it anyway. We also found that people who could serve as information sources comprised a major part of students' information-seeking behavior, but that the people consulted tended to be friends and family members; faculty and information professionals were largely absent. Students also demonstrated limited understanding of citation and plagiarism when summarizing and paraphrasing sources. Below is a fuller discussion of our findings and the other studies that they confirm or update.

The "Google Generation" Strikes Again

The students interviewed in this study reported research strategies that align with those found in other studies (most specifically Head 2013; Lee 2008; McClure and Clink 2009; Rowlands et al. 2008). This generation of students is heavily reliant on search engines, especially Google, for finding information. Common to all students participating in this study was the use of Google as one of the first, if not the very first, place they went to find information. Students were also highly unified in their reasons for using Google as one of their primary resources for information. One student summarized other responses well: "Quick. Convenient . . . I can find whatever I need through Google" (student 7). He went on to describe, as many other students did, that he was aware there were other ("more scholarly," as student 6 put it) ways to find information. In addition, students voiced the sentiment that they felt their current information-seeking behavior was adequate: "Right now, Google's working for me, and I'm not, uh, as smart, you know, with different databases and search engines as I wish I could be, so Google, right now, just works for me" (student 7).

The Information "Comfort Zone"

Our findings were also in line with those of earlier studies in that the students reported exhausting their searches once they had reviewed the information options they had used before rather than looking for new places to find information (Lee 2008, 214; Kim and Sin 2011, 180–84; Timmers and Glas 2010, 64; Warwick et al. 2009, 2412). Students probably only *perceived* that they had exhausted their sources, however, as four students admitted there was probably more information on their topic in the source but that they were unsure of how to locate it. Students in this sample used a relatively limited repertoire of information resources, primarily Google, news websites, friends and family, class notes, and select databases through their institution's library website, all of which appear to represent a distinct "comfort zone" in which they operated. Students tended to describe a linear process as they worked through their selected resources for information, starting at their preferred information resource—for all but one, Google—and proceeding to their next favored resource when no more satisfactory options could be found (students 1 and 3–11). They reported that when they felt they had enough information (usually, the minimum number of required sources for their paper), they simply stopped looking for any more information.

Use and Fear of Wikipedia

Michelle Twait (2005) found that undergraduate students' top criterion for finding a source useful was perceived content (students did not seem to read a source in its entirety before making these decisions), followed by familiarity with where the resource is housed (a website or database, for example). Other prominent criteria (in decreasing order of importance) were reputation or credibility; convenience; and format, type, or genre (Twait 2005, 569–70). Hur-li Lee arrived at similar findings three years later (Lee 2008, 214–16). Kyung-Sun Kim and Sei-Ching Joanna Sin (2011) studied the selection criteria students claimed to use and compared them with the methods they actually used based on characteristics of the sources they finally selected. From a list they provided as part of the study, Kim and Sin found students' favored criteria to be accuracy and trustworthiness, ease of accessibility, ease of use, cost (whether the resource is free or not), and currency. The characteristics of sources students actually used were ease of accessibility, cost (whether the resource is free or not), familiarity, ease of use, and content comprehensiveness (Kim and Sin 2011, 184–85). In all of these studies, familiarity was high on the list, and for current students, perhaps the most familiar resource is *Wikipedia*. Alison Head's more recent survey of 1,341 first-year students reports that while students describe moving away from Google and *Wikipedia* as they progress through their education, "learning to navigate their new and complex digital and print Landscape" (and struggling in the process), many others report that "they still relied on their deeply ingrained habit of using Google searches and Wikipedia, a practice that had been acceptable for research papers in high school" (Head 2013, 3). These findings mirror those revealed in our study.

Most students in our study reported that they had explicitly been discouraged or even forbidden to use *Wikipedia* as a resource of information in their writing by their high-school teachers and/or college instructors and professors. As a result, students were anxious about accessing *Wikipedia* in the course of their research, all the while feeling comfortable with the generalness of its content. Student 10 characterized the scenario this way: "*Wikipedia*'s always, like, the definition is what [Google] automatically goes to, and then I'll read through *Wikipedia*, but everyone always says don't always trust it, depending on the teacher, and so then, I'll try and find other sources." While it appears from the data that different teachers of writing feel differently about *Wikipedia*, on the whole, students perceive their teachers as disapproving of the site. This cautious use of *Wikipedia* was also reported by Lim, who observed that students use *Wikipedia* in the initial stages of their information-seeking process but fail to cite it (Lim 2009, 2200).

Engaging with Sources

Jamieson and Howard (2013) found that first-year writing students largely used academically appropriate sources in their papers (e.g., journal articles, books, book chapters, government documents, etc.), but these sources were used selectively. For example, 69 percent of the research had been drawn from the first page (46 percent) or second page (23 percent) of the source (see also Jamieson, this collection). Our pilot study further investigated both these findings by exploring the degree to which students engage with the information they choose. When asked question 8 (*How far into a source do you read before choosing something to include in your paper? Is it different for short sources and very long sources?*), students responded that they would "try" to read the entirety of the piece of information, but most admitted they limited the amount of time they spent on their essays, which subsequently limited how far they read into a source before choosing something and incorporating it into their papers. In many cases, rather than trying to find the best piece of information for their papers, students simply used the first they came across. Student 4 described some of the limitations in delving into sources, "It's just, if it's really long, I have a job, I have other homework to do, you know?" This finding is not altogether bleak, however. Students 6 and 9 both described reading their sources in their entirety. Student 9 even described printing all his sources and highlighting and annotating them.

Funneling

Question 2 on our interview guide explored why students engaged so briefly with their sources. We found that students searched in a way we describe as *funneling*. Students tended to begin their research with expansive search terms to find basic information on the subject. Toward the end of their research, they had more specific search terms and source expectations. Students tended not to browse for topics for their essays, instead choosing them *ahead* of their writing and information-search processes. Armed with a topic, students *then* engaged in browsing behavior, typically using the simplest form of their topic as their search term, such as "animal testing" (described by student 10), "religion in politics," (described by student 6) or "Johnny Depp films" (described by student 7). Only when their central search term returned too many hits or failed, in their perception, to turn up any more useful information, did students begin to add to or change their search terms.

Student 11 summed up his peers' and his own behaviors succinctly and clearly: "I tend to browse in the beginning, and then, as I get more specific in my paper, obviously, I'm going to search for more specific things to fit that exact topic." His description points to another finding of this study: students in this study largely tended to select resources that supported their predetermined stance or approach to a topic rather than letting the information they found in the course of their search process shape their perspectives. This finding is especially interesting given the earlier finding that students tend to select topics they are interested in but know little about. This apparent contradiction is worrisome because if this is the case, students are apparently choosing their sources out of convenience, learning little about their topics in the process of writing their essays; they are supporting limited repertoires of knowledge with limited information, found in limited *resources* of information, a finding that confirms what researchers such as Twait (2005, 567–73) and Lee (2008, 211–19) found.

Social Information Seeking

The students in Twait's qualitative study reported that in their information searches, they infrequently or never consulted people—whether friends, faculty, or librarians (Twait 2005, 571); however, others have found that students do appear to consult their peers during their information-seeking pursuits and do so more often than consulting faculty and librarians (Baro, Onyenania, and Osaheni 2010, 114–15; O'Brien and Symons 2005, 421). This finding may be the result of local contexts or the fact that not all students studied were first-year students, but it is an issue worth further exploration.

In our interviews, students readily and easily discussed the people involved in their information seeking, and when they chose to talk to people for information, students went to family members and friends unless being prompted or required to contact members outside their social circles by their teachers. Student 10, when asked whether she would cold-contact someone without being required to by an instructor, firmly replied that she would not; she would only contact friends and family in the course of her usual information seeking.

Students reported that they liked referring to friends and family members for a variety of reasons. Student 4 observed that his family members could be trusted to know good information on the kinds of subjects he tended to write on. While it was expected that some of the students would consult information professionals such as librarians and library information specialists, only one student, student 8, reported working with an information professional in the course of seeking information for her papers. Given that students tended to exploit information resources they had been taught about in academic settings, it is possible additional guidance and instruction is needed from writing instructors to guide their students to information professionals who could help them immensely in their search process (Head and Eisenberg 2009, 15).

Avoiding Plagiarism

A key finding of the Citation Project (e.g., Howard, Serviss, and Rodrigue 2010, 177–92) was that students tend to patchwrite (see Jamieson's "The Evolution of the Citation Project," this volume). In her 1993 article, Rebecca Moore Howard introduced the term "patchwriting," describing it as "copying from a source text and then deleting some words, altering grammatical structures, or plugging in one-for-one synonym substitutes" and arguing that patchwriting is "a valuable composing strategy in which the writer engages in entry-level manipulation of new ideas and vocabulary" (Howard 1993, 1). She called on faculty and administrators to stop classifying patchwriting as plagiarism, a lead the Citation Project and the Council of Writing Program Administrators have followed, classifying it as "misuse of sources" but not plagiarism (Council of Writing Program Administrators 2003). Our interviews reveal that this distinction has not reached the majority of students.

Students reported that they are well aware that they should not plagiarize and that they make clear attempts to avoid plagiarizing but struggle to incorporate sources, a finding also reported by Head (2013). Like the students in Head's study, students in this study reported needing a fuller understanding of the distinctions among quoting, paraphrasing, and summarizing sources and how to cite them. We asked students whether they tended to quote, summarize, or paraphrase in their writing (question 10). If they responded that they summarized or paraphrased, we probed the nature of that practice further by asking how much of the original sentence structure they preserved when they did so. Approximately half the students described keeping the original structure of the source to a large degree (generally defined as misuse of sources). One notable case was a student who believed that simply changing words in a sentence was plagiarism but still didn't fully understand how to paraphrase. Student 9 stated, "I completely change it when I paraphrase, I mean, it's plagiarism if you don't and so I just usually completely change it, and I won't cite 'em, I'll just use it, the information I found, and I'll just completely write it in my own words." Student 9 also stated, "I don't really like to summarize, 'cause I never really got how that . . . I know how to summarize it, but I never really got how you cite that." While students on the whole seemed to understand the proper way to attribute quotes, their understanding of summary and paraphrase was highly nuanced and seemingly incomplete.

CONCLUSION

While some of the findings of this study are inconclusive because of the small sample, many of our findings align themselves with and expand upon existing perspectives of undergraduates and first-year writers, suggesting that earlier research findings and findings from other small studies are generalizable in key areas. We hope others will build upon our research and expand the study to more students, especially first-year students, and more institution types. Such research should help key stakeholders, such as librarians, instructors, administrators, and developers of textbooks and digital products, identify important trends among this unique user group and develop appropriate pedagogies, policies, and resources. But in the meantime, we believe these findings will be of assistance to faculty and librarians helping first-year composition students develop their information-literacy skills, given that these students are still at the start of their academic careers.

Acknowledgments

The authors would like to thank the eleven students who volunteered their time and thoughts and Russ Winn for inviting his students' participation. We are also indebted to Brock Dethier and Keith Gibson for their terrific feedback on early drafts of this chapter.

Note

1. Due to differences in usage of terminology between the humanities and information sciences, this chapter defines *resource* as an encompassing source of information, such as a search engine or a database, and a *source* as a single published genre or piece of information such as a person, journal article, book, or webpage.

APPENDIX 7.A
Interview Guide

These appendices may be downloaded from https://upcolorado.com/utah-state-university-press/item/3188-points-of-departure and used or modified for teaching or research purposes with attribution.

1. The first thing I want you to share is a story. Think about research papers, that is, the essays where you have to incorporate outside sources. Think about ones you have written for your college-level English courses. If it helps, think about the next essay you have to write, too. Tell me the story of what happens from the time you get the research paper assignment to the time you turn it in. *As necessary during the story, inquire about where information/research/sources came from.*

2. When you do research for your English papers, do you go in search of something specific, or do you tend to browse until you find something? Can you try and describe what your search process is like from beginning, when you start looking for information, to end, when you have everything you need?

3. Generally speaking, where else do you go in terms of gathering research or sources for your English papers, thinking about both people and places?

    List sources here:
      a. Are there any other places you go for information? For instance, digital libraries, databases, library websites, news sites, Wikipedia, or other websites, for example?
      b. I'm not familiar with _____ (information place). Can you describe it briefly for me?

4. Why do you use _____ (source) for your writing research? (What is it about those information places that you find useful? What is special about them?) *Go through each source student mentioned, asking why student uses each source.*

5. How did you find out about these sources of information? (Were you taught how to use them? Did you hear about them from friends or roommates? Forums? Study guides? Just happen upon them?) *Go through each of the sources the student volunteers to learn how s/he found out about them.*

6. When you come across a potential source for your paper, how do you know if a source is useful or not? How do you know if a source is credible?

7. When you choose a source for your paper, what makes you decide to keep it or move on without using it?

8. How far into a source do you read before choosing something to include in your paper? Is it different for short sources and very long sources?
9. During the search process, do you tend to prefer primary sources or secondary sources? To clarify, primary sources are the first reports on data or original documents, and secondary sources tend to interpret, analyze, summarize, or paraphrase the original information. A medical study from Princeton would be the primary source, where WebMD, Wikipedia, and news articles would be the secondary sources.
    a. Why do you prefer primary/secondary sources? What is it about them that is helpful to you when you research and when you write?
10. When you add the source to your writing, how do you typically do it? Do you quote it, summarize it, paraphrase it, reword it? (*Whichever one(s) the participant chooses, ask them how they define that: How do you define summarizing?*) If they mention summarizing or paraphrasing, ask: When you summarize or paraphrase, do you keep some of the sentence structure of the original, do you move things around and change it completely, or what does that look like when you do it?
    a. (Ask why they do it that way, if it's not built into their answer.)
11. Is there anything else about the information you use as a writing student that would be helpful for people to understand?

References

Attfield, Simon, Ann Blandford, and John Dowell. 2003. "Information Seeking in the Context of Writing: A Design Psychology Interpretation of the 'Problematic Situation.'" *Journal of Documentation* 59 (4): 430–53. http://dx.doi.org/10.1108/00220410310485712.

Baro, Emmanuel E., George O. Onyenania, and Oni Osaheni. 2010. "Information Seeking Behaviour of Undergraduate Students in the Humanities in Three Universities in Nigeria." *South African Journal of Library and Information Science* 76 (2): 109–17. http://dx.doi.org/10.7553/76-2-74.

Boyatzis, Richard E. 1998. *Transforming Qualitative Information: Thematic Analysis and Code Development*. Thousand Oaks, CA: SAGE.

Boyd, Andrew. 2004. "Multi-Channel Information Seeking: A Fuzzy Conceptual Model." *Aslib Proceedings* 56 (2): 81–88. http://dx.doi.org/10.1108/00012530410529440.

Callinan, Joanne E. 2005. "Information-Seeking Behaviour of Undergraduate Biology Students: A Comparative Analysis of First Year and Final Year Students in University College Dublin." *Library Review* 54 (2): 86–99. http://dx.doi.org/10.1108/00242530510583039.

Council of Writing Program Administrators. 2003. "Defining and Avoiding Plagiarism: The WPA Statement on Best Practices." http://wpacouncil.org/positions/WPAplagiarism.pdf.

Downs, Douglas, and Elizabeth Wardle. 2007. "Teaching about Writing, Righting Misconceptions: (Re) Envisioning 'First-Year Composition' as 'Introduction to Writing Studies.'" *College Composition and Communication* 58 (4): 552–84.

Fescemyer, Kathy. 2000. "Information-Seeking Behavior of Undergraduate Geography Students." *Research Strategies* 17 (4): 307–17. http://dx.doi.org/10.1016/S0734-3310(01)00054-4.

Fisher, Karen, and Heidi Julien. 2009. "Information Behavior." *Annual Review of Information Science & Technology* 43 (1): 317–58. http://dx.doi.org/10.1002/aris.2009.1440430114.

Head, Alison. 2013. "Project Information Literacy: What Can Be Learned about the Information-Seeking Behaviors of Today's College Students?" In *Imagine, Innovate, Inspire: The Proceedings of the ACRL 2013 Conference*, edited by Dawn M. Mueller, 472–82. Chicago: ALA http://dx.doi.org/10.2139/ssrn.2281511.

Head, Alison J., and Michael B. Eisenberg. 2009. "Finding Context: What Today's College Students Say about Conducting Research in the Digital Age." Project Information Literacy Progress Report, University of Washington's Information School. http://www.projectinfolit.org/uploads/2/7/5/4/27541717/2009_final_report.pdf.

Hendley, Michelle. 2012. "Citation Behavior of Undergraduate Students: A Study of History, Political Science, and Sociology Papers." *Behavioral & Social Sciences Librarian* 31 (2): 96–111. http://dx.doi.org/10.1080/01639269.2012.679884.

Howard, Rebecca Moore. 1993. "A Plagiarism Pentimento." *Journal of Teaching Writing* 11 (3): 233–46.

Howard, Rebecca Moore, Tricia Serviss, and Tanya K. Rodrigue. 2010. "Writing from Sources, Writing from Sentences." *Writing & Pedagogy* 2 (2): 177–92. http://dx.doi.org/10.1558/wap.v2i2.177.

Jamieson, Sandra. 2016. "What the Citation Project Tells Us About Information Literacy in College Composition." In *Information Literacy: Research and Collaboration across Disciplines*, edited by Barbara D'Angelo, Sandra Jamieson, Barry Maid, and Janice R. Walker, 117–41. Perspectives in Writing Series. Fort Collins, CO: WAC Clearing House and University Press of Colorado.

Jamieson, Sandra, and Rebecca Moore Howard. 2011. "A Statistical Profile of 160 Students' Researched Writing, with Implications for Teaching." Paper presented at the Conference on College Composition and Communication, Atlanta, GA, April.

Jamieson, Sandra, and Rebecca Moore Howard. 2013. "Sentence-Mining: Uncovering the Amount of Reading and Reading Comprehension in College Writers' Researched Writing." In *The New Digital Scholar: Exploring and Enriching the Research and Writing Practices of NextGen Students*, edited by Randall McClure and James Purdy, 109–32. Medford, NJ: Information Today.

Kim, Kyung-Sun, and Sei-Ching Joanna Sin. 2011. "Selecting Quality Sources: Bridging the Gap Between the Perception and Use of Information Sources." *Journal of Information Science* 37 (2): 178–88. http://dx.doi.org/10.1177/0165551511400958.

Lee, Hur-Li. 2008. "Information Structures and Undergraduate Students." *Journal of Academic Librarianship* 34 (3): 211–19. http://dx.doi.org/10.1016/j.acalib.2008.03.004.

Li, Yongyan, and Christine Pearson Casanave. 2012. "Two First-year Students' Strategies for Writing from Sources: Patchwriting or Plagiarism?" *Journal of Second Language Writing* 21 (2): 165–80. http://dx.doi.org/10.1016/j.jslw.2012.03.002.

Lim, Sook. 2009. "How and Why Do College Students Use Wikipedia?" *Journal of the American Society for Information Science* 60 (11): 2189–202. http://dx.doi.org/10.1002/asi.21142.

McClure, Randall, and Kellian Clink. 2009. "How Do You Know That?: An Investigation of Student Research Practices in the Digital Age." *Portal: Libraries and the Academy* 9 (1): 115–32. http://dx.doi.org/10.1353/pla.0.0033.

O'Brien, Heather L., and Sonya Symons. 2005. "The Information Behaviors and Preferences of Undergraduate Students." *Research Strategies* 20 (4): 409–23. http://dx.doi.org/10.1016/j.resstr.2006.12.021.

Rowland, Fytton, and Iris Rubbert. 2001. "An Evaluation of the Information Needs and Practices of Part-Time and Distance-Learning Students in the Context of Educational and Social Change through Lifelong Learning." *Journal of Documentation* 57 (6): 741–62. http://dx.doi.org/10.1108/EUM0000000007105.

Rowlands, Ian, David Nicholas, Peter Williams, Paul Huntington, Maggie Fieldhouse, Barrie Gunter, Richard Withey, Hamid R. Jamali, Tom Dobrowolski, and Carol Tenopir. 2008. "The Google Generation: The Information Behaviour of the Researcher of the Future." *Aslib Proceedings* 60 (4): 290–310. http://dx.doi.org/10.1108/00012530810887953.

Schroeder, Charles C. 1993. "New Students—New Learning Styles." *Change: The Magazine of Higher Learning* 25 (5): 21–26. http://dx.doi.org/10.1080/00091383.1993.9939900.

Timmers, Caroline F., and Cees A. W. Glas. 2010. "Developing Scales for Information-Seeking Behaviour." *Journal of Documentation* 66 (1): 46–69. http://dx.doi.org/10.1108/00220411011016362.

Twait, Michelle. 2005. "Undergraduate Students' Source Selection Criteria: A Qualitative Study." *Journal of Academic Librarianship* 31 (6): 567–73. http://dx.doi.org/10.1016/j.acalib.2005.08.008.

Valentine, Barbara. 1993. "Undergraduate Research Behavior: Using Focus Groups to Generate Theory." *Journal of Academic Librarianship* 19 (5): 300–4. http://dx.doi.org/10.1016/0099-1333(93)90026-2.

Walker, John. 2010. "Measuring Plagiarism: Researching What Students Do, Not What They Say They Do." *Studies in Higher Education* 35 (1): 41–59. http://dx.doi.org/10.1080/03075070902912994.

Warwick, Claire, John Rimmer, Ann Blandford, Jeremy Gow, and George Buchanan. 2009. "Cognitive Economy and Satisficing in Information Seeking: A Longitudinal Study of Undergraduate Information Behavior." *Journal of the American Society for Information Science and Technology* 60 (12): 2402–415. http://dx.doi.org/10.1002/asi.21179.

Chapter 8
JUST READ THE ASSIGNMENT
Using Course Documents to Analyze Research Pedagogy

Elizabeth Kleinfeld

ABSTRACT

This chapter discusses a pilot study born from teacher-research methods that examines how course documents in first-year writing courses might shape student ideas about source use. Building on Dan Melzer's (2003; 2009) analytic method, publicly available syllabi, assignments, and handouts were collected from twelve universities and twelve community colleges and then coded for attributes related to source selection, use, and documentation, as well as allusions to plagiarism and academic integrity. The findings expand and confirm those by Head and Eisenberg's (2010) analysis of the guidance course handouts provide to college students to facilitate their understanding of the threshold concepts central to information literacy and academic research. This chapter suggests how future researchers can refine the methods of initial research to further explore how course documents frame research and writing from sources for students and explicitly or implicitly move them beyond essential-knowledge thresholds. Initial findings support other research suggesting that course documents may contradict what instructors value about academic research and writing from sources.

INTRODUCTION

In 2009, the Metropolitan State University of Denver's (MSU Denver) English department volunteered to become one of sixteen institutions that contributed first-year composition (FYC) students' research papers to the Citation Project's data pool. The preliminary findings of the Citation Project resonated with the composition program's leadership, and as an emerging Hispanic-serving institution (HSI) with modified open enrollment that attracts many first-generation college students and nontraditional students, we were eager to learn how our students' writing compared with the writing of students at other institutions.

One of the benefits of being a participating institution in the Citation Project study was receiving a report describing the data from each individual campus in comparison to the national data. When our report arrived in December 2011, we were relieved to see our students did no "worse" than other students in the data pool. We were heartened to see our students weren't doing anything students at better-funded institutions weren't also doing. Overall, our results were in line with the national findings, showing that MSU Denver students struggle with locating sources long enough to treat subjects in depth, seldom summarize, and overly rely on direct quotation (Jamieson and Howard 2011). Like faculty nationwide who have seen the Citation Project phase one findings, I was not surprised, but I was very, very disappointed to see quantifiable evidence that students, as Howard likes to say when she presents the findings, "have very little of their own to say."

Anecdotally, I find students generally give me what I ask for; if they submit work significantly different than expected, I need to examine my own assignment to discover how I might have miscued students. When I look at the Citation Project findings, I therefore ask myself, "Is there anything in our research-project assignments and handouts that could be contributing to how our students use sources?" My initial hypothesis that handouts and assignments may be miscuing students is supported by Alison Head and Michael Eisenberg (2010) of Project Information Literacy, who reveal that instructors' written guidelines and assignments are extremely important in how students write from sources. They characterize handouts as "a roadmap" of the research process for students, pointing out that students are much more likely to have an assignment sheet with them than the course syllabus as they complete an assignment (Head and Eisenberg 2010, 23), but they focus on handouts only. To investigate how the combination of course documents frames source use for students, I designed a pilot study of course documents—including syllabi, assignments, and handouts—from FYW classes. The study is not designed to be a complete rhetorical or content analysis of the course documents; rather, it focuses specifically on the instruction offered to students on source citation and closely related matters through teaching artifacts. The research questions guiding the study include:

- What language is used in syllabi and research-project assignments to describe what research is and its purposes?

- How are summary, paraphrase, and quotation described? Is one technique recommended over others, and if so, is a rationale provided?
- How do course documents indicate the relative value of different aspects of writing from sources, such as judging the appropriateness of a source; using summary, paraphrase, and/or quotation; and documenting sources?

Taken together, these questions get at the issue of how citation and source use are constructed and reinforced for students through course documents, expanding the work of Head and Eisenberg (2010) and adding to our understanding of how to respond to the findings of the Citation Project.

FRAMEWORK

In "The Aims and Process of the Research Paper," Schwegler and Shamoon (1982) suggest there is a "considerable difference between the way students view the research paper (and have been taught to view it) and the way most college instructors and other researchers view it" (818). The authors indicate that while students tend to understand research papers as informative, instructors have a much more sophisticated view, believing "the aim is to test a theory, to follow up on previous research, or to explore a problem posed by other research or by events" (819) and to be "interpretive" (820). When Schwegler and Shamoon (1982) studied research articles written by faculty, they found that research by others was cited to "provide an intellectual context for the study" (822), while students looked for sources that "support an argumentative thesis" (822).

Barbara Valentine (2001) found that while faculty who write with sources seek to theorize and build on the work of others, students are motivated less by a desire to build and share knowledge than to earn good grades. In fact, Valentine found students "focus much time and energy on trying to figure out what the professor wants" (108), noting that instructional artifacts, including syllabi, assignments, and handouts, were key pieces of evidence students relied on to discern what the professor wants.

In studying faculty assumptions about research processes, Gloria Leckie (1996) found that faculty imagine their students will conduct research much the same way they do: by following what Leckie calls the "expert researcher model." Faculty are expert researchers and are so removed from being undergraduates that they no longer remember how they researched when they were students. Leckie describes the expert researcher model as one that requires a long process of acculturation, an in-depth knowledge of the discipline, awareness of important scholars working in particular areas, participation in a system of informal scholarly communication, and a view of research as a non-sequential, non-linear process with a large degree of ambiguity and serendipity. (202)

Alvarez and Dimmock (2007) also found faculty expect their students to understand research the same way they do. In fact, Leckie (1996) found, students see research as an information-gathering exercise and have none of the background knowledge about which people and ideas are important in the field they are researching. The results of these beliefs are revealed in the Citation Project papers.

Conversations with my colleagues about the Citation Project data for our institution focused on the student output (Jamieson and Howard 2011), and many faculty expressed surprise at the fact that the data reveal students relying on quotation over summary while faculty report that in their own writing from sources, they tend to rely on summary over quotation. The findings of Alvarez and Dimmock (2007) and Leckie (1996) about disparity in faculty and student beliefs about the research process seemed, then, at least at my institution, to extend to the process of incorporating source material as well as identifying it.

Research like that by Alvarez and Dimmock (2007) and Leckie (1996) relies on interviews and focus groups, while the Citation Project research (Jamieson and Howard 2013) focused on student output. My research examines faculty input in terms of course documents, extending work done by Melzer (2003; 2009) and Head and Eisenberg (2010), who focused only on assignments and only on students in WAC courses. Dan Melzer (2003) conducted two studies of writing assignments from writing-across-the-curriculum courses at colleges and universities across the country, one of eight hundred assignments (2003) and another study of twenty-one hundred assignments (2009). Head and Eisenberg (2010) also studied writing assignments from across the curriculum, but they focused specifically on assignments for researched writing. While these studies examined assignments from non-FYW courses, I focus exclusively on FYW course documents, and I collected more than just assignments.

METHOD

I began my research with a single-institution study in which I examined the syllabi, assignments, and other instructional artifacts routinely collected by MSU Denver's composition program. I studied materials collected from fifty-six sections of our FYW writing-from-sources course during the 2010–11 academic year and developed a coding system that allowed me to code each document for attributes and features related to source selection, use, and documentation, as well as for more generalized treatment of plagiarism and academic integrity. These attributes and features grew out of a series of conversations with composition faculty at MSU Denver about the Citation Project results; I asked them to think about how their research experiences seem to contrast with their students' research experiences. Because the Citation Project does not identify participating institutions individually in their data analysis, I could not treat my own study as a further investigation of their findings. Instead, I used the same national/local comparison strategy deployed by the Citation Project to design my study of course artifacts from multiple sites. If a sample including course materials from a broad range of institutions showed traits roughly similar to the MSU Denver course materials, the study's findings would be more broadly applicable and therefore more useful to others.

Data Collection

To gather documents from universities, I used a variation on Melzer's (2003) method. Like him, I started at the University of Texas at Austin's online index of US universities by state. I selected the last institution listed for each state and located a syllabus for an FYC class involving writing from sources. In the instances in which I couldn't find one, I went on to the next-to-last institution listed, and so on. Once I found a course, I collected the syllabus, the first three writing-from-sources assignments I could locate, and any other materials available online for that course that mentioned *research, documentation, sources, summary, paraphrase,* or *quotation.* I kept documents from each course together in a packet. This constituted the first set of documents. I was unable to find documents connected to a writing-from-sources FYW class for one state, so this set represented materials from forty-nine states and institutions. Materials collected were used from 2008 to 2011.

Then I collected materials from community colleges using the University of Texas at Austin's online index of US community colleges by state and the same selection method as I used with the index of US universities. According to the American Association of Community Colleges, 44 percent of all US undergraduates attend a community college, so looking at documents from community college FYW courses is crucial if we are to gain a clear picture of the cumulative effect of course materials on FYW students. I was unable to find materials from three states, so the community college set represents materials from forty-seven states and institutions. Materials collected were used from 2007 to 2011. Because all materials were publicly available on the Internet, the MSU Denver IRB determined the study to be exempt from review.

Data Preparation

A research assistant removed all identifying information from the documents. I then used a random-number generator to select twelve packets of documents out of each set for analysis. I identified each document only by set, not by state, institution, or instructor. I examined the randomized pool of documents for clues about what we may be communicating to students about writing from sources and ways that communication might contribute to the type of source use the Citation Project found. Table 8.1 catalogues the genres of the 210 documents I analyzed across each data set.

Before I discuss how I coded documents, I want to acknowledge an important aspect of my collection method. Like the Citation Project researchers, I have adhered meticulously to the CCCC Guidelines for the Ethical Conduct of Research in Composition Studies (National Council of Teachers of English 2003). I have taken precautions to, as Kirsch and Mortensen (1999) suggest, "avoid embarrassing or otherwise stigmatizing participants in ways not covered by federal laws and regulations" (4–5). In adherence to the CCCC guidelines, I have "describe[d] the documents in the data pool] in ways that are fair and serious, cause no harm, and protect privacy." For example, I have chosen not to reveal whether a document I mention below is from a university or a community college; I identify which set a document came from only when necessary or obvious. When I describe documents below, I avoid quotation or any paraphrase that could potentially be linked to the instructor.

Despite the extra precautions that had to be taken with a nonvoluntary sample, I thought it important to the validity of this study that I examine documents that were as "authentic" as possible. The benefit of this type of data collection is that it circumvents the Hawthorne Effect in which voluntary submission of data may inspire a participant to share only those artifacts that create a flattering portrait of the participant or institution. While there may have been documents handed to students in class that were not made available online, and while undoubtedly the research process was the subject of in-class and perhaps one-on-one instruction and discussion, my focus on research documents that

Table 8.1. Summary of data pool

	Syllabi	Assignments	Handouts	Courses	Instructors	Institutions
SET ONE: universities	12	36	14	12	12	12
SET TWO: community colleges	12	36	28	12	12	12
TOTALS	24	72	42	24	24	24

students could access online is supported by Head and Eisenberg's (2010) finding that students are guided primarily by written assignments as they conduct research (23).

Data Coding

I coded each document for attributes and features related to source selection, use, and documentation, as well as more generalized treatment of plagiarism and academic integrity (see Appendix 8.A). In total, I coded for eleven different attributes and features within eight general coding categories. Two of the features I coded are very similar to a feature Head and Eisenberg coded. I coded for whether a type or quality of source was specified; Head and Eisenberg (2010) coded for whether specific research resources were specified. And I coded for whether a specific number of sources was required and whether a specific number of quotations was required; Head and Eisenberg (2010) looked for whether a specific number of total citations was required. Otherwise, the features I coded for are quite different from those Head and Eisenberg looked for, largely because their study examines how research is assigned in general across the curriculum, while I studied how source use is described and assigned in FYW courses focused on writing from sources. I discuss each coded attribute and some examples below (see Appendix 8.B for my coding guidelines).

Coding Category 1: Purpose of Conducting Academic Research
The first feature I coded in the 210 documents was whether the purpose of academic research was explained. Explanations of the purposes of academic research ranged from simply stating that students need to find sources to back up arguments to discussing the more complex concept of learning about an issue and the reasons behind different people's positions on the issue. If the purpose of research was addressed, I indicated in the coding the extent of the explanation.

Coding Category 2: Statement on Academic Integrity or Plagiarism

Focusing only on the syllabi, I looked for a statement about plagiarism or academic integrity. If I found a statement, I compared it with the institution's policy or statement as published in their student handbook or code of conduct. If a statement existed, I coded it in one of three ways: present and original, meaning the language did not adhere closely to the institution's policy or statement; present and cited, meaning it quoted from the institution's policy or statement and provided a citation; or present and unattributed, meaning it featured language from the institution's policy or statement but without attribution.

I did not code for how useful the statements would be for helping students understand, identify, or avoid plagiarism or breaches of academic integrity. Several examples among all three data sets had statements I categorized as original that simply indicated plagiarism would not be tolerated without defining plagiarism. The usefulness of such statements would be an interesting area for further research.

Coding Category 3: Source Specifications

As I looked at assignments, the first questions I coded for were, "Is the number of sources required specified? If so, is a reason for that number or type given?" I tracked instances according to each course packet, not individual assignments, so whether a packet included one, two, or three assignments that specified number of sources, it shows up as only one instance (a typical assignment might read "the final paper should include eight credible sources," so I coded the course as assigning a paper with a specific number of sources). I did not note the number of sources for each assignment or course because the types of assignments varied from short summaries to midlength syntheses to full-fledged research papers, so meaningful conclusions cannot be drawn from knowing what the average number of required sources was across such a disparate range of assignments. About half the assignments that specified how many sources to use also specified the type of source, such as, "Your sources should include at least one book and two articles from peer-reviewed journals."

Roughly 88 percent of all packets featured an assignment that included an adjective describing the quality of sources to be used, such as "credible," "academic," "reliable," or "current," or they described sources that could not be used, such as "articles from the popular press," *Wikipedia*, or "sources with no author listed." None of the assignments defined the adjectives used to describe the quality or explained why certain sources were off limits. Several assignments referenced class discussions that probably did define the adjectives or explain why some sources should not be used, such as, "As we discussed in class last week, only credible sources should be used."

Coding Category 4: Treatment of Summary, Paraphrase, and Quotation

Next, I looked at whether/how the terms *summary*, *paraphrase*, and *quotation* were explained or defined in assignments and/or handouts. Again, I counted any number of instances per packet as one instance. One handout, for example, explained that quotations should not be used to convey information. Another handout explained that every source citation, whether it is a summary, paraphrase, or quotation, should expound upon an idea presented by the writer.

There were several handouts that included lists of traits of effective summaries and/or paraphrases. One typical handout had a bulleted list of eight things a paraphrase should do, including being written in original language, being about the same length as the passage being paraphrased, being integrated smoothly into the paper, and citing the source.

Coding Category 5: How to Use Research to Support a Point

Every packet included one or more assignment that asked students to use "research to support [their] arguments," but only 13 percent explained what that meant or how to do it.

Many assignments directed students to "properly support all points with outside sources," or "support all opinions with fact." Several assignments did indicate how students should use research to support their points; for example, one explained that a research paper must go beyond being a collection of other people's ideas and should use the ideas of others to "verify, clarify, and support" the writer's ideas. The assignment then gives an annotated example of a "citation sandwich," with a signal phrase, a paraphrase from a source, and an explanation of how the paraphrase connects to the student writer's claim.

Coding Category 6: Excessive Research

Excessive research is the term I use to describe an idea modeled on Nancy Welch's (1997) concept of "excessive revision." Welch envisions the teaching of revision less as a narrowing and focusing process and more as a process of "getting restless" with a draft's initial meanings and looking for alternatives, "questioning the ideal of the . . . complete, contained, and disciplined text" (165). In this sense, Welch uses "excessive" not to mean too much of something but rather to mean more than the minimum needed. I extend Welch's idea of excessive revision to the idea of excessive research: helping students to see the initial sources they're drawn to as starting points and to resist the urge to immediately narrow and focus on the first few sources located. Excessive research results in more sources consulted and read as well as a longer, more complicated research process.

I looked at all the course documents I collected for any indication that excessive research was encouraged. One reference to excessive research was in an assignment that asked students to read and analyze several sources before selecting the best one to use for that assignment. Another assignment encouraged students to arrange several interviews even though the assignment only required that one be referenced in the final product.

Coding Category 7: Generative Use of Sources

I looked at assignments and handouts for references to generative source use, that is, using the Works Cited list of an article to find more sources. One assignment that encouraged generative use of sources directed students to locate two sources mentioned in a source's footnotes or bibliography. Another advised students to read all sources with an eye toward finding source ideas for future research projects.

Coding Category 8: Attribution of Borrowed Material

Because I've seen unattributed material distributed in classes I've observed, I wondered whether any of the packets would include unattributed material, such as handouts photocopied from textbooks without any bibliographic information included. However, none of the material I coded included unattributed borrowed material.

DISCUSSION OF METHOD

The collection of materials posted and circulating online came with its own problems. Many materials were several years old, and many had no date indications, but judging from the textbook editions those syllabi listed, I could assume the materials were five to ten years old. I recommend to anyone considering a similar study that only materials created within the last three years be included in the data pool to ensure the currency of pedagogical methods reflected. None of the materials I collected, for example, featured multimodal, multigenre, or social media-focused approaches to teaching first-year writing, all of which seem to now be more mainstream. Because writing from sources in genres other than the traditional research paper can feature source use and citation markedly different from the traditional research paper, courses that focus on writing in different modes or genres or for social media may also emphasize different aspects of source use and citation.

Another issue that came up in the collection of materials was labeling what kinds of material I was looking at. I kept the syllabus, assignments, and other materials (which I called *handouts*) for each course together in a packet. Occasionally, it was not completely obvious whether a document was an assignment or a handout. I considered a document to be an assignment if it asked students to produce a particular, discrete composition to submit for a specified number of points. I considered everything that wasn't a syllabus or an assignment a handout. A researcher interested in replicating this study might consider further categorizing handouts by genre. For example, handouts that are model documents or mentor texts could be considered a separate category from handouts that provide instructions for doing something, such as using a word processor's references function.

I would also recommend that researchers working with collected syllabi, assignments, and/or handouts interview instructors. This was a feature of Head and Eisenberg's (2010) research, and I believe being able to talk to instructors about their rationales for particular assignment requirements would offer valuable insights.

My analysis is based on a limited picture of the instruction students in a writing-from-sources course might receive. As noted above, I assume many of the students would have received other documents not available online, and many were also assigned textbook readings. In addition, class discussions and lectures and other scaffolding activities may also have helped prepare them for their research assignments. Analysis of the official documents of the class made publicly available via the Internet provides a narrower artifact base, but it also allows a focus on the documents that legitimate the research process for all students; we write down what we consider to be particularly important. A student may miss a class and therefore that day's lecture or activity, but the information we put in our syllabi, assignments, and handouts gets to every student and, as Head and Eisenberg (2010) show, guides them as they work.

FINDINGS

Because these are not the syllabi, assignments, and handouts necessarily connected to the classes and students whose work was coded in the Citation Project study of first-year writing, the analysis doesn't explain the Citation Project findings, but it does provide a context. Similarities and themes emerged from my data pool that seem to indicate larger trends; limitations in how the documents, as a group, portray research and its purposes coupled with the Citation Project findings at least suggest the need for an expanded pedagogy as well as additional research.

Students Are Asked to Research Differently from How Experienced Researchers Operate

A gap exists between what we teach students in FYW writing-from-sources courses and what experienced writers writing from sources know and do. The course documents I studied did not steer students toward making the kinds of choices and developing the kinds of practices experienced researchers deploy.

As I discussed in the literature review above, faculty researchers write from sources to test theories, extend research, and interpret (Schwegler and Shamoon 1982; Valentine 2001), and faculty researchers expect their students to use the same research model they use, what Leckie (1996) terms the "expert researcher model." My own experience facilitating workshops for professors who are writing from sources indicates that experienced writers have a very clear purpose not only for conducting their research but also for writing about it. This contrasts dramatically with the fact that only 17 percent of curricular packets indicated a clear purpose for conducting research. The professors I've worked with conduct excessive research, gathering many more sources than they will ultimately use, and never have I heard a professor say they were aiming for a particular number of sources; this contrasts with the fact that only 4 percent of packets held documents that encouraged students to conduct excessive research, and 88 percent specified the number of sources to use without specifying a reason. And finally, the professors I've worked with use sources generatively, using each source's list of references to locate more sources, while only 4 percent of the packets indicated that students are taught to use their sources generatively.

COIK

COIK is an acronym used by technical communicators to describe information that is clear only if known, shorthand for information that only makes sense to someone with prior knowledge of the topic being discussed. I saw many instances of COIK as I studied the packets, the most obvious being what it means to use sources for support. A student who doesn't know how to use sources for support will not likely find this exhortation helpful.

Some other examples of COIK I saw had to do with the oversimplification of differences between sources like *Wikipedia* and academic peer-reviewed journal articles. A handout that states that only peer-reviewed journal articles should be used for sources because only they are "verified" implies that peer review is a fact-verification process. Similarly, an assignment telling students to use only "credible" sources rather than reference works might imply to some students that not all (or any) reference works are credible.

No Sense of Priority

Many course documents did not indicate a sense of priority among concepts. For example, very few documents noted that in most cases, quotation should be used more sparingly than summary and paraphrase. I saw many lists of grading criteria and assignment requirements that did not clearly indicate any priority among the listed items. For example, one list of eighteen grading criteria for a researched argument presented formatting and sentence-level concerns in the first half of the list and then the tenth item referred to synthesizing sources smoothly, the eleventh item referred to using research to support points, the twelfth item referred to source attribution, and so on. The logic of that ordering was not explained, so many students would consider the list to have been created in order of priority while that is unlikely to have actually been the case. Many documents devoted more space to formatting information, such as font and margin sizes, than to substantive issues of source use. When we devote more space in a handout to a concept, we certainly imply to students that that concept is more important than concepts to which we devote less space.

Acontextual

Many documents presented seemingly acontexual requirements, the most obvious being a required number of sources. Eighty-eight percent of the packets included an assignment that specified a number of sources and not one single packet included an assignment that provided a rationale for that number of sources. It may be obvious to the instructor that the number of sources is an indicator of the breadth and depth of research that should be conducted, but as written in the assignments, the numbers appear to be entirely acontextual. Requiring a number of sources to be used also seems to further dim any possibility of students conducting excessive research, as I never saw any mention of gathering a particular number of sources and then selecting a smaller number to actually cite.

DISCUSSION OF FINDINGS

Although we coded for different attributes, my findings are in line with those of Head and Eisenberg, who ultimately recommend that research assignments should do more to help students understand the contexts in which research takes place. They comment that "few of the handouts in our sample peeled back the layers of the knowledge production process" (2010, 26), which is true of the documents I examined as well.

Although I did not include it in the coding, I also noticed that many syllabi listed a closed-book documentation quiz or exam in which students would need to have memorized many bibliographic formats. This is in stark contrast to what the faculty I've worked with have told me about how they document source material. Most have told me they have and use a reference guide—and more and more are telling me they use online format guides. Few report committing every documentation format to memory.[1] I would have liked to do more with this finding, but I didn't have a way to systematically code for it.

CONCLUSION

The findings of this pilot study suggest a need for more nuanced and focused pedagogy around research assignments, but further study is necessary to explore this question more broadly. This pilot study will help me fine tune the features I examine in a larger pool of documents representing a broader range of institutions. I anticipate collecting fifty to seventy-five packets of syllabi, assignments, and handouts from universities and fifty to seventy-five from community colleges, again using Melzer's method. The larger study will continue seeking to answer the questions of the pilot study, with a focus on how course documents portray the purposes of research, the value of different types of source material, and the development of research practices that will best serve students beyond the FYC classroom. If possible, it would be helpful to triangulate this research with interviews, focus groups, or surveys conducted on specific campuses and with coded papers; however, continuing to draw on, expand, and note overlaps with other published studies adds depth to my findings and suggests richer conclusions.

Note

1. In "The Faculty Problem," librarian Constance McCarthy (1985) laments that most faculty know very little about most aspects of bibliographic research, from finding sources to documenting them.

APPENDIX 8.A
Writing from Sources Syllabi Coding Sheet

These appendices may be downloaded from https://upcolorado.com/utah-state-university-press/item/3188-points-of-departure and used or modified for teaching or research purposes with attribution.

		Packet number				
Coding Category		1	2	3	4	5
1	Is the purpose of academic research unstated, stated, or explained?					
2	Is a statement on academic integrity or plagiarism nonexistent, present and original, present and cited, or present and unattributed?					
3	Is the number of sources required specified? Yes and a reason for that number is given, yes and a reason for that number is not given, or no.					
4	Is a type or quality of sources specified, yes or no?					
5	In any treatment of summary, paraphrase, and quotation, are the terms "summary," "paraphrase," and/or "quotation" defined, yes or no?					
6	In any treatment of summary, paraphrase, and quotation, is there an explanation of when to use these strategies, yes or no?					
7	Is the quantity of quotations to be used specified? Yes with a reason given, yes with no reason given, or no.					
8	Is how to use research to support a point explained?					
9	Is there any indication that excessive research is encouraged?					
10	Is there any indication that using sources generatively is encouraged?					
11	Is all borrowed material cited, yes or no?					

APPENDIX 8.B
Writing from Sources Syllabi Coding Definitions

1. The purpose of academic research is
   - stated: there is a statement that academic research should have a purpose. No accompanying discussion of possible purposes or rhetorical situations for academic research.
   - explained: 1+ sentences elaborate on purposes for academic research, including potential purposes and rhetorical situations.

2. A statement on academic integrity or plagiarism is
   - nonexistent: there is no mention of academic integrity or avoiding plagiarism.
   - present and original: there is a statement of 1+ sentences using the term "academic integrity" and/or "plagiarism" that differs from the college/university statement in both language and syntax.
   - present and cited: there is an exact word-for-word copying of all or part of college/university policy with an attribution of any sort (parenthetical, footnote, signal phrase) to the source material.
   - present and unattributed: there is an exact word-for-word copying of all or part of college/university policy without an attribution of any sort.

3. Is the number of sources required specified?
   - Yes, a number is given.
     - If so, is a reason for that number given?
       - Yes: there is an elaboration on source number that explains why that number of sources is appropriate for the rhetorical situation.
       - No.
   - No, a number is not given.

4. Is a type or quality of sources specified?
   - Yes, source type or quality is specified, either in terms of types of sources that should or should not be used. Source specifications may be particular categories of sources (peer-reviewed) or adjectives (credible).
   - No, source type or quality is not specified.

5. In any treatment of summary, paraphrase, and quotation, are the terms "summary," "paraphrase," and/or "quotation" defined?
   - Yes: a definition is offered, including synonyms and/or characteristics of effective summaries/paraphrases/quotations.
   - No.

6. In any treatment of summary, paraphrase, and quotation, is there an explanation of when to use these strategies?
    - Yes: 1+ phrases or sentences offer guidance about when to use a summary, paraphrase, or quotation.
    - No.
7. Is the quantity of quotations to be used specified?
    - Yes.
        - Is a reason provided for that number?
            - Yes: there is an elaboration on the quotation number that explains why that number of quotations is appropriate for the rhetorical situation.
            - No.
    - No.
8. Is how to use research to support a point explained?
    - Yes: 1+ sentences describe how to support a point with research, including examples and/or step-by-step instructions.
    - No.
9. Is there any indication that excessive research is encouraged?
    - Yes: There is a statement that more sources should be consulted than ultimately used.
    - No.
10. Is there any indication that using sources generatively is encouraged?
    - Yes: students are directed to use at least one source to find at least one additional source.
    - No.
11. Is all borrowed material cited?
    - Yes: all handouts that use borrowed material cite their sources with a parenthetical note, footnote, signal phrase, and/or full bibliographic entry.
    - No.

References

Alvarez, Barbara, and Nora Dimmock. 2007. "Expectations of Student Research." In *Studying Students: The Undergraduate Research Project at the University of Rochester*, edited by Nancy Foster and Susan Gibbons, 1–7. Chicago, IL: Association of College and Research Libraries.

National Council of Teachers of English. 2003. "CCCC Guidelines for the Ethical Conduct of Research in Composition Studies." ncte.org. http://www.ncte.org/cccc/resources/positions/ethicalconduct

Head, Alison J., and Michael B. Eisenberg. 2010. *Assigning Inquiry: How Handouts for Research Assignments Guide Today's College Students.* Project Information Literacy Progress Report. http://www.projectinfolit.org/uploads/2/7/5/4/27541717/pil_handout_study_finalvjuly_2010.pdf.

Jamieson, Sandra, and Rebecca Moore Howard. 2011. "Report of Citation Project Findings: Metropolitan State College of Denver in a National Context." PDF file.

Jamieson, Sandra, and Rebecca Moore Howard. 2013. "Sentence-Mining: Uncovering the Amount of Reading and Reading Comprehension in College Writers' Researched Writing." In *The New Digital Scholar: Exploring and Enriching the Research and Writing Practices of NextGen Students,* edited by Randall McClure and James Purdy, 109–32. Medford, NJ: Information Today.

Kirsch, Gesa, and Peter Mortensen. 1999. "Toward an Ethics of Research." In *Ethical Dilemmas in Feminist Research,* edited by Gesa E. Kirsch, 87–104. Albany: SUNY Press.

Leckie, Gloria J. 1996. "Desperately Seeking Citations: Uncovering Faculty Assumptions about the Undergraduate Research Process." *Journal of Academic Librarianship* 22 (3): 201–8. http://dx.doi.org/10.1016/S0099-1333(96)90059-2.

McCarthy, Constance. 1985. "The Faculty Problem." *Journal of Academic Librarianship* 11 (3): 142–45.

Melzer, Dan. 2003. "Assignments Across the Curriculum: A Survey of College Writing." *Language and Learning Across the Disciplines* 6 (1): 86–110.

Melzer, Dan. 2009. "Writing Assignments Across the Curriculum: A National Study of College Writing." *College Composition and Communication* 61 (2): 240–60.

Schwegler, Robert A., and Linda K. Shamoon. 1982. "The Aims and Process of the Research Paper." *College English* 44 (8): 817–24. http://dx.doi.org/10.2307/377338.

Valentine, Barbara. 2001. "The Legitimate Effort in Research Papers: Student Commitment versus Faculty Expectations." *Journal of Academic Librarianship* 27 (2): 107–15. http://dx.doi.org/10.1016/S0099-1333(00)00182-8.

Welch, Nancy. 1997. *Getting Restless: Rethinking Revision in Writing Instruction.* Portsmouth, NH: Heinemann.

Points of Departure 3
USING EXISTING RESEARCH TO THINK BEYOND THE LOCAL

Like the other research described in this collection, we present the chapters in this section along with their various appendices as part of the evolving research process that informs writing studies, with each serving as a potential point of departure for adaptation or development. As they plan a study or take existing research beyond preliminary, pilot, or local study, researchers can use what these chapters reveal to help them shape and refine questions, generate hypotheses to test, and replicate or revise methods and interpretations. We also hope these adaptations will be developed in ways that allow the studies to become part of larger transcontextual research with shared procedures and similarly transparent methods so others, in turn, can pick up the mantle.

As noted in the interchapter that introduces this section, what makes the research discussed in these three chapters intellectually interesting to us and, we hope, generative of further research to include other institutions, is the ways they each uncover threshold moments for the participants and offer a deeper understanding of the threshold concepts at work in writing studies and the field of information literacy. Like threshold concepts themselves, such research can be transformative, and as the interpretations of the findings become integrated into our way of thinking and doing, they change it irreversibly, "exposing the previous hidden interrelatedness" of things (Meyer and Land 2005, 373). Research into student writing, source-use practices, and information literacy might be characterized as always in some way seeking to uncover where and how students possess, resist, or have yet to incorporate specific threshold concepts and related skills, yet that research, especially

DOI: 10.7330/9781607326250.c008a

if it is empirically based, is difficult to plan and execute. The chapters in this section gesture toward further projects that are transcontextual, translocal, and data based and in so doing help us imagine such research and take us through the complicated process of developing it.

The main context for writing studies research remains the first-year writing class. It is to be found on most campuses across the United States, in both two- and four-year colleges, and the students are generally in the same college year and have experienced a similar course. Such a broad base makes possible cross-institutional research of student output (papers or reference lists) like that by the Citation Project and inputs (beliefs and practices) like those from Project Information Literacy; however, interpretation of the findings is also limited by the context. For example, many students dislike first-year writing courses and therefore do not necessarily produce their best work for the course or approach the work as we might wish, and it is possible that not all the papers studied were written by the students who submitted them (the question motivating other large-scale research by the Center for Academic Integrity). Multiple conclusions are drawn from the study of student papers, but they are based on what the writers of the paper *did* or said they did, not on what they might actually be capable of doing. The research described in these three chapters goes beyond that limitation by looking at papers produced in other contexts, asking students what they know, and exploring how instructors present information literacy to their students.

SAME QUESTION; DIFFERENT CONTEXT

In chapter 6, Lee-Ann Kastman Breuch and Brian Larson enter the tradition of writing across the curriculum to conduct research that expands our understanding of what students do in professional and technical writing courses and how it compares to what will be expected of them after graduation. Breuch and Larson take the popular IMRAD superstructure developed by John Swales and assigned in many technical and professional writing courses and use one of the rhetorical moves (Move 4: reference to previous research) to code papers written by junior- and senior-level college students for technical and professional writing courses at a single institution. Swales and others had conducted such genre analysis on published papers (Swales 1990), so Breuch and Larson replicate features of Swales's research by applying the same categories to a different context. In this way, the question they explore is both local and potentially transcontextual, but it also reveals problems with the method they developed. What could be harder than taking research that had been conducted on published papers and applying the same categories to student papers? The opportunity to compare professional and technical writing by experts and by novices seems to offer many pedagogical possibilities, yet their findings are less robust than they might have been, they tell us, precisely because they were studying writing by students. Students, it turns out, even when instructed to use a specific format (see chapter 6, Appendix 6.A), do not always do so—indeed, half the papers submitted did not use the IMRAD structure (188), meaning the rhetorical moves did not always map onto student writing. Yet *that*, in itself, is a valuable finding, as they point out, and led to productive faculty conversations on their campus.

Based on the papers they could code, Breuch and Larson report findings that are available for comparison with published papers and that might inform pedagogy and expectations on a local classroom level. They recommend against applying Swales's *collective* rhetorical moves to student papers, noting that coding for too many categories introduces too much possibility of coding error (a warning also offered based on early Citation Project coding—see chapter 1). They do suggest that future research might apply the same single category as they did and learn from their experience, and the chapter offers suggestions for those who might take up similar research. These recommendations are particularly important:

1. creating a coding guide and revising it to reflect changes (see chapter 6, Appendix 6.B);
2. narrowing a focus from the beginning rather than trying to code too many features, in their case all of the features of IMRAD (see chapter 6, Appendix 6.C);
3. revising the coding categories and unit sizes as the research proceeds and then recoding as necessary (see chapter 6, Appendix 6.D);
4. developing a method of training coders and achieving and testing inter- and intrarater reliability—an issue raised in several chapters within this collection and one that necessitates adjustment and further research into quantitative methods, especially in sociology.

SAME QUESTION; DIFFERENT METHOD

Breuch and Larson also suggest an expansion of the research to include an interview or focus-group component that would allow researchers to hear from students as well as coding their output. Other research might explore the gap between the textual features found—and not found—in technical and professional communications by students and in published writing, perhaps by conducting interviews to ascertain when professional and technical writers begin to take on the formats revealed in published writing (in college, in internships, in the workplace?) and how they learn to do so.

An example of interview-based research can be seen in chapter 7, in which Whitney Olsen and Anne Diekema discuss how they used this method to address questions about the ways students select sources. Their study also began with other research, but as they explain, rather than replicating any one single study, they designed questions "to be in dialogue with and, where relevant, to update other research" (216) in order to expand the value of those studies. Their research builds on the findings of previous studies in such a way that their findings overlap those of the earlier studies, allowing them to adapt methods from an age of primarily print literacy to take into consideration the changing notion of information-seeking in the digital age. Rather than exactly replicating questions that did not allow for the changing nature of information seeking, they describe developing questions reflecting the same areas of concern and then report their findings within the context of previous research. By using different questions to explore the same issue as previous studies, and by then mapping their results onto those previous findings, they demonstrate one way small-scale research can feed into larger-scale RAD research.

Those interested in conducting their own follow-up research using interviews and focus groups could replicate the questions used by Olsen and Diekema or use Olsen and Diekema's findings as another starting point for revised questions and further interpretation. Future researchers could also more intentionally place these and other findings within the threshold categories identified by the ACRL and use those as a starting point for questions. The method of coding findings based on the concepts that arise from studying transcripts is valuable in such research, but research that seeks to replicate this study might benefit from starting with the categories used by Olsen and Diekema and using them to explore findings within the research's framework, developing additional categories if necessary. Based on what Olsen and Diekema learned as they developed and modified their research, their chapter offers advice to those who might follow them in this line of inquiry, along with examples (in the appendix) of artifacts that might be replicable. Their advice includes the following:

1. creating an interview guide based on the research questions that shape the study and sticking to it exactly while allowing space for follow-up questions (see chapter 7, Appendix 7.A);
2. selecting a neutral space for interviews that is both quiet and available for all the interviews, having the same person present in the same way (in person or online) for all the interviews, and remembering to test audio or video recording software before the interview begins;
3. developing a process for selecting participants consistent for all and approved by the institutional review board ahead of the research;
4. developing a method of coding that is based on or replicates that developed by others where appropriate, and, in this case, transcribing the interviews as a way to discover emergent themes for coding.

Olsen and Diekema note the limitations of their small sample size, but the exploratory nature of this research allowed them to identify strategies for scaling up beyond two universities. They suggest that future researchers who build on their work might include a larger-scale survey or focus groups, methods we see enacted and discussed in the chapters in section 2 of this collection.

SAME QUESTION; EXPANDED DATA SET

In the final chapter in this section, Elizabeth Kleinfeld also describes research developed from and within the context of other studies. Having seen student output such as that described in chapter 6 and read the articles cited in chapter 7 about students' beliefs concerning research, Kleinfeld turned her attention to instructional input in terms of the written guidelines provided within courses to help students conduct research and understand crucial concepts of information literacy. Single-input studies had looked at syllabi (Melzer 2003) and handouts (Head and Eisenberg 2010), but Kleinfeld collected all the documents produced for specific classes and analyzed them within the contexts of these previous studies and the gaps in the documents they analyzed. Her findings reflect theirs, and viewed in the context of this larger research, they allow her to make broader claims about the ways faculty might better prepare students to understand college-level information literacy. By selecting an equal mix of two- and four-year institutions, and explaining how she identified them, Kleinfeld reminds us of the importance of not simply researching what we know but of also providing comparative data. Follow-up research might build on that already conducted by librarians at two- and four- year colleges to help readers imagine spaces for collaboration between librarians and classroom-based faculty in different contexts and institution types.

In addition to offering information that might guide pedagogical interventions, Kleinfeld's research is designed to explore the reasons students seek and use resources as they do. Like Head and Eisenberg's (2010) study of course handouts, her research invites the critique that written documents are only one part of a course and are not necessarily indicative of what is taught overall; however, Head and Eisenberg (2010) explored this question and reported that students pay more attention to written instructions than to class discussion, thereby validating the collection of course documents. This research is another example of how smaller-scale studies can be conducted within the context of larger studies and in significant ways can be validated by them. Follow-up research or studies that evolve from this one might include interviews in which faculty and students are asked to talk about course documents and how they use and understand them. Based on the experience described by Breuch and Larson, it might be wise for any larger-scale study involving multiple coders to focus on fewer features at a time and thereby increase the likelihood of inter- and intrarater reliability. Of course, if Kleinfeld is able to build the corpus of documents she describes at the end of the chapter, multiple research teams could use the same documents, each coding for different features and then combing or triangulating their findings at the end.

Advice future researchers might take from Kleinfeld's chapter, then, includes the following:

1. Even if there is only one coder, developing a simple coding sheet on which to record responses and revising it as necessary facilitates the process (see chapter 8, Appendix 8.A). As Citation Project coders found (see chapter 1), any such changes should be recorded and explained in a coding notebook as the research develops, as should information about any necessary recoding that results.

2. Developing and updating a detailed coding guide and revising it to reflect changes increases a single coder's (intrarater) reliability across documents and provides the basis for training and coding when the research expands (see chapter 8, Appendix 8.B).

3. Finding and using existing lists helps researchers develop methods to randomize data collection and facilitates replication. In this case, drawing from the list of institutions allowed Kleinfeld to create a broad and transparently derived database.

4. Incorporating other research that addresses possible limitations into the discussion of methods helps validate them and thereby the findings. In this case, the knowledge about student reaction to written documents increases the relevance of Kleinfeld's findings.

DEPARTURE POINTS: SOME PARTICULAR WAYS FORWARD

We argue that within the field of writing studies, the meaning of replication should be expanded; rather than viewing it simply as a blind copy of previous research, researchers should think of it as a response to the research question or hypotheses of previous research using modified methods and approaches as appropriate. This approach includes the inevitable revisions that are part of scaling up from a small local study to a national or international study. It also includes the realization that adding a survey or coding category to existing research may reveal information that fills gaps in the initial study. These three chapters offer the opportunity to build on and/or expand the three methods described—genre analysis, interviews, and rhetorical analysis—and also to build on and/or expand the research questions, the findings, or the interpretations offered. They invite analysis of the kinds of challenges each research method brings, and they highlight the messiness of research in process. They also all invite exploration of the threshold concepts that block students as they approach source-based writing along with those that may impede research in the field of writing studies.

References

Head, Alison J., and Michael B. Eisenberg. 2010. "Assigning Inquiry: How Handouts for Research Assignments Guide Today's College Students." Project Information Literacy Progress Report. http://www.projectinfolit.org/uploads/2/7/5/4/27541717/pil_handout_study_finalvjuly_2010.pdf.

Melzer, Dan. 2003. "Assignments Across the Curriculum: A Survey of College Writing." *Language and Learning Across the Disciplines* 6 (1): 86–110.

Meyer, Jan, and Ray Land. 2005. "Threshold Concepts and Troublesome Knowledge: Epistemological Considerations and a Conceptual Framework for Teaching and Learning." *Higher Education* 49 (3): 373–88. http://dx.doi.org/10.1007/s10734-004-6779-5.

Swales, John. 1990. *Genre Analysis: English in Academic and Research Settings*. Cambridge: Cambridge University Press.

Afterword

TEACHING HYBRIDITY IN GRADUATE RESEARCH COURSES

Rebecca Moore Howard

When Tanya Rodrigue, Tricia Serviss, Sandra Jamieson, and I began work on the Citation Project, we faced a steep learning curve. None of us had much (if any) specific training in research methods for writing studies, and all of us knew the hermeneutics with which we were familiar were of little use for persuading audiences outside our field. None of our training prepared us for conducting research that would be replicable, aggregable, or data based. All of us thought, though, that such research was valuable for understanding how college students work with source material. Too much had been written about the plagiarism plague, too much about nefarious students' determination to cheat. Too many of our colleagues were subscribing to such narratives. We needed data to support any counternarratives we might propose.

What we learned, as we developed the Citation Project, was that RAD research is valuable not only for supporting arguments but also for discovering them. Again and again our research turned up surprising data—insights we gained *from* the research rather than claims we brought *to* it.

Getting there, though, was a trial-and-error task. Sandra took some stats classes. We consulted a variety of methodological works. The social science models were helpful, yet we found ourselves adapting them to suit our purposes rather than faithfully adhering to the models. That produced some back and forth with editors and reviewers who read drafts of our first article (Howard, Serviss, and Rodrigue 2010). Any deviation—rhetorical, conceptual, or methodological—from social science norms was marked for revision. We were being schooled in the social sciences. If interpretation, reflection, and personal experience could not be shoehorned into the discussion section, it had no place in the article; it could not be used as evidence for claims. We got the article published, but not without several revisions and negotiations.

It would be easy to conclude that our difficulties were simply the result of our ignorance of social science methodology. Certainly that was an element. Deeper, though, was the element of our own familiarity with hermeneutic inquiry. I am not referring to a particular school or theory set, nor to a particular scholar such as Paul Ricoeur or Richard Rorty. Rather, I use *hermeneutics* as an umbrella term for inquiry that is variously text-based, reflexive, conversational, contingent, humanistic. What matters more in hermeneutics is the individual conducting the inquiry, rather than the method.

In recent years I've been teaching the research-methods course in Syracuse's PhD program in composition and cultural rhetoric. My experiences with the Citation Project have been very much with me as I've navigated the teaching of that course. In the field of writing studies today, how does one prepare doctoral students as researchers? Those who have sat in my classes have typically come from MA programs in English departments at other institutions, and like me, they are comfortable with hermeneutic traditions. So are the leading journals in the field. What, then, should I be teaching in this methods course?

My predecessors in the course taught it primarily from the hermeneutic perspective. When I first taught it, I focused on the empirical, addressing data-based methods of textual analysis, relying on guides such as *Methods of Text and Discourse Analysis* (Titscher et al. 2000). The second time I taught the course, though, the class explored both hermeneutic and empirical approaches to research in rhetoric and writing studies. We were still using Stephan Titscher et al., but we were also using the second edition of Gabriele Griffin's (2013) *Research Methods for English Studies*. While that edition retains a chapter in which Catherine Belsey (2013) assumes the synonymy of the terms *close reading* and *textual analysis*, the book as a whole pushes readers out of the insularity of traditional literary interpretation and toward a more expansive sense of researched inquiry in English studies.

It is that more expansive sense that I advocate here—not for English studies but for writing studies. And I am not so much interested in writing studies researchers' having a smorgasbord of established research methods available to them (though that is itself a fine thing) as I am interested in the possibilities for hybridized research methods developed for, rather than imported into, the field of writing studies. We need not pit humanistic research against social science models but instead figure out how we might draw on both as we forge research methods appropriate to a still-young academic field.

Which brings me to the present volume. *Points of Departure* addresses empirical RAD research, but it is written by and for people like me and my graduate students, people who are schooled in hermeneutic textual inquiry very much like what Belsey (2013) describes but who recognize the importance of empirical research. In her introduction to this volume, Tricia Serviss cites scholars such as Chris Anson (2008) and Richard Haswell (2005) who advocate RAD research. Anson's argument is of particular interest to me, as it speaks to the importance of RAD research for persuading audiences outside writing studies, outside the humanities, outside the academy. These are often stakeholders—administrators, legislators—who are in powerful positions to support (or not) the pedagogical work of writing studies. These are not stakeholders who make policy decisions based on educators' personal experiences, reflections on classroom experiences, or narratives of events. These stakeholders are persuaded by data and the analysis thereof. For these reasons alone, RAD research is of great value in writing studies.

This value is not to deny the powerful effect hermeneutic methods such as narrative, personal experience, reflection, and close reading can have upon readers, evoking the "narrative knowledge" Patricia Harkin (1989) once associated with "the kinds of tacit awareness that comes to teachers . . . as a consequence of the work that they do" (57). Such methods encourage a feeling of identity between writer and audience, a sense of shared revelation and understanding, one human being connecting to and being enriched by the emotions and experiences of another. Jacqueline Jones Royster (1996) has persuasively argued for the accumulation of individual stories as a way of making meaning: "My sense of things," she says, "is that individual stories placed one against another against another build credibility and offer . . . a litany of evidence from which a call for transformation in theory and practice might rightfully begin" (30).

As I work with graduate students now, I encourage them not to choose between hermeneutics and empiricism but to discover possibilities in the relays between them. This is not to say we should all pick and choose research methods that seem most convenient or comfortable at any given moment—the "serendipitous" research design against which Sonja Foss and William Waters caution graduate students (Foss and Waters 2007, 26). Rather, we should think about how we might not just mix methods but hybridize them in an effort to bridge (perhaps collapse?) the great divide of the empirical and the hermeneutic. It is in this effort, I believe, that writing studies scholars will find their most powerful research methods.

And it is here that we will gain our greatest insights. Certainly my own experience with RAD methods has demonstrated the limitations of my own hermeneutic reflections on my classroom experiences. As we launched the Citation Project research described in chapter 1 of this volume, for example, I expected (based on my own classroom experiences) that we would find undergraduate writers doing more patchwriting than paraphrasing. I was wrong: 16.01 percent of 174 students' citations included patchwriting, and 31.87 percent included paraphrase (see Table 1.1 on page 43 of this collection).

As we coded our data, I also learned far more about the rhetorical moves of undergraduate writers than I ever would have through the sort of textual analysis Belsey (2013) advocates, in which the vanguard scholar interacts directly with the text. Whatever the value of close reading—and that value is considerable—it's of little use for discovering repeated rhetorical patterns in student writing. A RAD method such as textual coding puts sufficient distance between the scholar and the text to allow her to see phenomena and patterns that might otherwise be obscured by the halo effect or by confirmation bias. Coding does not, however, remove the scholar from the equation, making her a mere servant of an externally imposed system. Quite the contrary: the result of textual coding, in my experience, is to foster a far greater intimacy with and understanding of the text than close reading (with all its attendant baggage of excessive researcher control) could ever provide. Nor does this RAD method obviate the interpretive element in textual scholarship; on the contrary, Johnny Saldaña (2013) refers to coding as itself an interpretive act (4). Back in 1992, Keith Grant-Davie observed that coding is the only research method in English studies for which reliability is demanded, whereas people actually value the differences in literary readings of texts (Grant-Davie 1992, 282). His assertions resonate with my own experiences with coding: close reading aims at difference—difference within the text, difference in the interpretation of it—and it foregrounds the individual scholar. Coding uncovers difference but searches for patterns. One individual scholar may conduct the entire research project, from developing the categories for coding to interpreting the results, but the research finds its greatest power when it is pluralistic, either in its production (cf. the twenty-five people involved in the Citation Project research) or in its transcontextual replication and aggregation, so eloquently advocated in this volume.

It feels potentially risky to suggest that graduate students in writing studies might be taught to imagine and pursue research that hybridizes empirical and hermeneutic methods. What if I'm leading them toward unpublishable scholarship? I'm not eager to line my students up for the sort of buffeting Tanya, Tricia, and I experienced in the editorial process of our first Citation Project article. (One reviewer, for example, remarked that our article must have been written by a very young scholar.) On the other hand, the article (Howard, Serviss, and Rodrigue 2010) resulting from all that back and forth is a good article. Our individual subjectivities are less present in it than we had originally imagined; that's a change that was necessary for us to publish in that journal. (By individual subjectivities I'm not referring to our egos on display, nothing as simple as whether we used the first-person pronoun, but more about our subjectivities present in the text as we ruminated over our research. Such authorial presence is very much a part of hermeneutic scholarship, and of course it is deliberately absented from empirical research reports.) But publish we did, in an empirical journal, and we learned a great deal in the process and benefitted enormously from the experience. We were outside our hermeneutic comfort zone, and we were learning by leaps and bounds.

What this volume offers is exploration of and reflection on RAD research within writing studies. What readers have seen in every one of these chapters, and in the intertexts and introduction, is hybridized research at work. Taken in its entirety and in its individual parts, this book demonstrates *how* one reports data-driven research with the author a rhetorical and phenomenological presence in the research and the reporting thereof. Nor is this the first time such a creature has been seen; increasingly, it is populating writing studies journals traditionally hermeneutic in their methodological commitments. The shift can be seen in a single issue of a single journal, *College Composition and Communication*. The June 2016 issue contains a humanistic essay that draws on personal experiences and secondary sources for its evidence (Tauber 2016). That same issue also includes an article that draws on the social science model: Blythe and Gonzales's (2016) headings faithfully follow the familiar conventions: "Research Methods," "Data Analysis," and so forth. The June 2016 issue of *College Composition and Communication* includes another data-driven report (Beerits 2016), and this one is very much a hybrid of the empirical and the hermeneutic. The headings are conceptual rather than conventional ("Analysis of Student Texts," "Categories of Self-Reference," and so forth); the argument is woven into the entire fabric of the article rather than being saved for a "discussion" section; and the author is present in the text, mulling over her data and findings as she builds her argument.

I point to these three articles to demonstrate the variety of research now being published in writing studies. I value both hermeneutic and empirical research and am confident of their continued vitality in our collective body of scholarship. And I see no danger whatsoever, no risk to graduate students, in encouraging the exploration of both traditions and of possible hybridizations of the two. I'm not talking here about "mixed" methods. I'm talking about bringing an explicit humanistic sensibility to working with data, about data-driven methods deployed within hermeneutic methodology.

For that humanistic sensibility, we can turn to some very fine recent methodological works in writing studies, such as Nickoson and Sheridan's (2012) *Writing Studies Research in Practice: Methods and Methodologies* and Schell and Rawson's (2010) *Rhetorica in Motion: Feminist Rhetorical Methods and Methodologies*. To the conversations established in such works, the present volume contributes a valorization of data-driven research, a transcontextual perspective, and a sustained attention to the articulation of research methods.

The last of these is a key piece—perhaps *the* key piece—to developing hybrid writing studies research. Hybridized methods invite scrutiny. For them to be deemed acceptable, they must be clear and sensible, honoring the research ethics and practices of both the hermeneutic and the empirical traditions. One's research methods may be reported in a social science methods section, all neat and tidy and cordoned off from the meaning-making parts of the publication, or it may be woven into the text, as an ongoing part of the action. (My own preferences are clear in the framing of the preceding sentence!) The contributors to *Points of Departure* demonstrate ways to make dialogic methods statements infused with reflexivity, narration, and contingency. Crystal Benedicks's description of her methods, for example, includes her *feelings about* her methods, descriptions of how she addressed her own insecurities as she worked with data. Elizabeth Kleinfeld's chapter speaks both to her classroom experiences and to her data analysis. Kristi Costello explains how her administrative responsibilities affected her research methods.

As Tricia Serviss states in her introduction to this volume, research in the *Points of Departure* essays is imagined as a process, not an event, and these essays model ways to make that principle explicit in reports of research. In their first interchapter to this volume, Serviss and Jamieson offer an understanding of *transcontextuality* that can motivate researchers to use RAD research methods. Even localized pilot studies that are never further developed by the designers have far-reaching potential value to other researchers if they are designed from a transcontextual viewpoint, with research methods fully explained, so other researchers might extend or revise the study. In such manner does *Points of Departure* provide necessary methodological and ethical principles. These principles are highly recommended for all manner of research. Establishing and teaching the authority of hybrid writing studies research is, I think, fully dependent on the committed embrace of these principles.

References

Anson, Chris M. 2008. "The Intelligent Design of Writing Programs: Reliance on Belief or a Future of Evidence?" *WPA: Writing Program Administration* 32 (1): 11–38.

Beerits, Laura. 2016. "Understanding I: The Rhetorical Variety of Self-References in College Literature Papers." *College Composition and Communication* 67 (4): 550–75.

Belsey, Catherine. 2013. "Textual Analysis as a Research Method." In *Research Methods for English Studies*. 2nd ed., edited by Gabriele Griffin, 160–78. Edinburgh: Edinburgh University Press.

Blythe, Stuart, and Laura Gonzales. 2016. "Coordination and Transfer across the Metagenre of Secondary Research." *College Composition and Communication* 67 (4): 607–33.

Foss, Sonja, and William Waters. 2007. *Destination Dissertation: A Traveler's Guide to a Done Dissertation*. Lanham, MD: Rowman and Littlefield.

Grant-Davie, Keith. 1992. "Coding Data: Issues of Validity, Reliability, and Interpretation." In *Methods and Methodology in Composition Research*, edited by Gesa Kirsch and Patricia A. Sullivan, 270–86. Carbondale: Southern Illinois University Press.

Griffin, Gabriele, ed. 2013. *Research Methods for English Studies*. 2nd ed. Edinburgh: Edinburgh University Press.

Harkin, Patricia. 1989. "Bringing Lore to Light." *PRE/TEXT* 10 (1–2): 55–67.

Haswell, Richard H. 2005. "NCTE/CCCC's Recent War on Scholarship." *Written Communication* 22 (2): 198–223. http://dx.doi.org/10.1177/0741088305275367.

Howard, Rebecca Moore, Tricia Serviss, and Tanya K. Rodrigue. 2010. "Writing from Sources, Writing from Sentences." *Writing & Pedagogy* 2 (2): 177–92. http://dx.doi.org/10.1558/wap.v2i2.177.

Nickoson, Lee, and Mary P. Sheridan, eds. 2012. *Writing Studies Research in Practice: Methods and Methodologies*. Carbondale: Southern Illinois University Press.

Royster, Jacqueline Jones. 1996. "When the First Voice You Hear Is Not Your Own." *College Composition and Communication* 47 (1): 29–40. http://dx.doi.org/10.2307/358272.

Saldaña, Johnny. 2013. *The Coding Manual for Qualitative Researchers*. 2nd ed. Los Angeles, CA: SAGE.

Schell, Eileen E., and K. J. Rawson. 2010. *Rhetorica in Motion: Feminist Rhetorical Methods and Methodologies*. Pittsburgh, PA: University of Pittsburgh Press.

Tauber, Daveena. 2016. "Expanding the Writing Franchise: Composition Consulting at the Graduate Level." *College Composition and Communication* 67 (4): 634–57.

Citation Project. n.d. "Findings—Source Use in Paper." http://site.citationproject.net/results/findings-source-use-in-paper/.

Titscher, Stefan, Michael Meyer, Ruth Wodak, and Eva Vetter. 2000. *Methods of Text and Discourse Analysis*. Los Angeles, CA: SAGE.

ABOUT THE AUTHORS

TRICIA SERVISS is the associate director of entry level writing in the University Writing Program at UC Davis. Recent articles appear in *Writing Pedagogy, College English, Assessing Writing*, and *Across the Disciplines*, as well as chapters in *Crossing Borders, Drawing Boundaries: The Rhetoric of Lines across America* (edited by Barbara Couture and Patti Wojahn) and *The Handbook of Academic Integrity* (edited by Tracy Bretag). Current research projects include a longitudinal study of first-generation college student STEM major literacy practices and longitudinal study of a transdisciplinary faculty development team leading a writing and research initiative to strengthen undergraduate learning. She is a principal researcher of the Citation Project (citationproject.net).

SANDRA JAMIESON is professor of English and director of writing across the curriculum at Drew University, where she teaches writing and writing-intensive courses including first-year writing, travel writing, writing for social media, civic engagement, authorship, and research writing. Her publications include two coedited collections, *Information Literacy: Research and Collaboration across Disciplines* and *Coming of Age: The Advanced Writing Curriculum*, and *The Bedford Guide to Teaching Writing in the Disciplines: An Instructor's Desk Reference* (with Rebecca Moore Howard). She has also published articles on information literacy, research, plagiarism, the vertical writing curriculum, writing across the curriculum, textbooks, and multicultural education. She is one of three Citation Project principal researchers, and is working on a book discussing findings from their first study, *Struggling with Sources*.

CRYSTAL BENEDICKS is associate professor of English and coordinator of writing across the curriculum at Wabash College, where she teaches classes on writing, literature, and gender/sexuality studies. In 2007, she coedited a book collection with Judith Summerfield titled *Reclaiming the Public University: Conversations on General & Liberal Education*. Her current research is at the intersection of disability studies, nineteenth-century poetics, and masculinity studies.

KATT BLACKWELL-STARNES is assistant professor in the Department of English, Modern Languages, and Philosophy at Lamar University. She received her PhD in rhetoric from Texas Woman's University and holds both a BA and an MA in English from Mississippi College. Her research focus is information literacy, and she explores both the cognitive side of students' information-literacy skills and pedagogical approaches to improving information-literacy instruction in the college classroom. Her current research projects include the LILAC Project and a faculty-librarian project focused on redesigning and expanding information-literacy instruction in first-year writing courses.

LEE-ANN KASTMAN BREUCH, is associate professor in the Department of Writing Studies at the University of Minnesota, where she is the director of undergraduate studies and the bachelor of science degree in technical writing and communication. Her research investigates rhetoric and digital writing in a variety of settings such as classrooms, professional organizations, and social media. She teaches courses in technical communication, digital writing, usability research, and evaluation of online interfaces. She has published articles in *Technical Communication, Journal of Business and Technical Communication, Technical*

Communication Quarterly, Journal of Advanced Composition, and *Computers and Composition.* She is author of *Virtual Peer Review: Teaching and Learning about Writing in Online Environments* and coauthor of the *Understanding and Creating Digital Texts: An Activity-Based Approach* with Richard Beach, Chris M. Anson, Lee-Ann Kastman Breuch, and Thomas Reynolds.

KRISTI MURRAY COSTELLO is assistant professor of writing studies and the director of the writing program and writing center at Arkansas State University. Her critical work has been published in *Composition Forum, Kairos: A Journal for Teachers of Writing in Webbed Environments, CCC IP Annual, Women in Higher Education,* and the recent collections *Ecologies of Writing Programs: Profiles of Writing Programs in Context,* edited by Mary Jo Reiff, Anis Bawarshi, Michelle Ballif, and Christian Weisser and *Teaching US-Educated Multilingual Writers: Practices from and for the Classroom,* edited by Mark Roberge, Kay M. Losey, and Margi Wald. She is a participating researcher on the Citation Project, recipient of a 2016 South-Central Writing Center Association Research Grant, and corecipient of a 2011 Conference on College Composition and Communication Certificate of Writing Program Excellence. Her research interests include WPA, WC/W, writing center studies, and GA/TA mentorship.

ANNE R. DIEKEMA is assistant professor of library media and instruction librarian at the Gerald R. Sherratt Library at Southern Utah University, where she teaches a general education class on information literacy to first-year students. Anne's research interests are in human-information behavior, information literacy, and personal information management. She is especially interested in how students find, use, manage and synthesize information from a variety of sources. Occasionally Anne can be found at the public library with therapy dog Mavis, a reading education assistance dog (R.E.A.D.). She is an organizing member of schoollibraryPALS: Parents Advocating for Libraries in Schools, which supports and promotes school libraries in Utah. She is also the embedded librarian for Southern Utah University's Semester in the Parks program.

REBECCA MOORE HOWARD earned her PhD in English at West Virginia University and is now professor of Writing and Rhetoric at Syracuse University. She is the author of *Writing Matters,* 3rd edition, and a variety of books and articles about plagiarism and pedagogy.

ELIZABETH KLEINFELD is associate professor of English and writing center director at Metropolitan State University of Denver. She teaches courses on rhetoric and composition theory and practice, including authorship studies and digital rhetoric. She has coauthored a textbook on multimodal and multigenre composition and has published articles on writing center work, digital rhetoric, and student source-citation practices. Her work has appeared in *Praxis* and *Computers and Composition Online.* She is currently working on an ethnographic study of first-year writing courses, focusing on how students' understanding of source-use strategies develops, and coauthoring a textbook for students writing from sources.

BRIAN N. LARSON is an associate professor in the School of Law at Texas A&M University where he teaches professional and technical communication, digital-media law, and research methods. He studies rhetoric and argumentation, especially in legal and professional communication. His communication research focuses on rhetorical and argumentation theory in context and practice, using text-analytic, computational, and cognitive methods. He attempts to draw explicit connections between legal philosophy or jurisprudence, argumentation theory, and empirical practice. His other research interests include digital-media law and research methods, especially as they relate to digital writing and digital humanities.

KAREN J. LUNSFORD is associate professor of writing and director of the PhD emphasis in writing studies at the University of California, Santa Barbara. She teaches courses in writing for science, technology, and the health professions. Currently, she and James Purdy are conducting an empirical study on how intellectual-property (IP) practices are affecting the work of teacher-scholars in writing studies.

M. WHITNEY OLSEN is an instructor of technical communication at Arizona State University, where she teaches technical editing to graduate and undergraduate students. Her research interests include the information behavior of English and writing students, encompassing information needs, seeking, and use. Her latest research is largely pedagogical for the sake of her students. Most recently, she took on a new role: mother, which daily keeps her reading in diverse literature.

JANICE R. WALKER is professor of writing and linguistics and chair of the Institutional Review Board (IRB) at Georgia Southern University. She has published journal articles, book chapters, and books about online research, documentation, intellectual property, and information literacy. She is founder and coordinator of the Graduate Research Network at the annual Computers and Writing Conference and co-coordinator for the Georgia Conference on Information Literacy hosted by Georgia Southern University. Her current research includes the LILAC Project (Learning Information Literacy across the Curriculum), and she recently published *Information Literacy: Research and Collaboration across Disciplines* coedited with Barbara D'Angelo, Sandra Jamieson, and Barry Maid, an open-access scholarly book available in full at wac.colostate.edu/books/infolit/.

INDEX

academic dishonesty, 41, 123, 131
academic honesty/integrity, instruction, 126, 130, 131, 228, 228–30, 242
academic honesty/dishonesty/integrity: perceptions, 126, 129, 130, 229, 133; policies/statements, 124, 133, 234; responses/penalties, 126
Academic Integrity, Center for, 246
ACRL (Association of College and Research Libraries), "Framework for Information Literacy for Higher Education," 53, 175, 177–78, 248
Adler-Kassner, Linda, 172, 176, 180
advice, for future research, 151, 191–92, 199–200, 237, 247, 249, 250; student—from family members, 216, 220, 241; students—from friends, 215, 216, 220
analysis: citation-context (*see* method, citation context analysis); genre, 184, 197; qualitative, xiii, xvi, 12, 53, 68–69, 73, 108, 133, 146, 211, 214; quantitative, statistical, xiii, xvi, 25–26, 35, 37, 53, 68–69, 108, 113, 133, 232; textual/rhetorical, 186, 187, 237, 253, 255 (*see also* Flesch-Kincaid readability measures); self-analysis, reflection, 117; thematic, 212, 214; unit of, 38, 47–9, 51, 65, 73, 188–9, 232, 237
analytical report. *See* papers, analytical reports/research papers
Anson, Chris, xvii, 4, 5, 37, 38, 42, 254
article, research. *See* papers, research/researched writing
assessment: institutional, xvii, 124, 134, 145, 151, 164, 182; of writing, 115, 163, 200, 201–2
assignment, research, 67, 74, 97, 133, 150, 185, 200, 223, 228; language, 132, 198–99, 227–44
Association of College and Research Libraries (ACRL). *See* ACRL
attribution of borrowed material. *See* citations/citation practices
audio recording, 69, 212
axial coding. *See* coding, axial

Bartholomae, David, 41, 172
Bazerman, Charles, 4, 5, 9, 183; *Handbook of Research on Writing*, 11
Benedicks, Crystal, 18, 98, 123, 164–67, 257, 259
Blackwell-Starnes, Katt, 17, 26, 53, 62, 259
Blum, Susan, *My Word! Plagiarism and College Culture*, 125
Brandt, Deborah, 16, 27–28; *Limits of the Local: Expanding Perspectives on Literacy as a Social Practice*, 27
Breuch, Lee-Ann Kastman, 19, 177–78, 182, 246–47, 259

citation context analysis. *See* method, citation context analysis
citation context coding. *See* coding, citation context
Citation Project, 15, 30, 33–61, 63, 73, 86, 87, 125, 132, 141, 177, 221, 227–28, 230–31, 237–38, 252, 256
citations/citation practices, 63, 86, 103, 116, 117, 124–34, 148, 152, 155, 190–99, 216, 228–29, 233–36
class notes, 215, 217
Clinton, Katie, 16, 27–8; *Limits of the Local: Expanding Perspectives on Literacy as a Social Practice*, 27
coders, training, xvi, 48–49, 107, 186, 188–91
coding, axial, 145; categories, 44–48, 145, 186–88, 191, 241; citation context, 38–39, 48–51, 107; confusion matrix, 188–91; double-coding, 50, 69, 109, 146; guide, 191, 200, 201, 250; inductive, 212; interrater reliability, xvi, 52, 111–12, 188–91; open, 145, 148; textual, 233
confirmation bias, 45–46, 115–16, 255
Cooper, Charles, xxii, 7, 8
Costello, Kristi Murray, 18, 98–99, 141, 164, 257, 260
course documents, 179, 227–244, 250

data, replicable. *See* RAD research
database, online, 147, 150, 215, 217

design-based research. *See* research, design-based
Diekema, Anne, 19, 178, 209–26, 248–49, 260
direct quotes, 113, 200

ecological validity. *See* research, design-based
Eisenberg, Michael B., 62, 132, 142, 144, 214, 221, 227–30, 233, 237, 240. *See also* Project Information Literacy
empiricism, xiv, 10, 254
engagement, 44, 94, 112, 163–4
Engagement, National Survey of Student (NSSE), xiv
excessive research, 235–36, 238–39

Flesch/Flesch-Kincaid readability measures, xvii–xviii, 52
focus groups, student. *See* method, focus groups
Framework for Information Literacy for Higher Education (ACRL), 53, 175, 178

genre, xviii, 4, 19, 134, 177–78, 182–208, 232, 236–37
genre analysis. *See* analysis, genre
Google, 70–72, 74, 87, 148, 150, 215–18
grounded theory, xvi, 12, 106, 145

halo effect, 45–6, 52, 116
Haswell, Richard, xiii, 4–5, 26
Head, Alison J., 62, 63, 72, 132, 142, 144, 214, 215–16, 218, 221, 227–30, 233, 237, 240. *See also* Project Information Literacy
hermeneutics, 252, 253, 254
Hillocks, George, *Teaching Writing as Reflective Action*, 116
Holmes, Richard, 186, 188, 189, 192
Howard, Rebecca Moore, 29, 33–61, 63, 110–11, 112, 141, 183, 184, 192, 210, 219, 221, 252–58, 260

IMRAD superstructure/research article (John Swales), 178, 183–208, 246–47
information/knowledge, background, 67, 73, 74, 118, 184, 187, 189, 193, 201, 202, 230
information: literacy, 44, 52, 62, 64, 65, 70, 72, 73, 74, 75, 87, 132, 147, 174, 175, 177, 180, 209, 214, 216, 222, 245, 249; professionals (*see* librarians/information professionals); seeking/behavior, 62, 65, 68, 70, 73, 209–26, 230, 248
informed consent, 65–67, 213

Institutional Research Board (IRB), 38–39, 40, 64, 66, 76, 106, 144, 185, 232
intellectual property, 38, 66
interrater reliability. *See* coding, interrater reliability
interview. *See* method, interview

Jamieson, Sandra, 11, 15, 17, 30, 34, 36, 44–45, 49, 52, 53, 54, 63, 105, 111, 184, 210, 214, 221, 228, 230, 252, 257

Kleinfeld, Elizabeth, 19, 177, 179, 198, 249–50, 257

Land, Ray, *Threshold Concepts*, 171–75, 245
language, assignments. *See* assignment, language
Larson, Brian N., 19, 177–78, 182, 246–47, 260
Latour, Bruno, xv, 16, 28
librarians/information professionals, 19, 62, 65, 69, 132, 142, 177, 179–80, 209, 215–16, 220, 221, 222, 250
library, 64, 70, 71, 72, 74, 75, 80, 210, 217
LILAC Project/Group (Learning Information Literacy across the Curriculum), 17, 26, 30, 53, 62–82, 86–87, 88, 263
Lunsford, Karen, xiii–xxi, 5, 14, 34, 84–85, 261

Melzer, Dan, 97, 179, 230, 231, 240
method: audio recording, 68–70, 212, 213, 249 (*see also* research-aloud protocol [RAP], audio and video); citation context analysis, 18, 35, 38, 40, 52, 102, 106, 107, 108, 111, 162, 163; design-based research (ecological validity) (*see* research, design-based); focus groups, 86, 123–40, 164, 165, 214, 230, 240, 247, 248–49; interview, 113, 177, 192, 209–26, 230, 237, 240, 247–49, 250; questionnaire/survey, 63, 64–67, 68, 70–73, 75, 76–81, 97, 107, 108, 110, 113, 123, 124, 125–27, 129–30, 131, 133, 141–61, 214, 251; reflective writing, 106, 108, 111, 113, 116, 120, 162, 192; video/screen capture, 64, 66–70, 81
methods, mixed, 65, 106, 113, 117, 123, 128, 133, 162
Meyer, Jan, *Threshold Concepts*, 171–75, 245

NSSE (National Survey of Student Engagement), xiv
North, Steven, 9, 83

Odell, Lee, xxi, 3, 5, 7, 8–9, 192
Olsen, M. Whitney, 19, 178, 209–26, 248–49, 261

papers: analytical reports/research papers, 183, 185, 198; research/researched writing, 29, 34, 41, 47, 87, 105, 141–43, 147, 148, 150, 178, 179, 185, 198–99, 218, 223, 227, 229, 230
paraphrase, 42–43, 45–46, 51, 53, 109–15, 119, 195, 200, 204, 216, 221–22, 235, 241, 255
patchwriting, 35, 38, 40, 42–48, 52, 53, 109–19, 183, 221, 255; definitions, 40, 46
Pecorari, Diane, 36, 38–39, 40, 41, 106
pedagogy: data collection as intervention, 74–75, 93, 95, 98, 108–9, 111–13, 116, 118, 163–66; graduate, 98, 102–7, 116–18; undergraduate, 39, 41, 53, 62, 73–75, 86, 91, 96, 116, 133, 171–76, 179–80, 183–84, 210, 222, 227–44, 247, 250, 252–58
PIL (Project Information Literacy). *See* Project Information Literacy
plagiarism, 35, 45–47, 78–79, 108, 114, 119, 124, 125, 130–32, 148–50, 156, 190, 210, 216, 221–22, 231, 234, 241, 252; detection software (PDS), 43; policy statements (*see* academic honesty/dishonesty/integrity statements)
Project Information Literacy (PIL), 30, 63, 132, 214, 216, 228, 246

qualitative analysis. *See* analysis, qualitative
quantitative analysis. *See* analysis, quantitative
questionnaire. *See* method, questionnaire/survey
quotation, 43, 78–79, 110, 233, 235, 239, 241

RAD research (replicable, aggregable, and data-driven), xiii–xix, 3–20, 25–31, 34, 44, 83, 88, 91–101, 130, 134, 167, 176, 216, 248, 252–58
reading, xvii–iv, 63, 65, 74, 102, 113, 116, 153–54, 174, 216–19, 236, 254; difficulty. *See* Flesch/Flesch-Kincaid readability measures
recording, audio. *See* methods, audio recording
research: action (defined), 162–63, 166; design-based (DBR), 91–101, 102–22; mixed method (*see* methods, mixed); replicable (*see* RAD research)

research-aloud protocol (RAP), audio and video, 64, 66–70, 72, 73, 81. *See also* method, audio recording
Rodrigue, Tanya, 29, 36, 38–42, 44, 48, 252, 256; *Writing from Sources, Writing from Sentences*, 63, 85, 105, 111, 141, 183, 184, 192, 221
Rose, Mike, 37, 41, 173, 175–76

screen capture. *See* method, video/screen capture
search: engine(s), 70–72, 217 (*see also* Google); process, xxi, 13–14, 28–30, 67–68, 72–75, 143, 162–63, 215, 219–21, 223–24, 228–30, 236–37; terms, 68, 70, 76, 209, 215, 219–20
sentence structure, 221, 224
Serviss, Tricia, 3–22, 29, 33, 36–38, 40, 41, 42, 44, 48, 98, 102–22, 127, 163–66, 252, 256, 259; *Writing from Sources, Writing from Sentences*, 63, 85, 105, 141, 183, 184, 192, 221
Shaughnessy, Mina, 9, 128, 173, 175
software: Atlas.ti, 69, 70; Audacity, 213; Camtasia, 62, 64; Flesh.app (Flesch reader), 52; plagiarism detection, 43; Qualtrics, 66, 69–70, 76; spreadsheet, 189
sources: primary, 80, 185, 187, 190, 193, 197, 203–4, 224; secondary, 80, 196–99, 209, 215–16, 224, 256
Spilka, Rachel, 183
statistical analysis and programs, SPSS, xvi, 25–26, 45, 53, 112–13, 146, 189, 191
summary, 29, 34, 40–43, 85–86, 112–24, 183–84, 222, 229–31, 235, 239, 242
survey(s). *See* method, questionnaire/survey
Sutherland-Smith, Wendy, 45
Swales, John, 182–202, 246–247

technical and professional writing, 182–200
textual analysis. *See* analysis, textual/rhetorical
thematic analysis. See analysis, thematic
theory, grounded. *See* grounded theory
threshold concept, 19, 113–15, 171–80, 227, 245, 251
transcontextual, xv, xviii, 14–17, 25–31, 86, 92–93, 106, 108, 163–67, 246
transcription, 68, 212, 249
transfer, 92, 104–5, 116–17, 176
translocal, 14–17, 25–31, 86, 92–93, 106, 108, 163–67

video: capture, 65–66, 87; release, 65, 68

Walker, Janice, 17, 26, 53, 62, 210, 261
websites, 211, 215, 217, 223
Wikipedia, 47, 78, 80, 124, 131, 150, 155, 160; use of, 70, 72–74, 215–16, 218–19, 223–24, 234, 239
Wolfe, Joanna, 183

writing: academic, 18, 103, 105–7, 163, 165; technical and professional, 184, 246–47
writing across the curriculum, 124, 230, 246

Yancey, Kathleen, 104, 172, 181
YouTube, 66, 71, 75–76

www.ingramcontent.com/pod-product-compliance
Ingram Content Group UK Ltd.
Pitfield, Milton Keynes, MK11 3LW, UK
UKHW021844140426
5217IPUK00022B/1580